The Bioregional Economy

In a world of climate change and declining oil supplies, what is the plan for the provisioning of resources? Green economists suggest a need to replace the globalised economy, and its extended supply chains, with a more 'local' economy. But what does this mean in more concrete terms? How large is a local economy, how self-reliant can it be, and what resources will still need to be imported? The concept of the 'bioregion' – developed and popularised within the disciplines of earth sciences, biosciences and planning – may facilitate the reconceptualisation of the global economy as a system of largely self-sufficient local economies.

A bioregional approach to economics assumes a different system of values to that which dominates neoclassical economics. The global economy is driven by growth, and the consumption ethic that matches this is one of expansion in range and quantity. Goods are defined as scarce, and access to them is a process based on competition. The bioregional approach challenges every aspect of that value system. It seeks a new ethic of consumption that prioritises locality, accountability and conviviality in the place of expansion and profit; it proposes a shift in the focus of the economy away from profits and towards provisioning; and it assumes a radical reorientation of work from employment towards livelihood.

This book by leading green economist Molly Scott Cato sets out a visionary yet rigorous account of what a bioregional approach to the economy would mean – and how to get there.

Molly Scott Cato is Professor of Strategy and Sustainability at Roehampton University, UK. She is the author of *Green Economics: An Introduction to Theory, Policy and Practice* (Earthscan, 2008) and she has written widely on themes concerned with mutualism, social enterprise, policy responses to climate change, banking and finance, and local economies. She works with Transition Stroud and Stroud Common Wealth.

The Bioregional Economy

Land, liberty and the pursuit of happiness

Molly Scott Cato

Routledge
Taylor & Francis Group

LONDON AND NEW YORK

First published 2013
by Routledge
2 Park Square, Milton Park, Abingdon, Oxon OX14 4RN

Simultaneously published in the USA and Canada
by Routledge
711 Third Avenue, New York, NY 10017

Routledge is an imprint of the Taylor & Francis Group, an informa business

British Library Cataloguing in Publication Data
A catalogue record for this book is available from the British Library

Library of Congress Cataloging in Publication Data
Cato, Molly Scott.
The bioregional economy : land, liberty and the pursuit of happiness / by Molly
Scott Cato.
  p. cm.
  1. Sustainable development–Social aspects. 2. Economic development–
Environmental aspects. 3. Regional economics–Environmental aspects. 4. Human
ecology–Economic aspects. I. Title.
  HC79.E5C3827 2012
  338.9'27–dc23
                        2012017740

ISBN: 978-1-84971-458-7 (hbk)
ISBN: 978-0-415-50082-1 (pbk)
ISBN: 978-0-203-08286-7 (ebk)

Typeset in Times New Roman
by Taylor & Francis Books

MIX
Paper from
responsible sources
FSC
www.fsc.org   FSC® C004839

Printed and bound in Great Britain by
TJ International Ltd, Padstow, Cornwall

In Memory of
Richard Douthwaite
You are so deeply missed
And yet every day your work helps us to build
a sustainable future.

Now, my co-mates and brothers in exile,
Hath not old custom made this life more sweet
Than that of painted pomp? Are not these woods
More free from peril than the envious court?
Here feel we but the penalty of Adam,
The seasons' difference, as the icy fang
And churlish chiding of the winter's wind,
Which, when it bites and blows upon my body,
Even till I shrink with cold, I smile and say
'This is no flattery: these are counsellors
That feelingly persuade me what I am.'
Sweet are the uses of adversity,
Which, like the toad, ugly and venomous,
Wears yet a precious jewel in his head;
And this our life exempt from public haunt
Finds tongues in trees, books in the running brooks,
Sermons in stones and good in every thing.
I would not change it.

    Duke Senior in *As You Like It*, II.1, on The Forest of Arden

Contents

PART III
Policies for a bioregional economy   **143**

Illustrations

Photographs

Figures

Tables

Preface

I have been thinking about this book for at least a decade, since I first began to wonder in my own mind what sort of economy might replace the profligate and essentially dissatisfying structure that globalisation has given us. Two beacons have come to light my way in thinking and writing: one to attract me; the other to repel. The first is best encapsulated in Doreen Massey's suggestion that we should be 'for place'. At the risk of any pretention to an academic career, I have to say that I take this as an inevitable assumption, a partial definition of the human condition. Just as we cannot live as isolated individuals, we cannot live without a sense of place. The second arose as a question following a talk I had given to an academic audience. 'What', my questioner asked, 'did Molly Scott Cato have to say to the people of Shanghai?' I felt quite aghast at first: I had nothing to say to them, nothing at all. But over the following days and weeks I realised this was a strength, not a sign of inadequacy. What right have I to create a message for Chinese people whose culture I do not understand? Our lessons must be grounded and they must be local. This is the philosophical motivation for the bioregional economy; the creative part is translating that into a strategy for acquiring resources, and for developing a locally based provisioning strategy.

To live in this way that would once have been commonplace now feels radical and exciting. In an age when the world's resources are available for a sum of money I have in my purse 24 hours a day within a 10-minute walk, there is a way in which it could be dismissed as playing. But something in me is not convinced of the power of that system, and the number of people queuing for allotments and learning the skills of growing, preserving and brewing, suggests that I am not alone in this. Playing is a child's work; it is a way of learning that is risk-free. It may be that, as a human community, and by a mixture of reason and intuition, we are rejecting progress and learning from an earlier way of being.

It is always difficult to know whether your sense of being at a pivotal point in history is real or fanciful. When I look at the history of humankind what I notice that is different about right now is that it is the first time we have had the information necessary to know for certain that we are making a terrible mistake. We are the first species that has been able to chronicle its own path to extinction. Can we use the same immense cognitive and communicative powers at our disposal to find a different and better way?

I believe that we can and that we must. My book is my commitment to this belief in the field of economics.

Molly Scott Cato
Stroud, UK
March 2012

Acknowledgements

I should begin with my friends in the Green House think tank and the Green Party, who have had the courage to challenge the neoliberal paradigm and dedicate their time and energy to working for something better. I feel I must say a special word about John Barry, whose work seems to interweave with mine in a way that I find at once inspiring and reinforcing. Developing a green political economy that will ensure secure and fulfilling provisioning for all the world's people is a demanding task, and I greatly appreciate sharing that task with John.

The writing of this book would not have been possible if I had not, at some point during 2011, decided to stop applying for research grants. After a series of time-consuming but unsuccessful applications I decided that the time spent could have produced the research, or at least part of it. I would like to acknowledge the following funding bodies that have declined to support aspects of this work: the ESRC, the Leverhulme Trust, the European Research Council, and the Joseph Rowntree Foundation.

For technical, emotional, intellectual and spiritual support and I would like to thank the following: Peter Richardson of Ethical Internet; Mike Munro-Turner of Jericho Partners; Helen Hastings-Spital; Rebecca Boden and Debbie Epstein of Edbrooke Careers Guidance and Moral Support Services; Jane Seraillier and Neil Buick; Jenny Jones, Michael Dunwell and Rhydian Fôn James. For helping me keep domestic body and soul together additional thanks to Angela Paine and Sue Dance.

For supporting my explorations in bioregional cosmopolitianism, my thanks to Nadia Johanisova, Lukaš, Eliška and other friends at Masaryk University, Brno; Pavla and Mark in Lučeč; Olga and Andrew in Helsinki; and Timur in Astana.

Finally, for reading parts of the typescript along the way: Jane Seraillier, Brian Heatley, Chris Hart, James Beecher, and Martin Large. And a big thank you to Rosa for her almost unfailing good humour (in spite of the crippling exam system) and for sparing my eyes.

Part I
Making sense of the bioregion

1

WHY BIOREGIONAL ECONOMICS?

> The world and I reciprocate one another. The landscape as I directly experience it is hardly a determinate object; it is an ambiguous realm that responds to my emotions and calls forth feelings from me in turn.
>
> (David Abram, *The Spell of the Sensuous*)

It has been a basic assumption amongst green economists for several decades that a green economy will be a local economy, or rather a system of self-reliant local economies that meet most of their own needs from within their boundaries. This might be seen as a reaction against globalisation, but in fact it is a reaction to the evidence of the destructive consequences of an economy that relies heavily on fossil fuel energy and, therefore, on the production of carbon dioxide. Less widely considered by policy-makers, although of equal and urgent concern, is the lack of resilience in our global systems of production and distribution. A globalised economic system heavily dependent on oil makes itself vulnerable directly, through depleting its own fundamental resource, and indirectly, through increasing the likelihood of destructive climatic events that would in turn threaten transport systems. The global economy as currently designed, therefore, is ultimately self-limiting. The primary task of a green economist in the era of climate change and ecological crisis is to consider how a system of self-reliant local economies might be designed, and how we might make a rapid transition towards such a future world.

This is fine to argue in theory; in practice the global economy is stronger than ever. The extraordinary ability we have to buy products from across the world for a normal person's wages at any hour of the day or night is dizzyingly impressive. Yet while civil servants struggle to find policies to both mitigate and adapt to climate change (this is a distinction I reject, for reasons that will become clear later), two different words are dominating the discourse amongst social scientists who are seeking responses to the crises that face us: transition and resilience. The experience of those who are attempting to make a transition to a sustainable way of living, particularly to transition to a sustainable system of provisioning, will be discussed in this book, and the theoretical discussion of why the current economy is unsustainable and what structures might facilitate our transition towards a more sustainable economy are covered at length in the succeeding chapters. While a theoretical treatment of the concept of resilience and its application to provisioning systems is beyond the scope of this book, I take it as understood that a sustainable economy will be resilient, in the sense that it will be able to deal with shocks in a responsive and creative way, rather than being catastrophically challenged by them (Barry, 2012).

For a green economist, the initial appeal of the concept of 'bioregionalism' and of the phrase 'the bioregional economy' is that it offers a way of adding some detail to the appealing but poorly theorised notion of the local economy. However, while developing this idea it has become clear to me that taking a bioregional approach, or 'living a rooted life', will have a profound impact on a whole range of other aspects of social, political, psychological and spiritual life. While aspects of the structure and organisation of a sustainable economy are covered in this book, I also focus my attention on the softer side of economics: what it means to work, and how the nature of our provisioning systems influences the kinds of people we are, and how happy we are.

This book is not the kind where you have nine chapters of critique and then a final chapter that sketches out a rough blueprint of a better world. Instead, it is a self-consciously utopian enterprise: an attempt to produce a plan for a sustainable and just economy. However, this is also a book that keeps an academic audience in mind, so I will argue my theory with as much rigour as I can muster, and I will present statistical evidence to support my case where this is available. I do not, however, necessarily accept that evidence, especially numerical evidence, is the only type of information that is relevant either in making an intellectual case or in academic learning and teaching. It is not possible to produce evidence to support the superiority of a world that does not yet exist; hence the recent exclusive focus on 'evidence-based policy-making' is in itself a conservative play (Levitas, 2010). Utopian thinking creates the possibility of imagining and achieving different and better worlds. This should not mean that it has no place in intellectual life and in the teaching of our young people; in fact, I would argue quite the reverse.

I use evidence where it is available, but I also unashamedly use the tools of argument and persuasion. In bioregional discourse the word 'home' has a particular resonance and one of my academic papers on the theme defines the bioregional economy as a system of 'home economics'. In English, 'home' is a word for which it is difficult to uncover negative connotations, no matter how dysfunctional families can sometimes be. Home is a place of safety. It is, famously, where the heart is and where charity begins. It is also, I believe, where a strategy for sustainable and secure provisioning begins.

1.1. Finding our place in space

The turning of a millennium brings us up short. After 2,000 years in our calendar even the most prosaic of us cannot help reflecting about the advances and failings of our species, the most reflexive that has yet evolved on this planet. As self-conscious social beings we are aware of these major historical breaks, even if the calendar that we use to mark them is our own construction imposed on a natural system that is cyclical rather than linear. It is in this context that I would like to place the extraordinary outburst of enthusiasm and hubris that is globalisation. What else could have persuaded us to accept such clearly mythical notions as 'the weightless economy' (Quah, 1999; Perraton, 2006) and the idea that we could somehow adopt a timeless, spaceless lifestyle? The high priest of financialised capitalism himself described the continued boom in global stock markets around the millennium as 'irrational exuberance' (Greenspan, 1996). To remind yourself of this time of supreme (and misplaced) confidence I would suggest that you read Thomas Friedman's book *The World is Flat*, a last-century paean to fossil-fuelled globalisation, whose very title suggests the loss of reality that accompanied our movement from the twentieth to twenty-first centuries, and then compare it with his later book, *Hot, Flat and Crowded*, written just three years later. Here we find Friedman coming down to earth with a bump after the millennial party at the end of the universe. This is a difficult transition and – like many who were both adherents and proponents of the hegemonic two-dimensioned myth of finance capitalism and the weightless economy – Friedman has moved rapidly to denial by now seeking, as he repeats countless times 'a free, cheap, renewable source of electrons' to make possible the continuation of his lifestyle in a climate-changed world.

Our attempt to escape our earthbound natures and live in the weightless, spaceless world of our shared imaginings was temporarily rather thrilling, but ultimately disappointing and inherently unsatisfying. Its dominance in western economies was accompanied by higher rates of mental illness than had previously been recorded (Angell, 2011). The establishment economist Richard Layard took up green economist Richard Douthwaite's (1992) theme that growth was 'an illusion' in the sense that, while apparently bringing more, after a certain level of development it actually reversed its munificence and ceased increasing our happiness, perhaps because it brought in its wake social consequences that we do not welcome: crime, family breakdown and environmental destruction, to name just three examples (Layard, 2006). Perhaps the source of this mental dis-ease can be found in the requirement of those who inhabit the weightless economy to indulge in permanent cognitive dissonance.

It is possible, in hindsight, to see the irrational exuberance that characterised the closing of the twentieth century, with its 'end of history' and other celebratory capitalist myths as a form of mass psychosis. We are living in two parallel worlds: one where we have never had it so good and human civilisation has reached an apotheosis of success where no further advance is possible; and another where we are confronted daily with evidence of the negative consequences of this same system for those in the poorer countries of the South, for other species and for our planet. Mary Mellor likens this denial of the negative consequences of our way of life to Dorian Gray's ability to ignore the painting hidden in his attic, which bears the marks of his dissolute lifestyle (Mellor, 2006).

A bioregionalist would argue that this sickness has arisen from our dislocation from physical reality. Their response to this mass delusion might be to replace its central ideas with more realistic ones: to be, in Doreen Massey's words, 'for space', or in the words of the bioregionalists, 'for place'. Gary Snyder has argued, 'Bioregionalism is the entry of place into the dialectic of history' (Snyder, 1990: 44), and while this flourish betrays his poetical origins it also suggests the importance of relocating ourselves in geographical reality.

The disconnection of people from their places is not a new process, and can be linked to the rise of capitalism as an economic system. The evidence that this is the case is not only found in the historical data relating to the mass movements of people from their small, rural communities into urban conurbations where they staffed the factories (Polanyi, 1944). It is also in the first question that is asked in many social situations: 'What do you do?' (Beck, 1992). In capitalist societies your survival depends on your work and your primary identity is in many cases also derived from it. The connection of identity with occupation (rather than place of origin) helps to explain why unemployment is so devastating even in societies where payments are made to provide for basic needs.

Some societies still retain the identification of person with place: in Welsh, for example, an initial question is often *O ble wyt ti'n dod yn wreiddiol?* (Where do you come from originally?). Part of the appeal of the bioregional economy is that it would make this question meaningful again. People would once again find a pride in place and a source of identity in the others they share that place with. This is one purpose of the book, then: to reconsider the nature of human life as a life spent in a place, in the context of economics. The bioregional economy is also an attempt to take forward the discussion around the importance of the resilient local economies that are often proposed as a solution to our problem with energy and the environment. The case for a more local view of provisioning has been strongly and repeatedly made (Douthwaite, 1996; Hines, 2000; Cato, 2009), and yet we still lack an answer to the questions that logically follow: how local is a local economy? How much of what we consume would be produced there? How would relationships between these local economies be mediated? As well as these questions, I consider what the impact of the transition to such a relocalised world might *feel* like – how it would affect our sense of identity, our relationships with each other and with the natural world.

So what is a bioregion? According to Sale:

> It is any part of the earth's surface whose rough boundaries are determined by natural characteristics rather than human dictates, distinguishable from other areas by particular attributes of flora, fauna, water, climate, soils, and landform, and by the human settlements and cultures those attributes have given rise to.
>
> *(Sale, 1991: 55).*

The intellectual move the bioregionalists make, then, is to challenge a world where the physical divisions of space we use for political decision-making and for the implementation of policy, are determined by human understanding, and to replace them with boundaries that are determined by natural systems, whether these relate to landforms and watersheds (topographical and hydrological delineation), or to the other species we share the planet with. With our notions of the 'global supermarket' and the 'weightless world' we have strayed from this natural system of habitation that was once typical of the interaction between the human species and the environment. Our present conception is that it makes no difference where you live: whatever the earth had to offer could be yours 24 hours a day, 365 days a year. The perceived limit is money, but as I will argue throughout this book, the insight of green economics is that, in reality, it is energy that is the real limit.

This globalisation view also relies on particular assumptions about the ownership of the earth's resources and how these are allocated. Our ability to buy Brazilian limes in November not only relies on abundant sources of energy but also on hard currency. The system that determines that countries like the UK and US have access to that currency and that Brazil will accept it in return for limes is not generally questioned, but in fact it raises fundamental moral concerns about the sharing of the value of global production. Indeed, rather than the same land being used to grow food for Brazilian citizens, it is being used to grow an export crop. It is beyond the scope of this book to engage in detailed theoretical argument about the way the value of natural resources is shared, but the distribution of per capita incomes on a global basis makes it plain that living in a country richly endowed with the resources that, together with labour, create value in the marketplace, does not guarantee you any particular share in the value that has been created: some of the world's wealthiest countries in resource terms are also some of its poorest in terms of living standards. A bioregional approach to economics would radically change these political-economic systems.

A consideration of the huge differences in wealth levels across nations, shocking though they are, is entirely anthropocentric. The most devastating consequences of our economic activity are being felt by other species as their habitats are destroyed and their resources are extracted for human consumption. Together with the rehabilitation of naturally defined geographical spaces, bioregionalism requires a radical reconceptualisation of community and the inclusion of other species as constitutive of a bioregional community:

> This larger community includes, along with the humans, the multiple nonhuman entities that constitute the local landscape, from the diverse plants and the myriad animals – birds, mammals, fish, reptiles, insects – that inhabit or migrate through the region, to the particular winds and weather patterns that inform the local geography; as well as the various landforms – forests, rivers, caves, mountains – that lend their specific character to the surrounding earth.
>
> *(Abram, 1996: 6–7)*

Abram continues his description of the bioregional ethic as one in which a fundamental respect for the earth inheres:

> Each place has its own mind, its own psyche. Oak, madrone, Douglas fir, red-tailed hawk, serpentine in the sandstone, a certain scale to the topography, drenching rains in the winter, fog off-shore in the summer, salmon surging in the streams – all these together make up a particular state of mind, a place-specific intelligence shared by all the humans that dwell therein, but also by the coyotes yapping in those valleys, by the bobcats and the ferns and the spiders, by all beings who live and make their way in that zone. Each place has its own psyche. Each sky its own blue.
>
> *(Abram, 1996: 262)*

Such writing verges on animism, and might be uncomfortable to academic readers. However, it is important to my argument to consider the impact such a deep sense of identification might impart to a new consumption ethic, which a bioregional economy might engender. It is also important to identify at this early stage that as part of this ethic the bioregionalist accepts that rational discourse is only one way in which human beings interact with each other and with their environment. As demonstrated by the quotation from Abram, part of the project of bioregionalism is to rehabilitate the intuitive and spiritual aspects of human life, in terms of understanding, public debate and policy-making.

1.2. Where did we go wrong?

While we are not short of lengthy and detailed reports and academic papers detailing the crises we find ourselves in, concrete propositions are becoming increasingly rare, especially amongst academics books, and we seem remarkably bereft of big ideas. In these pages I seek unashamedly to fill the gap. Replacing opposition with proposition will make me vulnerable to attack, of course, but vulnerability is one of many admirable human qualities that are in urgent need of rehabilitation, so I am prepared to take my chances. The intent of this book is to be propositional, not oppositional. However, I must begin by outlining the crisis of our economic system, what we might dare to call the crisis of capitalism. The threats to human life on earth are many, as we move into the twenty-first century, but they are all aspects of one crisis: the crisis that arises from our inability to live satisfied human lives within the boundaries set by nature.

I choose to begin my discussion of the crisis in what might be considered an unlikely spot: the Millennium Ecosystem Assessment, which used evidence and argument to conclude that:

> The changes that have been made to ecosystems have contributed to substantial net gains in human well-being and economic development, but these gains have been achieved at growing costs in the form of the degradation of many ecosystem services, increased risks of non-linear changes, and the exacerbation of poverty for some groups of people. These problems, unless addressed, will substantially diminish the benefits that future generations obtain from ecosystems.
>
> *(Millennium Ecosystem Assessment, 2005: 1)*

It is difficult to argue with the concept of an ecosystem assessment. It is a rational and evidence-based approach and yet it is simultaneously disgusting. My disgust cannot be counted, whereas the ecosystem assessors can put a price on the value of pollination 'services' at £430m. per year to the UK economy. An exercise that is supposed to convince me that nature is now being properly valued in fact does the reverse. Nature is being commodified so that the continuing process of trade in nature's bounty can continue at an accelerated pace. We can make more or less sophisticated arguments on this point (and some of the best are being made by Sian Sullivan (2010), but we will always be talking past one another. We are living in two separate paradigms: one where something is not valued unless it is costed; and the other where the most important aspects of life are priceless. A rational debate is not going to resolve this disagreement.

Environmental economists argue that the reason we are destroying our environment is that it does not have a market value. However, this argument seems to be undermined by the fact that the environments they would buy and sell, those that are not, as yet, destroyed, lie in parts of the world where the market form of economic activity is not dominant—perhaps most obviously the Amazon rainforest. Attempts to create a market exchange between those who seek trees to absorb their excessive carbon emissions and those whose environments are available to them in exchange for cash, for example under the Clean Development Mechanism, have met with only limited success in development terms (Disch, 2010), but have provided opportunities for better informed entrepreneurs to profit, sometimes at the expense of those living sustainable lifestyles and at the expense of their environments (Lohman, 2006).

Similarly, many of the world's poorer people continue to live in a co-operative relationship with their land, and it is in these areas that environments are surviving better than they are in the industrialised nations. Such people have better retained a sense of their dependence on natural systems, which more highly sophisticated civilisations believe themselves to have transcended:

> Indigenous people believe that if they cause harm to nature, then they will themselves come to harm, whether it is speaking without respect of certain animals, or whether it is overfishing a lake or hunting out a certain type of animal. This is something that we in the industrialized world have lost, and perhaps need to remember.
>
> *(Pretty, 2007: 159)*

But as environmental pressures increase, subsistence farmers in the world's poorer nations are threatened with displacement and loss of livelihood as their land is traded to provide carbon sinks and other 'ecosystem services' for the peoples of the richer world. (Norberg-Hodge, 2009)

The reason I begin my critique here, with the attempt to put a price on nature, is because it is the relationship between our human community and the resources the earth provides that enables its survival which is the heart of what an economy is about. The process of ecosystem assessment exemplifies the nature of the relationship at present: it is a market relationship, dominated by the human species and underpinned by principles of private ownership: '"Nature", it would seem, has become simply a stock of "resources" for human civilization' (Abram, 1996: 28). The market analogy is the hegemonic principle of our time: it is for this reason that Foucault identified political economy as the 'major form of knowledge' and within a liberal, bourgeois order the dominant ideology is one of 'economic truth' (Foucault, 2007; 2008). As Barry develops the theme, 'This naturalising of the market is of course not simply a way of empowering this economic order, but also crucially depoliticises the capitalist market and its relations and identities/subjectivities, thus effectively removing it from any critique which could potentially lead to its replace-ment or radical restructuring' (Barry, 2012: Ch. 4). The market is assumed and all problems must be translated into a market form before they can be solved.

Yet, in this era where policy should respond to evidence, where is the evidence that the spread of the market has protected the natural world? The past three decades have seen the market extended into all corners of the globe and all sectors of the globalised economy, and in parallel it has seen us achieve record-breaking rates of environmental destruction, threatening our very survival as a species. When Stern identified climate change as the 'greatest market failure of all time' (Stern, 2007) he was reinforcing the dominance of the market model: it would simply have been impossible for him to draw the much more obvious conclusion that the market itself was a failure.

The evidence that the widening reach of the market has exacerbated environ-mental problems is widespread and growing. Some of the most horrifying statistics and statements drawn from this large evidence-base are presented in Table 1.1. There is no need to emphasise these statistics since we are all aware of them. Our time would be better spent exploring how the economic system we live within is responsible for these destructive effects, and what sort of economic structures would enable us to live harmoniously on this planet. We are not short of evidence; what we are short of is an alternative model and the political courage to achieve it.

The data speak for themselves, but I will briefly consider one of the many crises in slightly greater depth: the crisis involving our most vital resource of water. Jeffrey Sachs sets the scene:

> Much of the world today is already in a water crisis … In many parts of the world we have exceeded sustainable limits on the withdrawals of water from groundwater aquifers and from rivers. The overuse of groundwater, at a rate much faster than the aquifers are recharged, is a pervasive problem, including in some of the most populous parts of the world.
>
> *(Sachs, 2008: 121–22).*

Sachs points to widespread irrigation and vast dam projects as two examples of what once appeared technological miracles but are now seen to have created the most fundamental ecological problem in terms of human survival on planet earth. According to United Nations (UN) figures, 1.4 billion people now live in 'closed' river basins, where use exceeds recharge, and these riversheds include the Yellow River in China, the Murray-Darling basin in Australia and southern Africa's Orange River.

TABLE 1.1. Indicators of ecological stress

Fisheries	85% of the world's fish stocks either fully exploited or over-exploited
Water	By 2025, 1.8 billion people will be living in countries or regions with absolute water scarcity
Forest loss	Expanded by 25% between 1990 and 2005
Species loss	The current extinction rate is between 1,000 and 10,000 times higher than the natural rate
Topsoil	285m. of total 1,500m. ha. lost between 1985 and 2000
Nitrogen Cycle	Human activities now contribute more (210m. tonnes) to the global supply of fixed nitrogen each year than natural processes do (140m. tonnes)
Coral reefs	75% of the world's reefs are threatened
Peak Oil	Most of the biggest oil fields have already peaked and the rate of decline in oil production is now running at nearly twice the pace calculated in 2007
Climate Change	Likelihood of significant warming already occurring at the continental scale in North America, Europe and Australia; medium confidence that some regions of the world have experienced more intense and longer droughts

Sources: Fisheries: Food and Agricultural Organization (2010), *The State of the World Fisheries and Aquaculture* (Rome: FAO); Water: FAO, Land and Water Division: http://www.fao.org/nr/water/issues/scarcity.html; Forest loss: Mongabay; Species Loss: International Union for the Conservation of Nature; Topsoil: University of Michigan's Global Change Program; Nitrogen Cycle: Gregory P. Asner, Timothy R. Seastedt, and Alan R. Townsend, 'The Decoupling of Terrestrial Carbon and Nitrogen Cycles: Human Influences on Land Cover and Nitrogen Supply Are Altering Natural Biogeochemical Links in the Biosphere,' *BioScience*, Vol.47, No. 4 (1997), p. 232; Coral Reefs: Burke, L., Reytar, K., Spalding, M. and Perry, A. (2011), *Reefs at Risk Revisited* (Washington, DC: World Resources Institute); Peak Oil: International Energy Agency, Paris, reported in Connor, 2009; Climate Change: IPCC Fifth Assessment Report, WGI.

The link between water and conflict is clear in some of the leading 'hot spots': the Sahel, the Horn of Africa, Israel–Palestine, Pakistan and Central Asia, the Indo-Gangetic Plains, The North China Plain, the US Southwest, and the Murray-Darling Basin.

I focus on this particularly because bioregionalists tend to define their bioregion in terms of waterways. While we may think of bioregional values as reconnecting people to land, the places they intend to reinhabit are often defined in terms of watersheds (Carr, 2004). As we will see in Chapter 8, a bioregional approach to economics raises questions about who owns the resources of our local places, and might have much to offer a world where it is possible for the land and water that are necessary for the basic survival of billions of people to fall into the hands of the executives of a dozen or so corporations.

1.3. We have taken leave of our senses

The central purpose of this chapter is to convince the reader that the human species is in peril, and that the economic system is deeply implicated in the threat to our future. Any academic or intellectual living in the early years of the twenty-first century lives with this horrifying prospect as a daily reality. Those of us who work in relevant fields (which now means almost all of us) are forced, by the conventions of our disciplines, to divorce ourselves from the emotional and spiritual consequences of this knowledge in order to do our work. Such a conflicted approach to intellectual work is nothing new: Darwin was famously a devout Christian. Yet surely the degree of effort required to exclude all emotional reaction from one's writing about the devastation of one's planet and the end of one's species is unprecedented, and perhaps intrinsically dishonest.

Paul Feyerabend, scourge of the methodological community and child of the 1960s, takes the phrase 'accept nothing; question everything' to its *logical* conclusion. In the manuscript called *The Conquest of Abundance*, which was left unfinished at the time of his death, he suggested that it may be our habit for analysing the world that has reduced our ability to show reverence and wonder. It has thus in a fundamental way limited our perception of the abundance of nature.

> Variety disappears when subjected to scholarly analysis. This is not the fault of scholars. Anyone who tries to make sense of a puzzling sequence of events, her or his own actions included, is forced to introduce ideas that are not in the events themselves, but put them in perspective … There is no escape: understanding a subject means transforming it, lifting it out of a natural habitat and inserting it into a model or a theory or a poetic account of it. But one transformation may be better than another in the sense that it permits or even explains what for the other transformation remains an unsolvable puzzle.
>
> *(Feyerabend, 2011: 12)*

Feyerabend develops his theme by exploring the point at which Greek culture underwent a shift from the mysterious, poetic understandings of Homeric times to the intellectually impressive mind-games of logic, evidence and proof. You might argue that this is the first step along the road that has led us to evidence-based policy-making and the impossibility of making anything change unless you can show that position B is better in terms of something measurable (and probably in money terms) than position A. In this world we cannot save hummingbirds unless they have a financial value, and hence they, and a thousand other species, must either pay their way or they are doomed.

Feyerabend describes how Socrates was concerned that the advent of writing would cause us to lose our memories, an interesting parallel to contemporary concerns about the impact on our cognition of computer-based technologies (Swain, 2011). Abram identifies the movement from oral to literary culture as a point of abstraction from our inherent connection with the earth:

> Alphabetic writing can engage the human senses only to the extent that those senses sever, at least provisionally, their spontaneous participation with the animate earth. To begin to read, alphabetically, is thus already to be dis-placed, cut off from the sensory nourishment of a more-than-human field of forms. It is also, however, to feel the still-lingering savor of that nourishment, and so to yearn, to hope, that such contact and conviviality may someday return.
>
> *(Abram, 1996: 196)*

Money is a similar abstraction, but this time in the field of material rather than spiritual value. Since its earliest days there has been a confusion about whether money was intrinsically valuable (because of being made of a precious metal, for example), or acquired its value thanks to a political or military authority, as in the phrase *fiat* money: money that is created at the behest of the ruler (Davies, 1997). Some forms of money are intellectually linked to particular resources, as in the derivation of the words *ariam* in Wales (from silver) and *argent* in French from the Latin word for silver. Our own pound sterling is apparently etymologically derived from the barrels of Easterling herrings, which formed the basis of trade in London (Black, 1997). However, these are exceptions that prove the general rule that money is an abstract form of value underpinned by political power. This fact has become particularly obvious since the 2008 crash but it is nothing new, as demonstrated by the massive stones called *Rai* used as a form of money by Yap people of Micronesia (Mellor, 2010). Of course this form of abstraction is particularly important to our theme since it has conspired in the abstraction of economic values from sources of natural wealth and hence supported the shift from provisioning to market economies.

My object here is rather to question the nature of argument that is appropriate. To choose, as a human community, to limit our decision-making capacity to that which can be justified rationally, and by preference statistically, is to exclude from discussion those aspects of life that we most value. We have made ourselves captive to the auditor, the accountant, the taxonomist. According to the division of the natural world created by the master taxonomist Linnaeus we are *Homo sapiens*. This tells us much about our post-Enlightenment self-image as a species, and perhaps some of the assumptions we need to challenge if we are to be a species with a flourishing future to match our glorious past. To what extent being a species that focuses so exclusively on one gender is a question that intrigues others. I am more interested in the 'sapiens' part of this formulation. Such a characterisation accords with our exaltation of the intellect, since 'sapiens' is usually translated as knowing. However, an alternative derivation suggests that it is actually from 'sapere', to be wise or to taste. To think of ourselves as a species that tastes the richness of life and does so with true appreciation seems to offer us a better hope than any amount of numerical analyses.

To question the exaltation of rationality and to rediscover and celebrate our human propensity for myth is a popular theme in bioregional writing. Kirkpatrick Sale is critical of the dominance of the very sort of strategy for mediation of the world that Feyerabend considers leads to 'the conquest of abundance', challenging 'the celebration of the mechanical, the tangible, the quantifiable, the utilitarian, the linear, and the divisible, as against the organic, the spiritual, the incalculable, the mysterious, the circular, and the holistic' (Sale, 1991: 19). This is not an attack on the scientific method *per se*, and indeed many proponents of bioregionalism are themselves ecological or biological scientists, but rather a concern to keep science in its proper place and to acknowledge that other modes of comprehension are equally valid. Like Feyerabend, Sale argues that the supreme role accorded to scientific conceptions of reality has diminished our sense of the mysterious power of life:

> The new [scientific] perception held – better than that, it proved – that the earth, the universe beyond it, and all within it operated according to certain clear, calculable, and unchanging laws, not by the whims of any living, sentient being. It showed that these laws were, far from being divinely created or spiritually inspired, capable of mundane scientific measurement, prediction, and replication, even scientific manipulation and control.
>
> *(Sale, 1991: 16)*

The power of this scientific method was such that it became hegemonic, and was even applied in areas where it could only generate category errors, as in Francis Galton's 'Statistical Enquiries into the Efficacy of Prayer' (Galton, 1872).

To call for rehabilitation of the intuitive aspects of human thinking is, therefore, not to undermine the importance of science, but rather to recognise its limits and to acknowledge the important role that myth, the argument of the intuitive mind, has always played in the advance of human culture. Myth is as central to our human culture as reason:

> Not to take myth seriously in the life of an ostensibly 'disenchanted' culture like our own is actually to impoverish our understanding of our shared world. And it is also to concede the subject by default to those who have no critical distance from it at all, who apprehend myth not as a historical phenomenon but as an unchallengeable and perennial mystery. As the great Talmudist Saul Liberman said when he introduced Gershom Scholem's lectures on the Kabbalah … Nonsense (when all is said and done) is still nonsense. But the study of nonsense, that is science.
>
> *(Schama, 2004: 134)*

For all our advanced statistics we are still subject to myths, but these myths are now implicit rather than explicit, which makes them both more powerful and more dangerous. Three interrelated myths are particularly relevant to the themes of this book: the myth of economism, the myth of the machine and the myth of the market.

A significant achievement of the bioregional movement is to combine the scientific understanding (which, after all, first gave rise to their concerns for the ecological crisis that their measurement tools were making them aware of) with a critical account of the inappropriate use of some of the metaphors that science has generated. McGinnis identifies the ubiquity of machine-imagery, especially in terms of the discourse of economics: 'Economic rationality opposes an organic life-producing view of natural systems and favors a vision of nature-as-machine that is economy-producing. The machine lacks self-sustaining, sacramental and life-giving properties.' (McGinnis, 1999: 65). Mary Midgley links the machine imagery to the conception of the economy as a system beyond human devising and human control:

> Another striking example today is the neo-Darwinist picture – now extremely influential – of evolution as essentially a simple projection of the money market.

> Here the noisy rhetoric of *selfishness, spite, exploitation, manipulation, investment, insurance* and *war-games* easily persuades people that this new form of Victorian social-atomist ideology must be true because it has the support of science.
>
> *(Midgley, 2002: 173)*

She is not alone in considering how the way economics thinks about itself is important in defining its power; nor in interpreting much of the way economists make their case as including elements of myth-making. In a critique of mainstream economic theory from the perspective of ecological economics, Kallis and colleagues characterise 'the myths of economism' as follows:

> Let us distinguish between an economy that is 'out there' and the complex of myths that people, both individually and in order to act together, have developed to aid them in living within the economy. This distinction is roughly parallel to nature as reality of its own and the complex myths traditional people hold about nature and their relation to nature. In traditional societies, myths provide explanations for natural phenomena, facilitate individual and collective decisions, and give meaning and coherence to life. As people act on their myths, their societies and the natural environment are shaped and co-evolved around them ... As modern people, we also act on comparable beliefs about our world (a world that is largely economic), that are rooted in the discipline of economics. We refer to this complex of myths as economism, and like traditional beliefs and scientific understanding, economism explains phenomena, facilitates individual and collective decisions, and gives meaning and coherence to our lives.
>
> *(Kallis et al., 2009: 18–19)*

The authors provide two insights that are supportive of my argument. First, that myths have power, and they guide human behaviour. While this is a basic understanding in the anthropological literature (as in the myth of the birdman in the ecologically challenged Easter Islands, or the cargo cults that replaced traditional religions in Pacific societies encountering more technologically advanced cultures), it is, according to Kallis *et al.*., equally true of our intellectually sophisticated, post-Enlightenment society. Second, they contend that the dominant myth of our culture is what they term 'economism', a suggestion that implies both the centrality and the hegemonic nature of the worldview of economics. (They do not make this explicit but they are referring here to neoclassical economics.)

Norgaard (another ecological economist) gives his own interpretation of economism in a paper that questions the deep dislocation from the natural world, which a myth of economism has given rise to:

> Let me expand on the term 'economism' (belief in the primacy of economics) by distinguishing between actual economic activity and the complex of myths we have developed that sustains our trust in the economy and makes it possible to keep it functioning – possible to keep people, capital, and land working

together. This distinction is parallel to the one between nature as a reality of its own and the complex of myths traditional peoples held about nature and their relation to it. Just as traditional myths provide explanations for natural phenomena, facilitate individual and collective decisions, and give meaning and coherence to life, so do modern beliefs about economics and the economy, in similar ways, make meaningful, coordinated life in industrial society possible.

(Norgaard, 2011)

Myths about the provisioning of resources are nothing new. In fact, as we will see in Chapter 3, the creation and maintenance of these myths has always formed part of the role in society that is now filled by economists. It is in its self-portrayal as an objective, rational endeavour that economics has done something radically new, and in its exclusive identification of its place in the scientific realm.

Yet economics, in spite of its protestations, is itself profoundly pre-scientific. The so-called 'laws' of economics were invented before some of the most basic laws governing the functioning of the universe – the laws of thermodynamics – were known. Although ecological and green economists may rail against neoclassical economists for their inability to understand the need to limit energy use, they are operating in a world where there is no requirement to accept that matter cannot be created from thin air, or that perpetual motion machines are a scientific impossibility. These points, first made by Georgescu-Roegen (1971) and expanded by his student Herman Daly, are at once both a devastating critique of mainstream economics as a science, and an explanation for its inability to be compatible with a stable life within this universe. In Chapter 9 we will come to see what a truly scientific analysis of an economic system looks like, and how it might influence policy.

In this era of ecological crisis, economists have much to learn from science, particularly from the science of energy, from ecology and from systems science. The concept of entropy could be particularly useful. Howard Odum (2001), perhaps the most scientific of those who have contributed to a green view of economics, attempted to measure energy flows through systems in order to provide for human needs with minimal disruption to natural systems. This, he believed, would facilitate an economic system that was life-enhancing rather than life-destroying, in accordance with Erwin Schrodinger's definition of life as 'that which attracts "a stream of negative entropy to itself, to compensate the entropy increase it produces by living, and thus to maintain itself on a stationary and fairly low entropy level"' (Sale, 1991: 190). While it has taken us several hundred years of elaborate experimentation and deep thought to realise the lessons of science, civilisations we might consider primitive have lived in this way for millennia:

Such cultures, much smaller in scale (and far less centralized) than modern Western civilization, seem to have maintained a relatively homeostatic or equilibrial relation with their local ecologies for vast periods of time, deriving their necessary sustenance from the land without seriously disrupting the ability of the earth to replenish itself.

(Abram, 1996: 94)

1.4. Conclusion: re-enchanting the world

The purpose of this chapter has been to raise an alert about the threats to our human community that arise from an economy that is growing out of control. While it is not my task to establish new myths to guide the future development of the economy, I have at least challenged some of those that pervade the current thinking of most economists, and the policy-makers they advise. These myths are important because 'our ideas about our place in the world pervade all our thought, along with the imagery that expresses them, constantly determining what questions we ask and what answers can seem possible' (Midgley, 2002: 173). The ecological crisis makes the ending of economic growth inevitable (Jackson, 2009) and we are therefore seeking new visions in which to ground our economic realities: 'Now is the moment to generate new social visions of living well and being happy without the imperative of economic growth. Visions that render compatible living well, working satisfactorily and maintaining our local and global ecosystems' (Kallis *et al.*, 2009: 22).

While it is scientific evidence that has led us to the realisation of the need for change, we will need deeper human wisdom to construct an alternative model for a provisioning system. Max Weber is respected for his sociological critique of capitalism as an economic system and in particular for the connection he described between the spiritual and ethical foundation on which the economic superstructure is based. In *The Protestant Ethic and the Spirit of Capitalism*, Weber describes how the qualities required by the Puritan sects – sobriety, thrift, and diligence – were exactly the characteristics that made successful capitalist enterprise possible. In particular, the inability of successful businesspeople to indulge themselves in material luxury facilitated the accumulation of capital for reinvestment in the business. Weber's critique involved what he called, quoting the German poet Schiller, 'the disenchantment of the world'.[1]

This disenchantment, or removal of magic from everyday life, worked at two different levels: internally it meant the divorce of people from their spiritual connection with the natural world. God was no longer manifest in creation but became a wholly transcendent, other-worldly creature. The process thus also involved a change in the nature of our relationship with a sense of place in space, together with the objectification of our sense of self, and the creation of linear time, with the consequences for the sort of meaning we could assign to our limited human lives. The external expression of this rationalist approach was the growth in bureaucracy and the scientistic and economistic worldview that predominates in our modern culture. Thus it was a system of myths, the Christian myths of the Protestants, that led us to view our world as concrete, material and external, and to view ourselves as cogs in a divinely inspired but not inherently divine machine (Balcomb, 2009). These myths have been instrumental in shaping an economy that follows this machine myth and that is increasingly divorced from the natural world. A bioregional approach to economics has the reversal of this process of objectification, disconnection and disenchantment as central to its project.

This removal of the sacramental from the physical world has been devastating for our relationship with what is now called, scientifically and with apparent absence of reverence, 'the environment'. We now see life as a series of chance events, rather than having a deeper meaning and for many of our leading thinkers, science itself has become their closest experience of religion (Midgley, 1985). Foremost among the leaders of this scientific revolution that followed the industrial revolution in England was Francis Galton, cousin to Charles Darwin and a man with a claim to be the inventor of statistics. Figure 1.1 illustrates his quincunx, a physical demonstration of his understanding of the world as governed by chance. The physical quincunx is like a child's bagatelle game, with a series of nails in a wooden board. When a ball is put in at the top it bounces off each nail and, by a random process, ends up in a certain position at the bottom. Galton used this to illustrate the way that discrete, random events combine to produce patterned and therefore predictable outcomes, a view of the world that has resonances of both the Protestant theories of providence and the benevolent and yet invisible hand of the perfect market. From the quincunx grew the binomial and then the normal distribution, the basis of all the regression methods so beloved of neoclassical economists and policy-makers. The quincunx, and the statistical system of thinking it gave rise to, provided reassurance in a world where religious conviction was breaking down; that there was still order – and perhaps meaning – in the random and apparently aimless sequence of events that made up our lives.

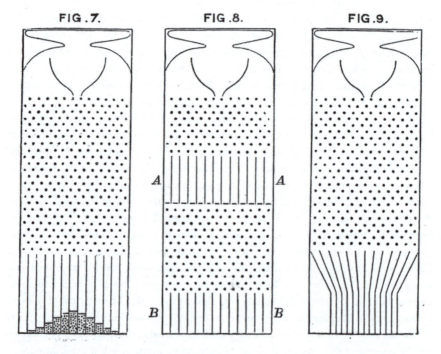

FIGURE 1.1 Francis Galton's quincunx
Source: This image is made available without copyright restriction by Wikimedia Commons.

Following hard on the heels of the statistician arrives the actuary, who can translate the statistical probability into financial terms. Insurance, which began its life as a socially embedded form of shared risk, provided by a 'Friendly Society', has now become a matter of risk calculations and a thin financial transaction. The inability of the industry to sell us the peace of mind it promises seems to be the obverse of the category error evident in Galton's paper about 'the efficacy of prayer'.[2] Similarly, the frustration of contemporary academics at their human subjects' inability to respond to risks in a calmly rational way (Adams, 1995) illustrates the continuing force of irrationality and superstition within the outwardly modern citizen. Determining whether it is the health and safety officer or the citizen who has 'gone mad' would take a different kind of study than that Galton was engaged in. Our inability to behave as rational utility-maximising agents may be frustrating for economists and policymakers, but I find it reassuring that we have not succumbed to the ways of modernity; rather we cling to our superstitious ways, whether these emerge in the form of the car-parking angel or the urban myth. I am less sanguine about urban myths that masquerade as science, such as the belief that human ingenuity will find a technological solution to climate change.

I will return to this argument in Chapter 3, where I address the role that an economist should have in a sustainable economy, and suggest that it would involve an inherent ethical, if not spiritual, dimension. I will end this chapter by considering how we might use our myth-making skills to our advantage in the days of transition that lie ahead. The prevalence of 'urban myths' and their rapid spread indicates how we build and reinforce our communities through stories. The most powerful British myth is one that is likely to prove useful in the times of change that lie ahead: the myth of the blitz. This is a myth that both constitutes and reinforces the kind of community spirit that is listed as a key factor in resilience by no less an authority than the US Homeland Security agency (Cutter *et al.*, 2010). Another is the Spitfire myth, which is frequently used by those campaigning for community responses to climate change to exemplify the way in which, in the period leading up to conflict with Germany in 1939, British politicians were in denial about the impending conflict. This left the country unprepared, particularly in terms of its lack of a skilful fighter plane. The Spitfire was designed and built by private citizens and saved the country in the Battle of Britain. In a similar way, the activists see themselves as building an alternative system of life that can survive the oil shocks and catastrophic weather events that they believe we will encounter as a human society over the next few decades.

And finally, I will share my own favourite story: the story of the Eddystone Lighthouse. The Eddystone Rocks were a danger to shipping off the Devon coast but the local storms were so ferocious that the first two designs of tower were rapidly destroyed. Between 1756 and 1759 John Smeaton produced a lighthouse whose basic design followed that of the oak tree, which is famously able to withstand forceful winds in spite of its bulk. He combined this observation and respect for nature with his own ingenious inventions of hydraulic lime (that could set under water) and hefty joints. The lighthouse protected shipping for well over a century until it had to be dismantled, not because its design proved weak but because the rocks it stood on had been undermined. The foundations were so solid they still stand next to the modern lighthouse on the site. Smeaton's tower was reconstructed on Plymouth Hoe as a beacon of hope, testament to the ability of the human species to work in partnership with nature.

In this chapter I have argued that the scientific evidence of the threats posed by our current economic system oblige us to rethink our relationship with the earth. In the field of economics the demand is that we reorder our provisioning systems so that they are compatible with a limited biosphere. In this context the most powerful myth that we need to challenge is the myth of freedom. This is often repeated in response to suggestions from green and ecological economists that we need to impose limits to growth, that the economy simply cannot be allowed to continue to grow, and that the ecological crisis provides evidence that we have already reached – perhaps sur-passed – ecological limits. The response is that to argue thus is to infringe human freedom, even that the right to own a car or take a foreign holiday is a human right. (The best recent example in this genre is Ben-Ami, 2010.)

This myth is not only destructive but misguided. It confuses freedom with licence; it suggests that limits are not a natural part of human existence, most obviously of course the inevitable limit of a human life-course. Bioregional thinking rejects this myth and replaces it with a challenge: the challenge of 'flourishing within limits' (Jackson, 2009). In other contexts modern citizens are prepared to see limits as a challenge to creativity rather than a restriction on the human right to always have more: take the example of the 140-character limit of the Tweet. The 17-syllable limit of the traditional Japanese haiku offers a similar challenge for poets to capture a complex meaning in a short verse that can be highly emotionally charged. In the Western poetic tradition the sonnet provides a similar creative opportunity and so I will close this chapter with an example from the romantic poet William Wordsworth, who certainly maximises its utility:

> Nuns fret not at their convent's narrow room;
> And hermits are contented with their cells;
> And students with their pensive citadels;
> Maids at the wheel, the weaver at his loom,
> Sit blithe and happy; bees that soar for bloom,
> High as the highest Peak of Furness-fells,
> Will murmur by the hour in foxglove bells:
> In truth the prison, unto which we doom
> Ourselves, no prison is: and hence for me,
> In sundry moods, 'twas pastime to be bound
> Within the Sonnet's scanty plot of ground;
> Pleased if some Souls (for such there needs must be)
> Who have felt the weight of too much liberty,
> Should find brief solace there, as I have found.

2

VISIONING THE BIOREGIONAL ECONOMY

> The little nations of the past lived within territories that conformed to some set of natural criteria ... That older human experience of a fluid, indistinct, but genuine home region was gradually replaced – across Eurasia – by the arbitrary and often violently imposed boundaries of emerging nation states.
>
> (Gary Snyder, *The Practice of the Wild*, p. 40)

Henry Ford coined the adage that best describes the ethic of the mass consumption-mass production era of the twentieth century: 'Any customer can have a car painted any colour that he wants so long as it is black'. I think we can usefully adapt this pithy phrase to help us vision the economy of the future. In this case it can be as colourful as human creativity can make possible but it has one fundamental limit: the energy limit. To put an exact number on the reduction in energy that we are looking for is a fairly unscientific process, but we need to reduce our current demand by something between 70 and 90 per cent.[1] So I might paraphrase Henry Ford by saying that you can have any economy you want so long as it is a low-energy economy and does not exceed the sorts of limits in terms of throughput of materials that have been identified by ecological economists. This book is about my vision of the most rewarding and satisfying economy we could create for the global human community while keeping within these planetary limits. Anybody is perfectly at liberty to create another vision, and in fact since Nature's way is one of diversity we are likely to have a variety of different local economies within and between the present nation-states of the world to replace the stultifying uniformity of the globalised monoculture. Designing future economies, and devising the political pathway to follow to arrive at them, offers both a challenge and an opportunity.

Since I have made it part of my life's work to share the idea of the bioregional economy, I have spent some time with fellow learners and designers of the sustainable future rethinking our local spaces – those parts of the wider world that we know best – in terms of a provisioning economy. What has genuinely surprised me is how good we all are at doing this. It is as though we are hard-wired to see our environment in terms of meeting our basic needs. In reality, why should we be surprised to find ourselves naturally skilled in this task, since it has obviously been essential to our survival as a species? When engaged in this bioregional planning we focus on key aspects of our very local environment – waterways, land, and species – as well as considering how these might provide us with energy, water and the raw materials for producing the necessaries of life. Needless to say, this sort of activity is fairly unusual for economics teachers or students in the twenty-first century.

In this chapter I try to open up some of the questions that have been closed down as a result of the ideological hegemony of globalisation. First I address the question of the territorialised nature, or otherwise, of economic activity, through a consideration of the recent history of the Icelandic economy. Section 2.2 then introduces the idea of a bioregion, provides a working definition and suggests how this might be used in reconceptualising economic life. Section 2.3 advances this discussion with a more fine-grained examination: analysing my own home community in terms of its own local bioregion. Finally, in Section 2.4, I offer some criticisms of the vision of the bioregional economy, as a word of warning and to pre-empt my critics.

2.1. So long and thanks for all the fish

The economy that provides an object lesson in the potential success and ultimate vulnerability of the rootless approach to economic life that characterises the global economy is that of Iceland. The collapse of the Icelandic economy in 2008 gave the first hint that the hubristic admiration for globalisation, and in particular the deterritorialisation of provisioning, was as fantastical as the South Sea Bubble or the belief in the value of tulip bulbs.[2] In those innocent days the idea of a country becoming bankrupt was so unusual that the response to the news was frequently a question: 'the supermarket?'

Barry's (1999) account of bioregionalism as a political philosophy identifies the changed relationship to the land that resulted from the process of industrialisation as central to the philosophical approach bioregionalists take to the economy, which for them entails a provisioning perspective. The loss of a close connection to nature that came in the wake of industrialisation and the movement of population from the land to the urban centres is, on his account, both ecologically and culturally destructive, leading to greater industrialisation of agriculture and a parallel alienation and social dislocation of people from their environment: 'Thus there is an increasing gap (both actual and cognitive) between the environment as a sphere of human production and the environment as a resource for human consumption, as a result of altered social-environmental relations' (Barry, 1998: 82).

In this section I develop an argument to support the bioregional view of the increasing disconnect between financial 'value' and economic product through a discussion of the recent history of the Icelandic economy. Iceland moved into the twenty-first century with an enviable record of social and economic achievement, and with the 11th highest life expectancy in the world (Wade and Sigurgeirsdottir,

2011). The country also appeared to have excellent credentials as a 'green' economy, with much of its energy being derived from geothermal and hydroelectric sources and extensive indigenous production of food, its sources of natural heat being used to achieve ambient growing conditions in a network of greenhouses. The government's aim had been to achieve self-sufficiency in food to support national security and, in spite of Iceland's position just outside the arctic circle, meaning that it has long, dark winters, the country had made remarkable achievements in terms of providing for its own need for a wide range of food products (Icelandic Agricultural Information Service, 1997).

These achievements began to be undermined from the late 1990s onwards when a group of young men schooled in neoliberal ideas at the University of Iceland formed a powerful network to bring their country into the globalised world economy. This led to the privatisation of the two major state-owned banks in 1998–2002 and a parallel establishment of private-equity companies owned by a small elite of Icelandic businesspeople (Wade and Sigurgeirsdottir, 2011). On the basis of using assets as mutual collateral to support the leveraging of large loans, Iceland massively expanded its available capital, and its banking sector grew to be of international significance, with Iceland's three main banks – Glitnir, Landsbanki and Kaupthing – becoming some of the largest in the world by 2006 (Ólafsson and Kristjánsson, 2010). This enabled the country's entrepreneurs, now proudly retitled the 'Viking raiders', to travel the world acquiring property and businesses, including some of the oldest and most high-profile retailers on the UK High Street such as House of Fraser, Hamleys, and Debenhams (Wade, 2009).

Iceland can be studied as a natural experiment in the ability of a country to divorce itself from its own geographical limits and to inflate its notional value beyond the capacity of the territory to which it belongs. By 2007 the nominal assets of the three large banks had expanded their value to some nine times the economic output of the whole of Iceland (Wade and Sigurgeirsdottir, 2011). Since these assets were in fact debts, it was only the peculiar nature of bank accounting, which enables debts to be accounted as assets and included on the positive side of the balance-sheet, that enabled Iceland to continue to appear solvent. From 2006 onwards, the banks' creditors began to be uncertain about the ability of the banks to make good on their borrowings. As was to become clear after the bubble had burst, the creditors' guarantees were only as a good as the government that was supporting them, and behind that the Icelandic people and the land they could use to generate goods and services of real economic value that could be sold.

The Icelandic financial crisis impinged on most people in the UK via the retail arms of the country's huge banks, which set up offering excellent rates of interest to lure in capital to support their need for further borrowing once the financial institutions had lost confidence in their ability to repay. Local authorities in the UK were also attracted by the promised returns, including some which deposited £33m. in Icesave accounts even after the fall of Lehman Brothers (Prince, 2008). By this time the banks' combined assets were notionally valued at 11 times the gross domestic product (GDP) of Iceland (Wade and Sigurgeirsdottir, 2011). Although Iceland's banks had been struggling to find further debt-money for some time, the seizing up of the global financial markets in September 2008 ended their ability to continue to leverage finance on the commercial markets. The consequences were immediate and catastrophic:

> The Icelandic krona (ISK) fell from about 90 to the euro at the start of 2008 to 190 in November 2008 ... The foreign exchange market stopped working. Foreign exchange became available only for government approved imports. The stock market collapsed by about 98% in 2008. By march 2009 the senior bonds of the banks were trading at between 2 and 10% of their face value. Average gross national income fell from 1.6 times that of the United States in 2007 to 0.8 times in February 2009.
>
> *(Wade and Sigurgeirsdottir, 2011: 66)*

The economic crisis rapidly became a political crisis, as the politicians and the people struggled over the question of who should pay the costs of the country's foreign creditors.

What was so disturbing about the recent history of Iceland, and in this it merely represents a microcosm of the globalised economy, is the way that there needed to be no apparent connection between the size of the real economy and the size of the financial economy. Nominally Icelandic businesses could use each other's collateral to borrow many times more than the country where they were based was worth. But the unravelling of the story demonstrates that this disconnect is more apparent than real, because when the financial intermediaries can no longer borrow the credit they turn to the government of the country where the bank is registered, imposing on it a duty to take on the losses and repay the creditors. Hence when British depositors in Iceland's banks lost their deposits, Prime Minister Gordon Brown immediately insisted that the Icelandic government should repay, leading to a lengthy legal battle the outcome of which is still undecided. This is a duty which the Icelandic people had no idea they had acquired, just as the British people in their turn had no idea that they were standing as implicit guarantors of their banks, which proceeded to become insolvent at the end of 2008.

The myth of deterritorialisation was created by the Vikings of various national origins who had found ways to create money from thin air by the process of mutually supportive bank credit. But when the bubble burst the creditors ignored this myth and targeted national governments to support the debts that had been taken on by companies registered in their territories. Far from floating free in a globalised world without governmental authority, those seeking repayment reverted to nationally based legislative frameworks (Mellor, 2010). The legally enforceable contracts between banks and the national governments who register them are, it seems, still valid in the post-geographical world of globalisation. The lesson that was learned from the collapse of financial institutions, in Iceland and elsewhere, was that geography matters very much indeed.

After the question of where the bank is registered and who should pay, there comes the question of how the economic value that the money can make a claim on is to be generated. Robert Wade (2009) has written of the Icelandic economy as Icarus, the Greek mythical hero whose hubris caused him to fly too close to the sun, and who was destroyed by his own arrogance. Following the bursting of the financial bubble in 2008, every economy that had lived well on the basis of the creation of credit was forced to come down to earth with a bump. The apparent severing of the link between finance and the real economy was only ever apparent. Now that those who are left holding credit come to make a claim for real goods and services it is the citizens of those countries whose banks generated the artificial financial value who have to pay for it, with their work, and the resources of those countries that have to be exploited to produce those goods and services.

In his account of the rise of the market economy, Karl Polanyi addresses this issue of the separation of economic systems from the social systems on which they inevitably depend. Polanyi conceived of the economy as 'submerged in social relationships'. To him the 'market economy' was a 'utopian myth', since it assumed that economic structures could prevail over social structures. Polanyi used the concept of 'embedding' to describe the need for the economy to be enmeshed within a complex system of social rules and cultural norms. He cites a wealth of evidence from anthropological studies, making clear that the majority of human societies have used material goods to establish status. An example might be the potlatch ceremony: a gargantuan and decadent feasting ritual that appalled Christian missionaries with its boisterous rejection of frugality. Its aim was for those with plenty to demonstrate their status by giving it away: Polanyi thus argues it to be a social rather than an economic form. In order for the great transformation from a provisioning society to a market economy to take place, a dehumanising process of commodification was necessary: people and the land needed to be turned into products that could be bought and sold:

> Machine production in a commercial society involves, in effect, no less a transformation than that of the natural and human substance of society into commodities. The conclusion, though weird, is inevitable; nothing less will serve the purpose: the dislocation caused by such devices must disjoint man's relationships and threaten his natural habitat with annihilation.
>
> *(Polanyi, 1944: 44)*

Polanyi is concerned not merely with the economic and social consequences of this creation of what he calls 'fictitious commodities' (land and labour), but also with the psychological distortions it gives rise to. The inherent motivation of human beings is fundamentally changed, he argues: 'for the motive of subsistence that of gain must be substituted'. This process changes the focus of human life away from gaining the respect of one's community and achieving a shared excellence in living and loving and towards the smaller and narrower objective of acquiring goods and exchanging them for the maximum amount of the key fictitious commodity in a market system: money.

Embedding the economy is important not only for purposes of security but also, and perhaps more importantly, because of the opportunity it offers for accountability:

'The rise of the market economy in everyday life, with exchange occurring over ever greater distance, can be thought of as a wedge between our contact with nature and with the moral consequences of the decisions we make' (Kallis *et al.*, 2009: 19). The bioregional economy is proposed precisely because of its ability to reconnect economic actors with each other and with their local environment: 'The only way people will apply "right behaviour" and behave in a responsible way is if they have been persuaded to see the problem concretely and to understand their connection to it directly – and this can be done only at a limited scale' (Sale, 1991: 53). Far from the rational economic man of the market, the bioregional citizen would act as a social being first, and an economic agent second. 'He does not act so as to safeguard his individual interest in the possession of material goods; he acts so as to safeguard his social standing, his social claims, his social assets. He values material goods only so far as they serve this end' (Polanyi, 1944: 48).

This reconnection is a necessary counter-move to the disembedding process of globalisation and one that was prefigured by Polanyi in his 1944 work. Rather than a dialectical process, Polanyi perceives of history, at least economic history, as being characterised by a tension between embedding and disembedding, a process he labels the 'double movement'. When the economy becomes too divorced from social restraint a political and social movement arises to force its re-embedding. It is the starting-point of the argument made in this book that we are urgently in need of a movement towards re-embedding and that we may conceive of the bioregional economy as the economy we would arrive at if we took the stricture to re-embed the economy seriously. We might find evidence of Polanyi's double movement in the rise of environmentalism and the novel approaches to provisioning that it has given rise to.

To ground our consideration of an economy we could move from the Icelandic model to the iceberg model of Maria Mies (see Figure 2.1). Mies is using the graphic to make a point about the distortion of real value that arises as a result of the monetisation of the economy:

> The layers making up that enormous invisible economy might be considered as built up in an order of increasing monetisation, with contracted and wage-labour exposed above the line ... Under the waterline are the 'colonies'. Both internal and external to a national economy, colonies may be defined by race, by gender, and by nationalism in the distribution of resources. They include nature. They exemplify the continuum of relationships based on violence, often with military oversight, which serve to extract resources for the benefit of powers outside the colony.
>
> *(Mies, 1999: 49)*

As we will discover in the following chapters, the bioregional economy offers a means of reconnecting us with the consequences of our decisions and thus offers the opportunity for a genuine accountability for our patterns of consumption.

A bioregional economy would return money to its role as the lubricant of a real economy made up of people, goods and services. It would be primarily a provisioning

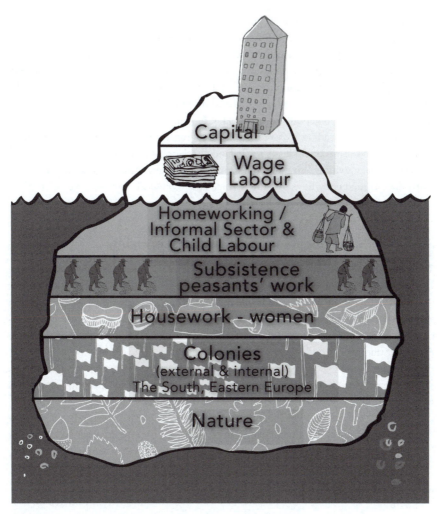

FIGURE 2.1 Maria Mies's iceberg model of the global economy
Source: Redrawn by Imogen Shaw.

economy, where the focus was on living a good life, with the acquisition of material items being only a means to this end. To achieve this we need to prevent the money system from becoming artificially inflated, creating the gap between economic activity, measured by GDP, and the money supply that increased so drastically in the years leading up to the financial crisis. As we saw in the case of Iceland, the creation of money through the credit-debt cycle facilitates the extraction of value by those who have power in the financial circuits, and they can translate this into a demand for goods and services. The uncontrolled expansion of finance creates a pressure for greater production and, hence, economic growth. If, as proponents of a steady-state economy argue (Daly, 1996; Jackson, 2009), ending economic growth is a fundamental first step towards ending the destructive impact of economic systems on the ecosystem, then creating a money system which is in balance with the level of activity in the real economy is a precondition of a sustainable future.

The growing gap between economic activity and money growth also gives rise to an inherent instability in the economy since, again as we saw in the case of Iceland, the struggle for the real economy to match up to the expectations created by the money supply becomes increasingly demanding until the financial bubble bursts, and then the pressure is reversed, with the sucking out of credit depressing useful economic activity and leading to a reduction in aggregate demand and economic recession. Hence we can conclude that a balanced relationship between money creation and economic activity is also a precondition for economic stability. It is for this reason that I have argued elsewhere that the finance and ecological crises are two sides of the same coin (Cato, 2009*b*).

2.2. Defining and mapping the bioregional economy

The concept of bioregionalism grew out of work undertaken by environmentalists in California and the US West Coast in the late 1960s and early 1970s. The focus was the need to respond to the environmental crisis by developing a different, more embedded relationship with their landscape. This included deepening their knowledge of local climate, ecology, species and culture and drew heavily on the native American tradition:

> A bioregion is literally and etymologically a 'life-place' – a unique region definable by natural (rather than political) boundaries with a geographic, climatic, hydrological and ecological character capable of supporting unique human and non-human living communities. Bioregions can be variously defined by the geography of watersheds, similar plant and animal ecosystems, and related identifiable landforms and by the unique human cultures that grow from natural limits and potentials of the region.
>
> *(Thayer, 2003: 3)*

Amongst proponents of bioregionalism, globalisation is seen as a system that divorces people from their locality; bioregionalism helps them to relearn their place in space, a process that is inherent in restructuring our relationship with our planet (Drenthen, 2009).

Political economist John Barry provides a critical account of bioregionalism as a social theory, which focuses on the view bioregionalists have that citizens in complex modern societies:

> have 'forgotten' that the economy and all its works is a subset and dependent upon the wider ecosystem ... Modern citizens have not only lost contact with the land, and their sense of embeddedness in the land, but at the same time they have lost those elemental social forms of more or less intimate and relatively transparent social relations. Thus a basic aim of bioregionalism is to get

>people back in touch with the land, and constitutive of that process is the
>recreation of community in a strong sense.
>
>   *(Barry, 1999: 9)*

A system of strengthened self-reliant local economies has long been constitutive of a sustainable society as theorised by green economists (Robertson, 1990; Hines, 2000; Woodin and Lucas, 2004; Douthwaite, 2006). The bioregion is proposed as a natural geographical unit that could form the basis for these local economies. A bioregional economy would be embedded within its bioregion and would acknowledge ecological limits (Cato, 2011a). The ambition of bioregional planners would be to achieve the maximum possible level of local demand from within the limits of the bioregion, thus reducing the use of scarce energy supplies in unnecessary trade-related transport. As we will see later, this attempt to achieve self-reliance (rather than self-sufficiency, which would imply an ideological rather than pragmatic commitment to local production) has considerable implications for the way production and consumption are organised, as well as fundamentally changing the way we conceive of ourselves, our work and our community.

But how are we to define our local provisioning areas? The founders of the original bioregionalist movement, in West Coast USA in the 1970s, focused heavily on watersheds. From the point of view of an orthodox economist this makes little sense. Water that is bought and sold arrives in pipes or plastic bottles; its origin is a source of little concern. However, as human populations have increased, have chosen the places of residence without regard to water availability, and have adopted increasingly luxurious lifestyles, the water crisis has been steadily building (Brown, 2011). The intense interest in watersheds in California must be an inevitable part of a consideration of provisioning in a semi-arid landscape. In the historical record, there are numerous examples of civilisations that have collapsed because they have failed to value and maintain their sources of water (Diamond, 2011). One of the most intriguing is the cave of swimmers in the Sahara desert, which was made famous in Anthony Minghella's film *The English Patient*. Photo 2.1 shows Malden Island in the Pacific Ocean, which is believed to have been abandoned due to repeated droughts.

So in defining the bioregion we begin with the watershed, but other geographical, biological and cultural features are also important. Early writing on bioregionalism suggested that bioregions could be defined in terms of marker species, watersheds, landforms and elevation (Andruss *et al.*, 1990). However, the definition rapidly expanded to include social forms so that 'the cultural dimension of the bioregion concept is integral to its very definition' (Carr, 2004: 76). In describing natural features that help us to define bioregions it is important to note that bioregional boundaries are designed to be flexible, and to be defined differently in the case of different goods or services. They have a self-producing character, which leaves their boundaries open and evolutionary: 'Unlike a bureaucratically and mechanically constructed boundary that divides the natural world into parts to manage, the boundary of a particular autopoietic system, like a cell, emerges as the system's components interact' (McGinnis, 1999: 73).

PHOTO 2.1 Malden Island, in the central Pacific Ocean, which was believed to have been abandoned due to repeated droughts.
Source: This image is made available without copyright restriction by Wikimedia Commons.

For the purposes of mapping the bioregional economy it is inevitable that we will each begin close to home. In my case this leaves me at something of a disadvantage, since bioregionalism has not proved a particularly popular concept amongst British policy-makers or academics. The situation is different in the North American continent, where regional planning has had much overlap with a bioregional approach to economic and social life, particularly in the work of Turner, who attempted to bring geographical awareness into US political and economic life (Turner, 1932); Mumford (1938), the originator of regional planning and Odum, whose early attempts to map regions' resources for the US prefigured much of the economic planning that would be necessary for a bioregional economy (Odum, 2001). (Sale – 1991 – identifies these three US theorists as proto-bioregionalists and provides helpful summaries of their contributions.)

The bioregional movement in North America has been deeply influenced by the land ethic of the continents' native peoples; and it is interesting that in another country where primarily white, European settlers confronted an autochthonous culture – Australia – bioregionalism has received positive engagement from the policymakers. Although they are not linked with provisioning, Australia's Department of Sustainability, Environment, Water, Population and Communities has mapped the country's bioregions and uses them to plan environmental protection and to support threatened eco-systems. The map of these bioregions was drawn up by state and territory agencies and based on 'vegetation communities and land systems'.

Thayer suggests that New Zealand has moved furthest towards an ecologically responsive planning system through its Local Government Reform Act and Resource

Management Act, which passed responsibility for strategic planning to the local regions, which were themselves based on hydrological basins. Thus we see that bioregional boundaries already feature in policy-making, although they have not yet crossed the divide from environmental to economic policy.[3]

2.3. The journey home

When your magnifying glass reaches your own backyard it is easy to lose a sense of perspective, and so I hope I am right in suggesting that a bioregional map of Britain would be rather more dense than those of North America or Australia. The British Isles are busy and diverse, a culture reflected in the ethnic diversity of our historic population groups, and now extended by a range of immigrant communities absorbed from our former colonies. The mapping exercise carried out by Natural England to create national 'character areas' is a useful start in creating a visual sense of our landscape,[4] although the 159 thus produced are too small and specific for the sorts of self-reliant provisioning units required for a bioregional approach to economic life.

It appears that the cultural diversity of these islands has been mapped onto a peculiarly diverse geology, which may prove a better starting point for determining our bioregions:

> In England and Wales we are singularly placed to appreciate the relationship of scenery and structure, for few other parts of the earth's surface show in a similar small area so great a diversity of rock types and of landscape features: 'Britain is a world by itself'; its mountains are not high, nor its rivers long, but within a few hundred miles of travel from east to west one may see more varieties of scenery than are to be found in many bigger countries.
>
> *(Trueman, 1938: 17)*

To what extent this view suffers from the myopia of self-observation is hard to determine, but Trueman's account of the relationship between the geological and morphological structures of England and Wales, and their related watersheds and landscape features, could provide a useful basis for mapping the British Isles in terms of their provisioning bioregions. He identifies 20 areas from the Valleys of South Wales to the Scottish Border Country that appear to be coherent territories identified by rock types and natural hydrological features. A simplified version of his geological map, which forms the bedrock for his regional distinctions, is reproduced as Figure 2.2.

Coming closer still to home, and to Stroud where I am typing these words into my computer, I shall dwell for a while on the area in which Trueman locates me: the Cotswold Stone Belt.[5] Local patriotism notwithstanding, it might provide some context for this discussion to reproduce a quotation from the acerbic and well-travelled clergyman Sydney Smith:

> The sudden variation from the hill country of Gloucestershire to the Vale of Severn, as observed from Birdlip or Frocester Hill, is strikingly sublime. You travel for twenty

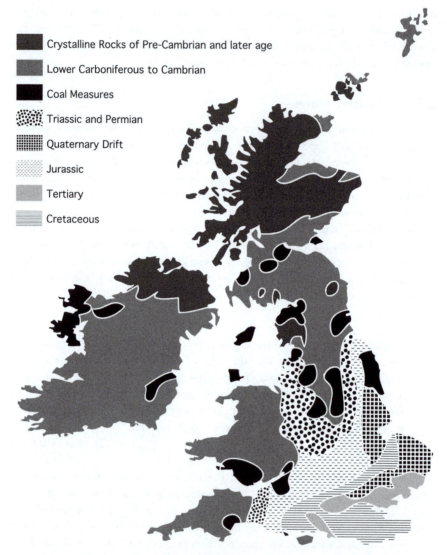

FIGURE 2.2 Geological map of the UK as suggestive of bioregional boundaries
Original artwork by Imogen Shaw.

or five-and-twenty miles over one of the most unfortunate desolate countries under heaven, divided by stone walls and abandoned to the screaming kites and larcenous crows: after travelling really twenty and to appearance ninety miles over this region of stone and sorrow, life begins to be a burden, and you wish to perish. At the very moment when you are taking this melancholy view of human affairs and hating the postilion and blaming the horses, there bursts upon your view, with all its towers, forests and streams, the deep and shaded Vale of Severn.

(quoted in Trueman, 1938: 20)

Smith, we may rapidly ascertain, lived in a time when high and bleak ground was considered barren and before the Romantic poets had relabelled it sublime. He communicates effectively, however, the dramatic nature of the Costwold landscape and especially of the escarpment which marks the break between the hills themselves and England's most mystical and lively river: the Severn. Alongside the oolitic stone that forms the Cotswolds and so clearly delineates its vernacular architecture, the river valleys also help to define this area as a distinct bioregion. As Figure 2.3 demonstrates there are three main river systems: the Gloucestershire Avon, the higher reaches of the Thames, and the north-western arm of the Kennet.[6] In addition, the (Stroud) Frome drains the edge of the Cotswold westwards, into the Severn.

These natural features begin to define the bioregion, and influence not only its architecture, as already identified, but also its traditional crafts and cuisine. This can be better explained in the case of our neighbouring bioregion of the Somerset Levels, an

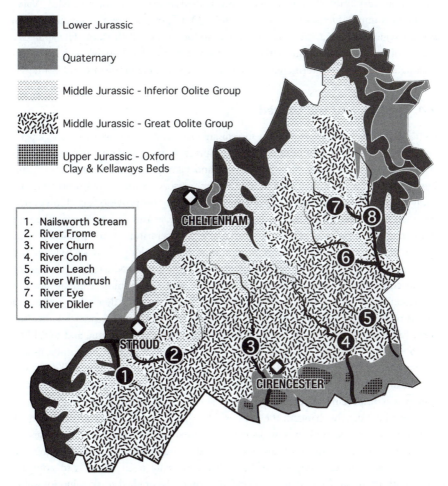

FIGURE 2.3 Riversheds and geological formations of the proposed Cotswolds bioregion
Source: Original artwork by Imogen Shaw.

area of wetland that I describe in detail elsewhere (Cato, 2011*a*). Here the local climatic and soil conditions perfectly suited various native willow species (especially *Salix triandra*), giving rise to a tradition of basket-making and related crafts. One particular form of basket was designed particularly for fishing for eels in the River Severn which, with its enormous tidal range (the second highest in the world), offers great opportunities to catch fish as it rises and falls twice daily. This begins to give an idea of the way human communities traditionally interacted with the local landscape to develop particular cultures; how those cultures might play a role in creating alternative consumption identities is discussed further in Chapter 7.

In the North American bioregional movement the species we share our landscapes with can also be used to define their boundaries, as in the example of the Salmon people of the American West Coast.[7] The UK, being much smaller, has more uniform animal life, although the chough is sufficiently distinctive to be used as the symbol of the county of Cornwall and the Red Kite is used as a local marker in Mid Wales. Domestic animals, such as the Gloucestershire Old Spot pig, are also identified with specific regional areas, as are crops that thrive in local soils and climates. The apple is a source of local identification in the area where I live and is widely used for cider-making in England's western counties of Gloucestershire, Herefordshire and Somerset.

2.4. The raw and the cooked

As a whole this book represents an interdisciplinary endeavour, and so some aspects of research into what I hope will become a priority, namely defining ourselves differently in relation to the place we inhabit and taking our local natural places, our bioregions, more seriously, can have only a very cursory treatment. I am situating my study in the field of economics and focusing primarily on provisioning. However, I have always conceived of the study of the economy as the first economic theorists did – in terms of political economy – hence the political nature of the proposals made in Part III of the book. I am aware, however, of the limitations of my knowledge and capacity in this field and so I want to identify now, in this introductory section, some of the concerns that have been raised about the social and political implications of bioregional thinking. I identify three, not to address them in depth but more as a means of alerting readers to them; and then leave them aside as we proceed with the more propositional aspects of the bioregional conception of economic and social life.

To conclude this survey of the bioregional vision I will address these dubious and potentially dangerous aspects of bioregionalism under three headings: balkanisation, parochialism and stagnation. When debating the value or otherwise of an alternative system it is important to remember that what we have at present is not sustainable and must be radically changed: the reasons why this is so were outlined in Chapter 1 and have been rehearsed in a wide range of other publications in recent years. A friend of mine once said about false teeth that if you compare them with having real teeth you are deeply disappointed, but what you really need to do is to compare them with no teeth. I feel that a similar lesson might be applied to sketching possible economic futures, and offer these critical thoughts in that spirit.

Balkanisation

Part of the ground on which I am arguing for a bioregional economy is the strong connection people can have to their local place, which, as I argue in Chapter 7, must be able to substitute for the very real delight and identity they currently find in an energy-intensive lifestyle. However, there is a fine and rather unsettling line between this strong sense of local community and the rejection of outsiders that has been such a threat to liberal values throughout human history. Essentialist versions of bioregional philosophy are particularly unhelpful here, as in Sale's suggestion that 'Outside or asystemic agents are normally detected and rejected, so that total population is stable, and within the system population levels of the species are maintained in a dynamic equilibrium' (Sale 1991: 73). He is writing here of ecosystem dynamics, but such comments could easily be misrepresented by proponents of exclusivist political philosophies, which is why maintaining a commitment to cultural diversity and social openness is of critical importance.

An equally unsettling strand of bioregional thinking celebrates the wildness of nature and ourselves as part of the pre-rational philosophy that links soul and soil in creating an ecologically responsive culture. The wild is eulogised, whether in nature or in culture, with little sensitivity to the achievement of taming wilder human impulses. Wild behaviour might, indeed, provide a source of entertainment and identification to rival the electronic games console, but we need to think seriously about how wild might be too wild.

Perhaps the most powerful example of the distortion of the link between the revival of the wildness of our European past and destructive social and political responses is provided by the Nazi regime in Germany. The case for a close intellectual link between green political thought and Nazism was first made by Bramwell (1989). In his *Origins of the Organic Movement*, Conford (2001) traces the connections between the British proponents of local self-reliance based on ecological principles in Britain in the 1930s and some of the more unsavoury views of race and place prevalent at that time. Evanoff is concerned that 'the emphasis bioregionalists place on localism might be construed as promoting insularity, ethnocentrism, and racism', and concludes that 'such worries are legitimate and point to the need for bioregionalism to develop a wider perspective that transcends a purely local focus and promotes greater cross-cultural understanding and cooperation' (Evanoff, 2007: 152).

In his 1995 book *Landscape and Memory*, Simon Schama provides an extended analysis of the link between the 'hunt for Germania' that underpinned Nazi ideology and the 'horrifying barbarism' that Tacitus identified with the German tribes who successfully resisted Imperial Rome. As Schama argues, 'it is these morbid associations, described by a not altogether neutral Latin commentator, between blood sacrifice, prostrate servitude, primitive woodland freedom, and a myth of ethnic origins that would cast the longest and darkest shadow over the fate of German nationality' (Schama, 1995/ 2004: 85). While, as Schama concludes, 'Green politics is sited in the present and the future, with only the very remote past (at least in Europe) invoked as a sacred ancestor', we should not be sanguine about the very strong and potentially destructive passions that identification with local land can arouse: 'Democracy ... averts its face from these myths at its peril. To exorcise their spell means, to some extent, understanding their potency at close quarters.' (Schama, 2004: 133)

It is exactly this ability of the local, and especially the local land, to evoke powerful responses that makes it an appealing substitute to the consumer culture that green economists tell us cannot be maintained. Local identification with place can provide a strong identity in a positive sense. Indeed, 'the desire of ancestral belonging' that Stephens (2001: 176) claims Bramwell identifies as key to Nazi ideology could, rather than being read as predictive of any particular form of political engagement, be read as a result of the economic dislocation that characterised Weimar Germany. In this sense, the post-globalisation world of economic insecurity and confused identities could be argued to be more conducive to far right social and political ideology than a firmly embedded and locally rooted social system of the bioregion.

Parochialism

If the first concern about living at a bioregional scale is about its capacity to encourage us to be too wild, the second concern is that it would fail to be wild enough. Our minds turn to the narrow judgementalism of fictional communities such as George Eliot's *Middlemarch* (subtitled 'A study of provincial life') or the factual but none the less oppressive accounts of communities such as that in Ronald Blythe's *Akenfield* (1972). The value of these bleak accounts of the cultural poverty that is possible within small, rural communities is a necessary balance to the environmentalist's temptation to romanticise the rural idyll. The lifestyle of many who currently inhabit our village communities, which they reach for weekend breaks by 4-wheel-drive vehicles or leave for a daily commute in similar luxury, is more dependent on lengthy supply chains than the life of the city resident, in spite of their many leisurely hours spent in the garden. What we are seeking to do here is not to replicate this lifestyle a million-fold but rather to design a life that involves genuine subsistence from the land of a rural community while maintaining as much of the global connectivity and cultural cosmopolitanism as energy limits permit. This point has been repeated from the early days of eco-design:

> Although we believe that the small community should be the basic unit of society and that each community should be as self-sufficient and self-regarding as possible, we would like to stress that we are not proposing that they be inward-looking, self-obsessed or in any way closed to the rest of the world.
>
> *(Blueprint, quoted in Sale, 1991: 66)*

How much we welcome this inclination, as Evanoff (2007: 143) writes, 'The cross-cultural dimension of bioregionalism remains relatively undertheorized … leaving bioregionalism open to the charge that it is inherently parochial and thus unable to effectively address problems that cut across cultural, political, and natural boundaries'.

Dobson (1989) criticises the bioregional worldview on the basis that there is no guarantee that if political power is devolved to the lowest level, all bioregions will be democratic and just. This follows the suggestion of the earliest theorists of bioregionalism, who were heroically optimistic in their requirement for the smallest communities to be responsible for all aspects of political power. What is argued here, rather, is a system of subsidiarity, where bioregional, national and global bodies are empowered to act in matters that are most appropriately dealt with there. A discussion of what those matters might be is reserved for Chapter 10, but a further examination of this critique is necessary here, as part of the very real risk posed by a bioregional approach.

This critique raises cultural as well as political concerns, with fears of a loss of cross-cultural awareness and a narrowing of intellectual horizons (Meredith, 2005). In this context the 'bioregional cosmopolitanism' called for by Thomashow (1999) can feel like a bit of an intellectual stretch. Heater reminds us that as far as cosmopolitanism is concerned, in the original Greek sense, 'A person thus described [as a cosmopolitan] was ... someone conscious of being part of the whole universe, the whole of life, the whole of nature, of which all human beings, let alone just the community of the person's political state, were but tiny portions' (Heater, 1999: 137). While this breadth of consciousness would be welcome in the midst of ecological crisis, perhaps we might wish for something more along the lines of Meredith's (2005: 84) bioregional communitarianism:

> Bioregionalism may be a set of values, but the bioregion itself is not an 'object': it is a 'terrain of consciousness' ... This terrain of consciousness has a capacity for self-development. As bioregional philosophy is modified by the very changes occurring in the bioregion itself, a more pragmatic approach which includes the concept of cosmopolitan communities and multiple rootedness may over-come a parochial personal commitment to a particular bioregion, in isolation from all that surrounds and passes through it. Part of this pragmatic approach will encompass the mobility of modern life, in which people move because they are compelled to, whether for employment, education, or family reasons. A robust inclusivity and a more liberal version of bioregionalism would have its practitioner apply a bioregional sensibility to each place that one inhabits.

In conclusion, perhaps what we need to seek is a creative dichotomy between the local and the global, between our close embedding in a local place and our accep-tance of the multiplicity of cultures that have enlivened and enriched all our lives.

To what extent this remains possible as access to energy supplies wanes is an urgent question. Again, bearing in mind my analogy of the false teeth, our aim should be to maintain the maximum interchange between cultures and to preserve as much of a cos-mopolitan outlook as is possible while keeping within the strict energy limit that the scientific evidence suggests is necessary. The huge technological advances that the 200-year oil bloom has brought us will support us well in this task. The global connections that are offered by the world wide web are already being used as a substitute for global economic and cultural exchange, and these substitutes for travel need to be extended and deepened.

However, I cannot concur with the arguments advanced by Monbiot (2006) and others about the justification of foreign travel on the basis that the distances travelled are 'love miles'. The climate scientists are implacable about the limits of CO_2 emissions that the planet can withstand and we have no alternative but to face these limits with equanimity and grace. Those who are reaching the ends of their lives now were the first generation who were able to enjoy the delights of rapid global travel, and those currently in their youth will be the last. As I discuss in Chapter 8, a limited trade in luxury goods will still be possible; annual trips to the antipodes to visit relatives will not.

Stagnation

As already discussed, the word 'home' is a popular one amongst bioregional theorists and one almost devoid of negative connotations. Home automatically communicates a sense of safety and of rootedness, but can also imply a lack of dynamism. As long ago as 1977 Herman Daly proposed a steady-state economy to replace the growth economy, yet the concept has an unfortunate implication of stagnation. Such stasis seems entirely at odds with the mutability of natural systems as the sense of 'homely', that might mean comfort but might just as easily mean a tedious regime of slippers-and-pipe, is in tension with the clear suggestion from the bioregionalists that the world they envisage will expect us to be self-reliant, skilful, perhaps even heroic citizens. In Sale's writings, and in a US context, bioregional citizens are exponents of 'Jeffersonian values', distrusting authority and control, enjoying first-hand experience of nature 'in the raw', and with a commitment to individualism within community.

The intellectual impulse towards developing the concept of a bioregional economy is to perceive that the system of globalised capitalism of the early twenty-first century cannot stop growing, and that its heedless and exponential growth is incompatible with the survival of the human species. In discourse terms the phrase 'dynamic equilibrium', first coined as an economic ambition by Lewis Mumford (1934/1963: 429) and later adopted by the leading ideologue of bioregionalism Kirkpatrick Sale, may be a better description of what we are seeking to achieve than Daly's steady state. Mumford identifies 'the fact of change itself' as the justification for the 'gigantic changes' that occurred during the nineteenth century. He called for a period of 'consolidation and assimilation' and made an intellectual connection between the closing of the US frontier and the need for the human species as a whole to 'settle down and make the most of what it has'.

This brings us to an important practical consideration that arises from a more local approach to economic life: the fact that if a system of local economies is designed around bioregions specifically because they share geographical and biological similarities, this means that their products – the basis that they offer for provisioning – will be specialised. I address this question of specialisation specifically in Chapter 9, where I consider it in conjunction with the issue of trade. However, at this initial stage of definition I should state that I consider the advantages of identification and solidarity offered by a bioregional conception of provisioning to outweigh the reduction in choice and drawbacks of specialisation. In Chapter 7 I offer evidence that the twin peaks of modern life, acceleration and individualism, have not brought human well-being and are now threatening human survival.

The process of creative destruction that has given rise to the turbo-capitalist model of economic life is now being openly questioned and compared with other cultural forms distant from us in time and space. The bioregional economy is likely to be marked by more stable and fixed identities than the globalised capitalist economy. Like the traditional societies that are discussed in the following chapter, it is likely to grow out of place and value having its roots in that place, in contrast to the spaceless, weightless mirage of the millennium. Change is likely to be evolutionary, rather than economic development being punctured by sudden and far-reaching shifts. However, it remains an open question what sort of motivation we will find to replace the financial and consumption-based incentives of the growth-based economy. This is especially difficult in the period of transition, when the need to make fundamental changes is not universally apparent. Once a crisis strikes, evidence suggests that human communities are actually both ingenious and co-operative (Quarantelli and Dynes, 1977). However, maintaining this level of engagement and creativity, particularly in a culture that has learned to rely on fairly instant and powerful rewards, is likely to prove a challenge, whichever path is chosen to lead us out of our current crises.

2.5. Conclusion

It is a tension we will return to throughout this book that, while intellectual discourse takes place at the global level, the bioregion must, of necessity, be defined locally. One of the questions that the concept of bioregionalism raises is to what extent we are empowered – intellectually, morally or politically – to make judgements and propose policies or provisioning strategies for places with which we do not have the deep connection that bioregionalism requires and presupposes. Being an ecological citizen (Dobson, 2003: ch. 3) imposes on us an awareness of the global situation and the necessity to abide by the rules that international citizenship and ecological literacy (Capra, 1995) demand, and yet we cannot be truly rooted in more than one small space on this earth; and so our duty also requires us to enhance and prioritise that relationship. I have tried to balance this tension by bringing into the discussion in the following chapters the sincere commitment to their local place of a range of colleagues and collaborators who call different countries 'home' and who do so in different languages. The fact that I no longer fly means that most of these colleagues – at least those whom I know well and whose local places I also know – are based in Europe. Perhaps this is also legitimised by the fact that much of the theorising about bioregionalism has emerged from other continents, and so part of the role of this book is to apply those theoretical and philosophical principles in a European cultural and geographical setting.

This chapter has provided an outline of the concept of the bioregion and an application of this concept to the discussion of the economy, that is to say the provisioning of the needs of citizens. I should also repeat in this conclusion that the bioregional economy is not offered as a blueprint or a prescriptive view of how economic life in the densely populated and heavily industrialised economies of the West *must* evolve. Rather it is one possible model that conforms to the necessary rules of a sustainable life, particularly in terms of its well-being to energy ratio.

3

THE ECONOMIST AS SHAMAN

The others, who are called the *Economists,* do not have the welfare of the people in mind. They think only of enriching empires without worrying themselves about the fate of the individual. Thus the theories of the Economists have greatly enriched England without enriching the English.

(Charles Fourier, from Lettre de Fourier au Grand Juge, 1803)

Introduction

Economists have not had a comfortable time in recent years, a period during which criticisms of their inability to predict, much less to find solutions for, the most significant economic crisis of the century, have been made widely. This culminated in the unedifying spectacle of a group of British economists finding themselves unable to find adequate answers to their sovereign's questioning about how they justified their existence after being asleep on watch during the most serious economic crisis in a century. At the opening of a new building at the London School of Economics in late 2008, Queen Elizabeth inquired: 'It's awful – why did nobody see it coming?' The director of management research, Professor Garicano, immediately replied that the crisis was not anticipated because 'everyone thought they were doing the right thing' (Montgomerie and Williams, 2009: 99).

Economics is a notoriously unreflexive discipline. Despite the best efforts of the *Journal of Economics Methodology* there is little evidence that the mainstream economics profession has questioned its methods, focus or orientation. There is a vocal minority of heterodox economists calling for pluralism in the discipline in terms of both research and pedagogy, but its self-identification as heterodox makes clear the nature of the problem. Unlike other disciplines, economics is not a contested terrain where different approaches wage more or less seemly academic battles. Rather it is a unified, pro-market, neoclassical majority, whose method is almost exclusively mathematical, against which dissidents launch periodic guerrilla attacks (see Mirowski, 2010). The failure of the discipline to operate in a reflexive way is best demonstrated by the fact that the accepted wisdom holds that, far from their discipline being in need of rapid and radical revision, what the economic crisis proved was the need for more markets, and more neoclassical economics, rather than a change of focus and more variety of method and theory (Barry, 2012: ch. 4).

I would suggest that economics is a discipline in crisis. Its inability to predict the tumultuous events that have devastated the Western economies from 2007 onwards is the most obvious example of this crisis. Yet the more persistent and ultimately more threatening demonstration of the crisis of the discipline lies in its inability to find a mediated settlement between our economic system and our environment. If, as we will explore in the following section, the most central issue of economics is about resources, then to allow a system of resource exploitation that is destroying the richness of life on earth, as well as threatening the future of humanity, is worse even than a dereliction of duty: it is an act of treason. It is a betrayal of the special – I might even argue sacred – duty that economists have been accorded by society.

Given the way that the academic economists have made themselves irrelevant with their self-referential number-crunching, and the professional economists have put themselves beyond the pale through their economical approach to ethics, it is understandable that the role of an economist might not be an attractive one to today's generation of young people. So my aim in this chapter is to begin to save the discipline of economics from itself; to rescue the project that led to the investment of time and energy by generations of clever men (and a smaller number of clever women);[1] to find a way for economists to discover again a sense of self-respect. This consideration is not about what economists do in our current society; instead I want to operate more like a social anthropologist, taking a step back and consider what an economist might be for in a general sense, rather than in the sense of a capitalist society in the early twenty-first century. Social anthropologists have the advantage of developing an in-depth knowledge of human societies vastly different from our own. They can thus develop a sense of what is essential about the way humans live together in community, and what is just superficial.

Perhaps I can illustrate this best by using an example. At a recent conference I encountered an American citizen with a headache. He asked me if I had any Advil. This is a very culturally specific request but, because US culture has encroached so far into our own, I was able to work out his problem and try to help. I asked if he preferred painkillers based on aspirin or paracetamol. He couldn't answer this question but just repeated his request. To him headache pills were just called Advil and it had never occurred to him that this was just a brand name that might not exist on our side of the Atlantic. A social anthropologist might encounter a whole range of possible treatments for headache based on plant extracts or physical manipulations. Or perhaps they might encounter societies where pain is highly valued by certain members of society, as a way of enabling especial insight or messages from the supernatural realm (see Carod-Artal and Vazquez-Cabrera, 2007). In a similar way, in this chapter

I want to stand right back from what economists do today in our universities and companies and consider, instead, whether there might be a role that we can sketch out for a person who has a particular expertise in the discovery and allocation of resources. In a sustainable world where we have a deep and sacred connection to our environment, what might be the role of such a person in negotiating our relationships with that world and our fellow creatures?[2]

3.1. Losing my religion

Economics defines itself as the study of 'how scarce resources are, or should be, allocated' (*Oxford Dictionary of Economics*: Black, 1997). At the risk of seeming academic in the pejorative sense, I would like to explore most of the words included in this short, and fairly consensual, definition.

The word 'how' appears fairly innocuous at first sight, but the effort of exploring precisely how economists study the mechanisms of allocation is, in fact, worthwhile. It is a fairly limited exploration, since the overwhelming focus of economists is on the economic system as we know it in industrialised, Western democracies. Economic history has been largely eliminated from university curricula and from funded research (a point recently made by Harvard economist Ken Rogoff: Reinhart and Rogoff, 2009) so that what economists are left studying and describing is the way the economic system we live with today in the industrialised, Western economies functions. The prevailing description within the neoclassical paradigm is one based around numerical and formalised 'models'. While economists in the institutionalist, and more recent behavioural, schools, consider the motivations of the individuals who populate this economy, they are marginalised within most economic work and are largely absent from teaching texts. When they do appear they often do so as carriers of 'expectations' (since expectations could not exist without a human agent), and their expectations are often found to mirror the economic models that their creators use to explain 'how' the economy works. We thus have a rather small, decidedly narrow, and determinedly closed circle. It is not the purpose of this book to critique neoclassical economics; this has been done convincingly elsewhere (Ormerod, 1994; Keen, 2001; Hill and Myatt, 2010). My purpose here is rather to add to the growing volume of pluralist work in economics.[3] So in conclusion to the discussion of the 'how' of our definition, I would suggest that it is precisely this which is being opened up to critical scrutiny in the remainder of this book.

The 'scarcity' of our definition is a key concept in neoclassical economics. It may be characterised as concept on a mission, so central is it to the functioning of the market system. Markets use the price mechanism to enable the efficient allocation of resources. The role of prices is to communicate to potential buyers and sellers how scarce a resource is, relative to the demand for it. If there were an infinite supply of the good in question, it would have no price; hence the fundamental importance of scarcity to the market understanding of economics. Hence, also, scarcity as a relative rather than an absolute concept, and one that should be explored rather than assumed (Daoud, 2011; Panayotakis, 2011). The absolute quantity of a resource is irrelevant if there is no demand for it, since no matter how scarce it may be there will be no price and hence no market. Conversely, if a resource is abundant but there is little demand for it, again the price mechanism will fail and market allocation will not be possible.

Regardless of the demand, to the neoclassical economist resource scarcity is unproblematic, since if one resource becomes depleted another can be used as a substitute:

> If it is very easy to substitute other factors for natural resources, then there is, in principle 'no problem'. The world can, in effect, get along without natural resources. Exhaustion is an event not a catastrophe ... If, on the other hand, output per unit of resources is effectively bounded – cannot exceed some upper limit of productivity which is, in turn, not too far from where we are now – then catastrophe is unavoidable ... Fortunately, what little evidence there is suggests that there is quite a lot of substitutability between exhaustible resources and renewable or reproducible resources
>
> *(Solow, 1993: 74, quoted in Gowdy and Hubacek, 2000).*[4]

Economists with a more deliberate focus on the planet – that is, the source of the resources which economics is established to allocate – see this Promethean approach to resources to be environmentally threatening. They critique the social construction of scarcity (Panayotakis, 2003), the creation of an artificial desire for material goods and a felt need to acquire them to be a fulfilled member of a human community. Scarcity thus defined plays a crucial role in driving the economic growth that threatens environmental security. (For more on the creation of needs and desires see Section 7.2.)

The issue of allocation is left fairly open in the definition, although in reality most economists will discuss allocation within the framework of the Pareto principle: 'Allocations are said to be Pareto optimal if no other feasible allocation could benefit some people without any deleterious effects on at least one other person' (Tietenberg, 2000: 27). This means that a distribution of whatever resource is efficient if no one person who is receiving some of that resource cannot receive more without another person receiving less. This principle operates as a strict limit on the acceptability of attempts to equalise distributions by allowing socially motivated interventions. For example, a policy that heavily taxed owners of second homes to create an incentive for them to sell and make a home available to a person without one would fail on the Pareto principle, since the owner of two homes would clearly have their utility reduced. Efficient allocation is one of the key claims for superiority of the market system and so it is rather disappointing that it is generally considered in this very narrow and rather static sense. It omits to consider two aspects that are of critical social importance. First, the equity of the allocation, and second, how the initial allocation, from which distributions of resources may stray only if they do not reduce any individual's utility, was arrived at. These questions, the crucial questions of political economy, are generally left outside the discussion.

Which brings us, finally, to consider the sub-clause of the definition, the question of normative economics, or how things should be, a question that is relegated to the end of many textbooks and many economics courses (Hill and Myatt, 2010). This is the point at which economics as it operates now, is forced to leave the safety of its modelling and accept that it inevitably finds itself inextricably entwined with the much messier disciplines of politics and ethics. Just as the Human Rights Act requires all new policies to have been assessed in terms of their impact on the most vulnerable (Hocking, 2010), so economic theorising and policy-making should not be able to be made without paying heed to distributional consequences. Yet, the primary measure of economic activity – gross domestic product (GDP) per capita – is defined in terms of an average amount of economic value per person, precisely sidelining the question of how equally this value is allocated in reality.

To conclude this section we need to have a new definition of the role of an economist in a sustainable society to frame the argument that follows. We have established that description of the process of allocation of resources (including in their complex form as products and services) is important, but it should be an explanation that encompasses the inherently social nature of economic interactions and is not naïve about the fact that questions of power will always be important when resources are being allocated. An economist should also take account of the ethical aspects of his or her work: justice is as important as efficiency when questions of resources are to be considered. But perhaps the most fundamental shift of all that needs to take place is the reappraisal of the relationship between people and the environment from which their resources are drawn. It is in his or her role as a mediator between people and their environment that the economist is most important in the context of a sustainable society. This role will also, therefore, require an understanding of the spiritual quality of that relationship. While this may be a demanding job description, it does begin to suggest the centrality of the role of the economist in the transition to sustainability,[5] and the quality of people we are looking for to fulfil this role.

3.2. Losing our way

The London underground map is perhaps the most beloved schematic drawing of all time. Produced in 1931 by London Underground employee Harry Beck (Garland, 1994), it has guided generations of Londoners across their city with clarity, speed and precision and without their ever having to emerge into its damp and formerly smoggy skies. Yet read from the opposite perspective, the London tube map has contributed to the divorcing of generations of Londoners from the physical reality of their city, so that they have no idea that instead of a sweaty and stressful ride on a packed train, they could be strolling across a sunny park or enjoying the pleasure of a journey on the river ferry, the traditional highway of choice before the Victorian era. The tube map is praised for eliminating the geographical element from the links between the different lines that make up the underground network. It is lauded for abstracting people from their environment in order to ease their passage through it from one building (their home) to another building (their workplace) and back again. It thus facilitated the movement of people in service of the economy without exploring the consequences of this for their deeper knowledge of the place where they spent their lives.

I raise this issue to highlight the question of the relationship between modern human culture and the physical world, which I take to be a question that economists should consider to be within their purview. In the new role for an economist that was sketched out in the first section of this chapter the question of resources remained central. Economics is about resources, and from a sustainability perspective we recognise that all those resources come from the natural environment. Hence the need for a discussion of how we relate to our environment is a necessary precursor to a consideration of how the economist might mediate this role. Polanyi's role in fore-grounding the importance of embedding economic transactions within social relationships has been discussed in the previous chapter. His notion of the 'double movement', which operates as an in-built pressure to bring the economy back into line with social needs, provides a useful counterbalance to the theorising of the placeless, weightless economy.

Ecofeminist theorists have expanded this notion of embedding to encompass the physical embedding of our economic systems within the natural world. Mellor characterises the argument as follows: 'The core argument of ecofeminist political economy is that the marginalisation of women's work is ecologically dangerous because women's lives as reflected in domestic and caring work represent the embodiedness of humanity, the link of humanity with its natural being' (Mellor, 2006: 142). Drawing on the work of feminist economics, this is partly an argument about the marginalisation of women's work, much of which takes places outside the market, and the monetised, economy (Mies, 1998). However, at a more fundamental level it is an argument about the distinct nature of women's work in being more closely connected to bodily existence, as in the caring work for human bodies, and particularly the vulnerable human bodies of the young, the old and the sick. Mellor argues that 'the capitalist market is disembodied and disembedded, carved out of the totality of human existence within the natural world'; a sustainable economy, by contrast, would be a provisioning economy, focused on provisioning for the meeting of embodied needs rather than the production of market goods for sale.

Mellor also draws attention to the temporal disembedding of work, especially to the nature of women's work as relating to the body and being intrinsically related to biological time. The movement to an industrial economy from a peasant economy has meant a parallel movement from the cyclical time of the seasons to the linear time of the clock (Mellor, 1997). As Mumford would have it, 'The clock, not the steam-engine, is the key-machine of the modern industrial age' (Mumford, 1934: 14). According to Griffiths (1999: 165), this has also meant a dislocation of our lives from their natural basis:

> In the thirteenth century, clocks became increasingly important for commerce. The urban commercial population often learned to count money by counting the bells of clocks and then used that arithmetic skill in shops and early businesses. Feudalism conceptually linked money with land and livestock, as language remembers, so *stock* market comes from *livestock*, and an annual *yield* originally meant a crop yield. The value of land rests in its immoveability, its

constancy; and as the land was a steady plenty of eternal cycles, so time was considered plentiful in those same everlasting rounds. But the rise of capitalism linked money to *time* and, in contrast to land, money's value comes from its circulation, not its hoarding. The value of money – currency – depends on its *movement*: the word currency comes from the Latin *currere* – to run.

We can extend Griffiths's insight by considering physical measures and the extent of their abstraction. Elsewhere (Cato, 2010) I have raised the question of how the abstract metric measure (the metre itself being defined as one ten-millionth of the distance from the Equator to the North Pole as measured by its passage through Paris) contributed to our disembedding from the natural world. In contrast, traditional weights and measures were based on specific distances of the human body and hence derived from our interaction with the world, an example being the Medieval cloth measures of spans and bolts, which were both derived from the ell. As its name suggests, this measured the distance between two elbows, hence the (later corrupted) expression 'Give him an inch and he'll take an ell'. Ancient China provides an example of these two more abstract forms of (dis)connection with the locale. According to Neil MacGregor (2010: 193), the consistency of the bronze bells of ancient China was such that they could be used to measure standard volumes, while their weight was so accurate they could also be used to provide standard weights for the purposes of 'bringing harmony to commerce as well as society'. Macgregor's expert witness Isabel Hilton finds this typical of Confucianism's aim of seeking balance and perhaps especially balance between people and nature.

The dislocation of our selves from our local environment, and the increasing distances between our bodies and the landscapes where the food that nourishes them is produced, has left us physiologically as well as psychologically vulnerable (issues I address in further detail in Chapters 5 and 9). The proposal of the bioregional economy implies a reconnection of ourselves with our environment via both time and space. This embedding – whether social, as proposed by Polanyi, or environmental, as proposed by the ecofeminists – is not a thin, theoretical business. As we will discover when we reach Chapter 6, it implies a wholly different approach to our work, which will also be much more strongly embedded in social relations and will bring us closer to the environment – the source of our raw materials – rather than separating us from it. By extension, our identity will be related to this work, rather than being found almost in contradistinction to it, in the escapes we make to foreign holiday destinations, for example. As we will see in Chapter 7, a bioregional economy implies significant changes to the way we conceive of ourselves and how we access and consume our resources, both individually and within communities.

But to continue the argument of this chapter, let us contrast for a moment the way we know our local place with the way that the Australian outback is known by its people: through a system of spiritually resonant songlines (Chatwin, 1988). The initial interpretation of these songlines, or tracks followed by totemic ancestors as they followed their creative journey across the land, is as a way of making geographical sense of place. They enable native peoples to find their way and to find sources of food and water. But they are also systems of meaning, of myths that enable individual identities, that build communities, and that facilitate relationships between human communities, animal communities, and the resources they share (Rigsby, 1999). Harvey (2006: 76) is concerned that we should not conceive of this understanding of land in terms of 'Just-so stories'. Rather:

> They encounter intimations of themselves in the country, places and lands that are both theirs and themselves. In realising the full richness of that which came from that foundational or formative world into this one, Aboriginal people increasingly live through and live out the expression of their own emplaced, located and embodied reality.

Taçon identifies in the songlines a process of using landscape to facilitate connection and relationship, concluding that:

> History and archaeology have repeatedly shown that cultures that fail to maintain sustainable connections to large stretches of land do so at their folly. Perhaps if we focused less on computer superhighways and paid more attention to looking after the diversity found along Dreaming Tracks, water courses and resource routes, our own survival would be less threatened.
>
> *(Taçon, 2005: 2)*

Such a deep and spiritually resonant connection between human communities and place is not specific to Australia. Jaye Griffiths (2007) found a similar relationship during her travels in Amazonia:

> Under Western eyes, the Amazon is an un-understandable wilderness, an undifferentiated green of undefinable plants, a bewildering forest of obscurity where not only your body but also your comprehension can become fatally lost. It confuses and perplexes and is perceived as almost pathologically pathless for the mind. But indigenous people know how to 'think' the forests, know that the paths through this wilderness are songs, the song that each plant has. Song makes a thread of light, a path of the mind; each song tells of one plant's relationship to other plants and not only differentiates one plant from another but distinguishes between the uses of, for example, stem or leaf or root of the same plant. There is practical wisdom here but also psychological wisdom: you find your way and learn how to live unlost, not through the wild forest but within it. The songlines harmonize people with environment. There is no divide. Mankind is a full-singing part, not discordant but as necessary – and as beautiful – as a violin to an orchestra.

It is superfluous to point out that this sort of understanding enhances human wellbeing in a range of ways that is impossible to fully comprehend by those of us raised in the dislocated, rationalist culture of the contemporary West. However, perhaps we might find an inkling of it in the way that urban myths are always located in local places. When we hear about the dog that was killed in the microwave or the escaped, psychopathic criminal, the story always takes place in a locality close to where we hear the story, suggesting a lingering need to pin stories to places. This refusal to allow stories to float free of their geographical settings is reminiscent of what Basso (1996) found amongst the Western Apache for whom 'wisdom sits in places':

> Animals, places, and whole landscapes have meanings, sometimes sobering, sometimes uplifting, but always with a moral dimension ... every story begins and ends with the phrase 'it happened at' ... and this anchoring of narrative to places means mention of a place evokes a particular story, which in turn carries a moral standard, and implication for certain types of social relations.
>
> *(quoted in Pretty, 2007: 160)*

There is a risk here of falling into the trap of romanticising or patronising the way of life of people in exotic foreign lands. Yet there are suggestions that we might find traces of a similar embedding in sacred landscapes of our own, in the history of these islands. Chatwin finds hints of the remnants of European songlines in the Greek myths. Perhaps we can find similar hints in some of the Celtic festivals and myths that made aspects of our own landscape sacred. Certainly the worship of natural features persisted until the twentieth century, in local well-dressing rituals (for details see Ross, 1967: 107) and the wassailing ceremonies that are still popular as life begins to reawaken following the winter. Deakin (2007: 122), in his eulogy to our native woodlands, suggests that Wessex demonstrates patterns of Neolithic barrows and stone and timber circles that could represent something similar to songlines: 'If rituals are a way of enacting a story, [...] the narrative of the Neolithic monuments in Wessex is about history, origins and people's place in the world. The story may well have been a creation myth, a singing up of the songlines on the land.'

In questioning the dislocation of people from their environment we have travelled a long way from the abstract coloured lines of the tube map towards ancient British songlines. We can imagine a time when the Tube was a refuge from bombing or from life-threatening smogs, but can we also imagine a time when most Londoners would value their city and its environment so highly that they would prefer to cycle or walk its streets and parks than to spend hours of their life in its fetid tunnels? In this book my aim is to broaden this thought to consider the many ways we interact with our environment and how we have lost our real sense of connection with it, whether in travel, in what we eat, or in how we spend our social lives. I try to rethink the role of the economist in this process and I seek to explore how an economist might act as some sort of mediator between people and their physical environment. If the capitalist economist, with his love of efficiency, would worship the tube, I ask how a green economist, focused on sustainability, might play a different role and find strikingly different answers to the questions about resources and infrastructure. Perhaps s/he might adopt a perspective that includes some of the wisdom of the Aboriginal shaman as well as the twentieth-century planner.

3.3. Losing our mojo

My proposition of the economist as shaman is a provocative one, and in some sense a thought experiment. To justify that it is an experiment worth conducting requires some evidence that the perception of economists by themselves and by others demonstrates their occupying a peculiar social position and playing a specific cultural role. In a paper musing on the distance between economists' view of the world and those of 'the general public' Mankiw (prominent pro-market economist, author of an undergraduate textbooks studied by millions, and adviser to the Bush White House), refers to the latter as 'muggles', implicitly suggesting that he and his fellow economists are the possessors of supernatural powers (Mankiw, 2009). Another gesture towards the supernatural powers of the financial function is found in the labelling of a plan to gain agreement about future action by British banks as 'Project Merlin'.[6]

More critically, and from outside what is often referred to as the 'charmed circle' of finance, Henderson long ago engaged in what she called 'Unfrocking the priest-hood' of economists, sarcastically referring to the 'snake oil' salesmen she considered presently indulged in the dark arts of modelling and prediction (1996). More recently, and particularly since the collapse of the Western capitalist model in 2007/8, similar critiques have spread (Keen, 2001; Barry, 2012) in a way it is tempting to see as the overthrowing of a powerful mythological system and its replacement with another – the move from the traditional religious ways to the birdman cult amongst Easter Islanders who found their own survival threatened by the over-exploitation and exhaustion of essential resources, perhaps.

To a Western, rational mind there is no place for the shaman and his or her very role is difficult to comprehend, as the conflicting terms witch-doctor, medicine man and wise woman testify. Is this person a healer, a wizard, a seer? Where does his or her power come from that she considers herself the equal of the chief and can strike terror into the hearts of her countryfolk? We can imagine that in societies where survival is considerably less secure than it is in the modern West, people who know where resources are, or how to access them, are important members of society.

Giddens (1991) suggests that a characteristic of modernity is a process of creating institutions and routines that shelter us from the uncomfortable reality of our own human dependence. We 'sequester' this reality, to protect us from these aspects of our lives that would prevent our optimal functioning within society. Barry (2012) views such sequestration as part of a strategy for dealing with the vulnerability that we, as modern humans, feel incapable of acknowledging. The pressure of modern society requires us to inhabit a realm of performed invulnerability, with our risk of sickness, dependence and eventual death being excluded from everyday life. One traditional role of the shaman is to manage the liminal spaces between socially and culturally public categories so that the peculiar behaviours that are needed in response to them and our own selves at times of transition and during rites of passage are not damaged or harmfully exposed (Harvey, 2006).

I would like to suggest that the role of the shaman is to inhabit this realm of what Barry calls 'the occluded': the aspects of our humanity that are taboo within a modern society. One aspect of this is the vulnerability of our physical selves and another our dependence on the natural world. Thus the sequestration of our dependence is closely tied to our disembedding from the natural world that ecofeminists theorise as central to our environmentally destructive behaviour. The role of a mainstream economist is to reinforce this disconnection by frequent and public statement of the strength and power of the global capitalist economy. Perhaps we see here a deeper explanation of the irrational exuberance that always seems particularly pronounced when market conditions reach their most challenging. In his role as shaman the economist is required to maintain the separation between the everyday and the taboo, between the whole and the polluted. His social role is to protect us from the risk of exposing our destructive and occluded vulnerability.

In traditional societies the role of the shaman was a two-faced one. While they were responsible for ensuring the provision of resources, they also had duties connected with protection and propitiation. Non-rationalist societies that recognise their dependence on the natural world but do not have the scientific understanding that permits an aspiration to control are conscious of the importance of their relationship with the environment and the other species they share it with in a way we are not. An important part of the role of the shaman was to maintain this relationship and to inhabit the liminal space between humans, their environment and other species.

We can find a reminder of how the religious code regulated the use of land in the book of Leviticus, the book of the bible that deals with law. The ancient Hebrews had precisely the kind of reverential and awe-filled relationship with their Almighty that typifies pre-scientific societies. In Chapter 26 (vv. 2–5) we find the Lord's promise of abundance, no doubt communicated to the faithful by a priestly figure:

> Ye shall keep my sabbaths, and reverence my sanctuary: I am the LORD. If ye walk in my statutes, and keep my commandments, and do them; then I will give you rain in due season, and the land shall yield her increase, and the trees of the field shall yield their fruit. And your threshing shall reach unto the vintage, and the vintage shall reach unto the sowing time: and ye shall eat your bread to the full, and dwell in your land safely.

We can interpret this as a divine guarantee of security of resources, so long as religious strictures are maintained. In the previous chapter we find the linked necessity of sharing this bounty fairly, the concept of jubilee from which modern economists might learn and which campaigners use to draw attention to the grossly unequal allocation of resources in our modern world (Busby, 2007). Here, the clear injunction is that land remains in sacred, non-personal ownership and that this shall be made manifest in a reallocation every 50 years (Chapter 25, vv. 8ff.):

> And thou shalt number seven sabbaths of years unto thee, seven times seven years; and the space of the seven sabbaths of years shall be unto thee forty and nine years ... ye shall hallow the fiftieth year, and proclaim liberty throughout all the land unto all the inhabitants thereof: it shall be a jubilee unto you; and

ye shall return every man unto his possession, and ye shall return every man
unto his family … And if thou sell aught unto thy neighbor, or buyest aught of
thy neighbor's hand, ye shall not oppress one another.

The jubilee presents an opportunity to return allocations to a socially determined
system, removing unfair distribution that will inevitably develop over time on the
basis of luck rather than judgement, but also to recognise that there are sacred constraints on the use of the land and that the relationship between people and their land
is a mutual one.

 This spiritually guided approach to the use of resources is not only found in historical societies but also in contemporary societies. Harvey (2006) describes the
Maori's approach as follows:

> Maori do not predicate the right to use Earth's natural resources on claims to
> human difference and superiority, and certainly not on the presumption that
> we alone in the world are living persons … the key theme and experience is of
> the etiquette of relationships. Offerings must be made, gifts given, exchanges
> made, excess profits returned. Life givers must not be abused or ignored,
> especially when they provide such inestimable benefits.
>
> *(Harvey, 2006: 63)*

3.4. Losing our minds

How have we come to a be a species which, while capable of minutely documenting
its own imminent extinction, has undervalued our connection with the earth, which
is the source of all well-being, and of our connection with the other species we share
it with? My contention is that the answer to this question is found in the move from
intuitive and embedded thought to abstract and rational conceptualising, as discussed
in the previous section. In this section we will proceed further to address the question
as reframed by Abram:

> How did civilized humankind lose all sense of reciprocity and relationship with
> the animate natural world, that rapport that so influences (and limits) the
> activities of most indigenous, tribal peoples? How did civilization break out of,
> and leave behind, the animistic or participatory mode of experience know to
> all native, place-based cultures?
>
> *(Abram, 1996: 137)*

Famously it was John Locke, the English 'empirical' philosopher – he who is often
held responsible for providing an intellectual justification for the ownership of land
(Haddad, 2003) – who argued that 'beasts abstract not' and therefore are not deser-
ving of respect equivalent to that accorded to other humans. As is clear from the
argument in the previous section, it should be clear that I wish to argue against
this on two grounds, of which the first is that abstraction can be considered to be a

self-evident proof of intellectual or moral progress. Second, what are we to make of his apparently 'empirical' conclusion that animals are not capable of intellectual abstraction? A slew of authors emerging from the perspectives of deep ecology and animal rights have vigorously contested this conclusion. Carl Sagan (1977) argues that chimpanzees at least demonstrate the ability for abstract reasoning. Other authors make a distinction between the moral status of animals who have been tamed and whose 'domestic' status implies that they owe their lives to human intervention, and wild animals (Callicott and Baird, 1980; Leopold, 1949).

The argument about the intellectual and moral capacities of animals is only a tangential concern of my discussion here, but the relationship we have with animals, and especially how we negotiate this relationship with other species when our provisioning requirements demand their deaths, is of great concern to the economist conceptualised as shaman. Part of the role of the economist as shaman, then, is to overcome the taboo that we intuitively associate with killing other animals who, however irrationally, we experience as our kin. How else are we to explain the repeated accounts of indigenous peoples' ceremonies to accompany the death of animals in the hunt:

> Animals had souls, of course, so in all hunting societies some form of ritual apology and forgiveness was necessary before the kill: hence the Navajo praying to the deer before the hunt, the Mbuti cleansing themselves by smoke each morning, the Naskapi pledging to the hunted 'You and I have the same mind and spirit'. But plants and flowers and trees had spirits, too, every bit as sensate, so almost all early peoples had elaborate ceremonies connected with cutting and harvesting, asking exoneration for the painful removal of some of the Earth's children, and most had stories like the Ojibways', which speak of 'the wailing of the trees under the axe', or like the ancient Chinese tales which mention cries of 'pain and indignation' from fallen branches.
>
> *(Sale, 1991: 6)*

Hunting, the killing of our fellow species to meet our need for food, has its myths and what Snyder refers to as its 'etiquette' in all indigenous societies. Harvey reports the communication from an Iglulik shaman that it is a great peril to human communities that their sustenance requires eating food that consists entirely of souls (2006: 146):

> The maintenance and furtherance of human community with the wider community of life – of persons only some of whom are human – requires enormous efforts to establish, safeguard, repair, stabilise and enhance relationships threatened by various everyday acts of intimate violence. That is, ordinary nutritional needs assault the community of life and require vigorous action to prevent the reciprocal endangerment of human communities.

This consideration seems helpful in drawing a line between the concerns expressed amongst those who consider that animals have 'rights' – that consuming them is immoral or unjust – and those who are more concerned about the relationship between human animals and the non-human animals they consume (Harrison, 2008). Perhaps considering animals as having souls – and that this requires a respectful relationship while not making impossible the taking of life and the consumption of animals' flesh – could help to progress this seemingly intractable argument.

Basso (1992: 164) cites a story of the Apache people to convey a similar point:

> Long ago, a boy went out to hunt deer. He rode on horseback. Pretty soon he saw one [a deer] standing by the side of a canyon. Then he went closer and shot it. He killed it. Then the deer rolled all the way down to the bottom of the canyon. Then the boy went down there. It was a buck, fat and muscular. There he butchered it. The meat was heavy, so he had to carry it up in pieces. He had a hard time reaching the top of the canyon with each piece. He left the last leg behind. On his way home the boy got dizzy and nearly fell off his horse. Then his nose twitched uncontrollably, like Deer's nose does. Then pain shot up behind his eyes. Then he became scared. He went back to the canyon to look for the leg but it was gone. He was very sick and nearly died and always had bad luck in hunting.

The moral of the tale is clear, and its retelling reminds young hunters that they must kill respectfully and use resources wisely.

A similar technique to bridge the gap between species was the story-telling connected to metamorphosis between humans and animals. These examples of the interchange between species, whether in physical or narrative form, play an important role in mediating our relationship with the environment:

> By invoking a dimension or a time when all entities were in human form, or when humans were in the shape of others animals and plants, these stories affirm human kinship with the multiple forms of the surrounding terrain. They thus indicate the respectful, mutual relations that must be practiced in relation to other animals, plants, and the land itself, in order to ensure one's own health and to preserve the well-being of the human community.
>
> *(Abram, 1996: 121)*

We might think that we have developed a long way beyond a belief in the possibility of metamorphosis or a sense of kinship with non-human animals, such as that evident in totemic cultures, yet there are hints of this closer relationship with animals in our own names. The former Russian president's name, Medvyedev, for example, is derived from the Slavic word for a bear (*medved*), as is the familiar English forename and surname Arthur (from the Celtic *ardd*, a bear), while the familiar name Ralph is derived from a Scandinavian root meaning 'counsel of wolf'. These names of people – as well as those of places which abound with animist references – remind us of a time when we knew ourselves to be animals and recognised the horse and bear as our siblings. This connectedness extended so far as enabling an experience of metamorphosis, where the space between different species and between the animate and inanimate worlds could be bridged.

The concept of totemism has lost credibility amongst social anthropologists, although evidence for cultures that experience relationships with animals that resembles kinship is widespread in their accounts of other societies. While art is not considered academic evidence as such, I cannot resist sharing some examples of artworks that demonstrate the closeness of observation between ourselves and our fellow species, and are suggestive of a closer relationship than that of 'dominion', which dominates the culture of the industrialised West. In the first (Photo 3.1), a detail from the cave-paintings at Pech-Merle, we see the shape of the rock being incorporated into the extraodinary drawing of a horse's head. This painting dates from 25,000 years BCE. The second example is a sculpture of a swimming reindeer, to be seen in the British Museum, where the shape of the animal's body is incorporated into the mammoth tusk, which provides its physical essence. (The artwork is described in detail in MacGregor, 2010: 19ff.) The third illustration is a modern example of metamorphosis: a young woman becoming transformed into a roaring lion (Photo 3.2).

In spite of the nervousness of the social anthropologists, Arne Naess (1986/1989) carried out research into what we really think about the moral importance of other species and found that some understanding of the relationship between different species has survived the rational revolution in the generalised belief that 'every life-form has its place in nature which we must respect'. Midgley (1996: 126) interprets his findings as suggesting that:

PHOTO 3.1 Picture of horses and hands from the Pech-Merle cave, Cabrerets, France
Source: This image is made available without copyright restriction by Wikimedia Commons.

PHOTO 3.2 Young woman in metamorphosis
   Source: Original artwork by Rosa Cato.

people are not orthodox individualists … they feel that they live within a vast whole – nature – which is in some sense the source of all value, and whose workings are quite generally entitled to respect. They do not see this whole as an extra item, or a set of items which they must appraise and evaluate one by one to make sure whether they need them. They see it as the original context which gives sense to their lives … From this angle, the burden of proof is not on someone who wants to preserve mahogany trees from extinction. It is on the person who proposes to destroy them.

This may be one role for the economist as shaman: to remind us of our commonality with other species and to limit our freedom to exploit them freely and without any recognition of the reverence due to their life. We might be encouraged to learn our place in the family of creatures, as we are reminded by Gary Snyder:

> The lessons we learn from the wild become the etiquette of freedom. We can enjoy our humanity with its flashy brains and sexual buzz, its social cravings and stubborn tantrums, and take ourselves as no more and no less than another being in the Big Watershed. We can accept each other all as barefoot equals sleeping on the same ground.
>
> *(Snyder, 1990: 26)*

This is a hard rather than a soft lesson. An understanding of ecology reduces the risk of romanticising nature, since the food web is a simple illustration of the harsh fact of natural life: we live because others have died. We do not know whether a fox feels guilt as it kills a vole, but for humans who are closely embedded with their natural environment, to live life consciously as part of a family of other creatures, to know that your survival requires the death of your brother or sister, is spiritually challenging. Part of the role of the shaman is to undertake the mediation that makes this daily life-and-death interaction more comfortable. The shaman exists in the liminal space between species, and between the worlds of life and death. S/he therefore has the ability to propitiate and to remove the risk of contamination.

3.5. Conclusion: economist as guide and mediator

The purpose of this chapter has not been to draw a strict academic parallel between the role of a shaman in a traditional society and that of an economist in a modern society. I would not be equipped to undertake such a comparison, especially in view of the wealth of ethnographic and other studies in the field (DuBois, 2011). Rather I have sought to identify the particular role of the shaman – that of mediation – as one that might usefully be applied to an economist in a sustainable society. In this final section I begin to sketch out how the notion of a shaman might give us a starting-point to consider what the role of an economist might be: taking seriously my suggestion about the necessity of mediation between human communities and the resources of the environments on which they depend suggests one important role for a green economist.

The first role, I would suggest, would be to acquire and exercise the authority to impose the boundaries to the acquisition of resources. As we saw in the previous section, in traditional societies this was a role of priestly figures, and is a role that we are in dire need of today, when politicians shy away from attempting to persuade us of the hard truth that we cannot continue to consume resources as we have in the past.

Once these boundaries are clearly established and maintained, the economist would be required to act as a mediator between humans and their environment, enabling the process of re-embedding, that would support our respectful relationship with the planet and our fellow species. Whatever the appropriate rituals might be in a twenty-first-century society, I would suggest that the role as described by Abram might provide a template: 'The traditional or tribal shaman, ensures that the village never takes more from the living land than it returns to it – not just materially but with prayers, propitiation, and praise' (Abram, 1996: 7). Recalling Schrodinger's view of life quoted in Chapter 1, as that which attracts 'a stream of negative entropy to itself', we might develop a view of the economist as an expert in this process of minimising the entropic disturbance caused by human lives, balancing our need for joy and flourishing with our impact on natural systems. Perhaps such a low-entropy lifestyle might be considered a part of a necessary approach to civic virtue on the part of the ecological citizen (Dobson, 2003). Just as there is 'bad medicine' in causing too much disruption to natural relationships and the balance of creatures with the planet, so the modern shaman might negotiate our way to access resources so that it causes the least entropic disorder. In the terminology of today's economics, he or she would be responsible for managing the trade-off between entropy and well-being.

And finally, I would suggest that we might assign to economists the role of relearning a relational, embedded approach to the way we live our lives. As we will see in later chapters, this will mean redefining who we consider to be part of our community, and rethinking how we share the common wealth of our local bioregion. How we use those resources – carefully and respectfully – would also fall within their scope of expertise. Nobel Prizewinner Wangari Maathai made much of the ancient Japanese concept of *mottainai*[6] and, although it has not attracted academic attention, it may help to guide economists focused on sustainability and remaking our relationship with resources. It is a difficult concept to translate but links to the intrinsic value of a resource and the wastefulness – perhaps even in a spiritual sense – when that resource is not used to its full. There is clearly a link here to ancient times when the earth itself had a sacred meaning, so that waste of resources was a demonstration of irreverance rather than just fecklessness.

What would economists who took seriously their role in the transition to a sustainable society be like? Not, I would suggest, the typical young man with expert statistical and econometric skills but little knowledge of life and no interest in human relationships or the exercise of judgement. Rather, we might expect our economists to demonstrate a courageous engagement with the environment guided by John Ruskin's useful motto: 'there is no wealth but life'. Hence the primary role of an economist in a sustainable society would be changing our relationship with the earth, its resources, and other species from one of exploitation to one of mutual respect. Far from the computer and the regression model, the training for such an economist would require a direct experience of the wholeness of life, such as that described by Glass-Coffin during her researches into shamanic practices:

> There, beneath a waning gibbous moon on a cool Florida winter night, the scene before me was completely ordinary except that every plant, from the tallest coconut palm to the smallest blade of grass acknowledged and honored my presence ... I suddenly realized, viscerally, what I had been writing about

for many years: that all Life is co-created as willing humans interact in reverence with the very Ground of Being that sustains us. This co-creation is reflected and nourished by the ways in which we interact with one another, by the ways in which we care for the material world that provides for us, and by the ways in which we relate to a firmament which both inspires and humbles us as we journey.

(Glass-Coffin, 2010: 210)

Part II
Bioregional resourcing

4

FIRMS, FARMS AND FACTORIES

Liberal economists, as usual, saw merely a romantic aberration inducted by unsound economic doctrines, where in reality towering political events were awakening even the simplest minds to the irrelevance of economic considerations in the face of the approaching dissolution of the international system.

(Polanyi, 1944: 198)

In Part I we have explored the theory of bioregionalism and considered how we might apply that particular *Weltanschauung* to the economy and to economics. In this chapter and the one that follows we move on to more bread-and-butter concerns: how will we produce and distribute the goods and services that we need and expect; how will a bioregional economy provide? I look at these questions from two differing perspectives: those of the old and new paradigms of economic life. In this chapter I consider the question from within the mental framework of the existing economy. I thus discuss issues of production and the 'factors' that are required to enable that production. This includes a discussion of the nature of organisation of the firms within which that production takes place. I then move to an initial brief consideration of exchange – that is, exchange within the bioregion. (Consideration of exchange on a grander scale must await Chapter 9, which includes a critical discussion of trade as currently undertaken – and theorised.) Although the nuts and bolts of the bioregional economy are discussed in this chapter it cannot really come to life until we shift our attention away from the central concerns of capitalism – exchange, profit, and capital accumulation – towards the central concerns of a human-focused and sustainable economy. Hence in Chapter 5 I address the same questions from the perspective of a provisioning economy.

In *Akenfield*, his ethnographic account of life in a Sussex village in the late 1960s, Ronald Blythe (1972) seeks to convey the relationship between farm-workers, their employers (the landowners) and the land itself. The younger men seek a 'clean' contract where money is exchanged for labour to replace the complex and emotionally involved system of loyalty and connection that farm-workers had lived with since feudal times. The trainer in the local Agricultural School explains the approach to work of agricultural labourers like this:

> When they get to the factory they will work in a way your ordinary conventional industrial worker will never work – really hard. The factory won't change their country natures … A wonderful worker. You will find that nearly every man in the village likes to be considered part of the atmosphere on the farm where hard work is the thing – the good thing! He never really gets used to the kind of 'average' day's work which has to be put in in a factory and he can't understand the kind of bargaining which goes on in industry between the workers and their employers.
>
> *(Blythe, 1972: 195)*

On the other side of the equation, the authority of the landowner is different, perhaps because behind him stands the implacable reality of nature herself. A factory worker can argue with the manager over how the value of his product should be shared between himself and absent shareholders, but there is no such argument with poor soils or bad winters. The intransigence of the global market is nothing to the intransigence of nature herself. There is no arguing with the weather – or with the changes that climate change will bring. Thus the humility of 'the peasant', while repulsive to our intellectual and urban gaze, may have some important lessons as we develop the ability to live within limits.

This is not to romanticise the life of the soil, which is relentlessly hard in all seasons, although Blythe's account makes clear, as does that of Flora Thompson (1939/2000) in *Lark Rise to Candleford*, that it was the introduction of market forces into rural production, and especially the stripping away of ownership and use rights from the 'common people' that reduced their lives to hopeless drudgery. As we shall see in the following chapters, it was the factory system that removed people from their sense of space as well as of time. It brought a productivist ethic where more was necessarily better and where access to resources came in exchange for money. The agricultural ethic of production, with its responsiveness to the variability of the earth and its seasonal approach to work was also lost. Work became a nine-to-five activity, and later a 24/7 activity, with the link to diurnal rhythms being lost.[1]

In spite of the tone of these introductory musings, this chapter begins in fairly conventional economic vein, by addressing the nature of production and its reliance on various factors. I then move on in Section 4.2 to consider an issue of contention between mainstream and green accounts of economic organisation: the issue of scale. Then in Section 4.3 I suggest a form of business that might provide a building-block of the bioregional economy – the co-operative firm – and discuss why it might offer higher efficiency levels as well as a greater commitment to sustainability. Section 4.4 concludes the chapter by considering how a rural ethic might provide a useful framing for rethinking production, a theme that is taken forward in the next chapter.

4.1. The impact of the fictitious commodities and shadow markets

When economists address the issue of the production of goods they begin with the concept of 'factors of production': these can be thought of as akin to resources, but fundamental productive resources that are necessary to make anything that can later be sold in a market. This is important because, as Polanyi points out, labour is not labour until there is a labour–market. Before this momentous transformation people are people or citizens or even workers, but not labour. Land also undergoes a trans-formation when it becomes available for sale in a market, although it does not undergo a change of name. What an economist means by land, however, is not what the layman means by land. As a factor of production land includes everything that can usefully be extracted from land (including from deep beneath it) to become part of a productive process. Thus 'the economic notion of resources is strictly *anthropo-centric*. That is, the economic value of any resource is defined by human needs and nothing else.' (Hussen, 2000: 4) There is no space in this definition for land to have a spiritual or relational importance – what economists would call an 'intrinsic value' – as it does for the Xiximeka people, for example, who see the land as their mother (Zapata and Schielman, 1999).[2] Polanyi (1944) referred to land and labour as 'ficti-tious commodities'. Real commodities are 'objects produced for sale on the market' (Polanyi, 1944: 75). Land, by contrast, 'is only another name for nature, which is not produced by man' while labour 'is only another name for a human activity'. He thought it a fiction to refer to these basic economic elements as equivalent to goods that were produced specifically to be sold.

The third conventional 'factor of production', capital, confronts us with even greater definitional problems. Within a market system, some additional force is required to harness the two fundamental factors to useful production: this factor is capital. In everyday discourse, capital might be considered akin to money, but again it has a different meaning for economists: '*Capital* refers to a class of resources that is pro-duced for the purpose of creating a more efficient production process. In other words, it is the stock of produced items available not for direct consumption, but for further production purposes. Examples include machines, buildings, computers and education (acquired skill)' (Hussen, 2000: 4). This is a somewhat confused definition combining intermediate goods and plant with human capacities. More recent dis-cussions of factors of production often include 'entrepreneurship' as a fourth factor (Naples and Aslanbeigui, 1996), although this merely illustrates the confused nature of the discussion, since human skills and abilities are clearly different in kind from the basic resources of the land and people's phisical work.

The definition from Hussen also excludes any consideration of money and the power money conveys to acquire productive resources and to encourage people to work to transform them into products. For Polanyi money was the third basic ele-ment of economic production: he addressed the issue of money directly and con-sidered it 'merely a token of purchasing power which, as a rule, is not produced at all, but comes into being through the mechanism of banking or state finance' (1944: 76). While this 'merely' may appear dismissive, we should be clear that on Polanyi's account capital-as-money plays a crucial role in the structure of a market economy: 'Yet if profits depend upon prices, then the monetary arrangements upon which prices depend must be vital to the functioning of any system motivated by profits' (1944: 201). His disparaging view is of the equating of money, as a factor of production, with land and labour. Land and labour are both fictitious commodities in the sense that they are not produced directly for sale, but money is surely an even more fictitious commodity since it is called into being to enable exchange and is maintained by credibility. It therefore has the strongest claim to be a fiction. The definition of capital is merely the most confused and confusing aspect of a fairly confused discussion.

Ecological economists have challenged this view of the nature of production, which they take to be a transformation of matter and energy; hence their focus on the importance of the physical laws of thermodynamics (Cato, 2011b: 74–78). Their closer attachment to the physical realities of production has also influenced their definition of the elements that make it possible:

> The basic factors of production are taken as being raw materials, energy, information flows, and the physical and biological processes within the ecosystem that are essential to sustaining life. Thus, except for information, the natural ecosystem is the ultimate source of all material inputs for the economic subsystem. In this sense, then nature can rightfully be regarded as the ultimate source of wealth.
>
> *(Hussen, 2000: 154)*

In his 1992 work *Wealth Beyond Measure*, Paul Ekins sought to combine the best of these two approaches by developing a four-capitals model, an attempt to expand on the concept of capital to enable the rights and needs of other economic 'actors' to be better represented in these negotiations. For example, the concept of 'natural capital' can bring land back into the discussion, but broaden its definition to include resources contained in the earth (as was true of classical economics) and other aspects of the environment which have traditionally been considered freely unconstrained, such as the sea, the atmosphere, and natural systems that support human life, such as pollination or nitrogen cycling (Ekins *et al.*, 1992). Human capital can broaden out consideration of the skilled worker beyond the thin vision of the utility-maximising individual found in economic theory. Social capital can to a limited extent (Fine, 2001) bring the community of workers into the discussion as a group who relate to each other with more or less success, rather than a collection of unassociated individuals.

By broadening our consideration to include these additional capitals we arrive at the four-capital model proposed by Ekins *et al.* (1992: 49):

> In this model, only the definition of manufactured capital is substantially changed from the three-capital case. Ecological capital embodies a more realistic perception than 'land' as to how the biosphere sustains the economy. Human capital emphasizes the roles in wealth creation of health, knowledge,

skill, and motivation. And the new category of social and organizational capital reflects the importance of many kinds of groups in helping people working together to be more productive than they could be as isolated individuals.

Porritt questioned the four-capital model, on the basis that it did not include the financial interest, the prototype 'capital' on some definitions. Once Ekins had gone so far as to re-label other basic factors as capital, capital itself appeared to have left the discussion altogether, in spite of its central importance to an economic system called 'capitalism'. The inclusion of 'financial capital' yielded the Five Capitals Model developed by Forum for the Future and reproduced as Figure 4.1 with the meaning of the capitals explained in Table 4.1. Such a model can facilitate a discussion of the relative importance of each capital in an absolute (i.e. in terms of human survival) and relative (i.e. within the economy as currently structured) sense. As illustrated here the model prioritises natural capital and Porritt makes clear that the earth, as the source of all value, must be protected (Porritt, 2005).

A key debate between environmental and ecological economists concerns whether these different types of capital can be substituted one for another. An environmental economist would argue that it is efficient to compensate for the diminishing stock of non-renewable resources by increasing use of renewable resources. This can drift into arguing that substitution between different types of capital might be possible, so that natural capital can be expended so long as this is compensated for by an increased level of manufactured or even financial capital. An ecological economist would, in contrast,

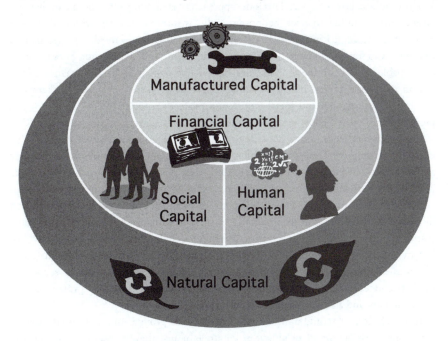

FIGURE 4.1 The Five Capitals Model
Source: Original artwork by Imogen Shaw.

TABLE 4.1 The five capital stocks explained

Type of capital	Description
Financial	Comprised of shares, bonds, or banknotes and useful to facilitate exchange of the other capitals. Has no intrinsic value
Manufactured	Infrastructure created by human effort
Social	Civil society organisations and the relationships of trust they create
Human	Health, knowledge, skills, motivation and spiritual ease of individuals
Natural	The environment, the resources available in the environment, and the natural systems it provides that support life

Source: Summarised from Parkin, 2010: Table 8.3.

defend the primacy of natural capital. While technical improvements can lead to more efficient use of resources, the substitution of capital for natural resources is problematic. The conclusion from the ecological economists is thus that sustainable development requires careful stewardship of all forms of capital and that this must take an equal place in economic calculations alongside considerations of maximizing productivity and utility.

Whatever the motivations of the theorists who together have contributed to this discussion, the decision to equate nature linguistically with money, through the use of the term 'natural capital', has facilitated the exploitation of natural resources. Underlying Ekins's decision to re-label all the factors of production as different forms of 'capital' was his understanding of the distinction between capital, as a fixed asset, and income, as a flow of value. This is the approach of an accountant, who has to draw up balance-sheets, rather than an economist, who is interested in theorising about the most efficient way to produce goods. Ekins believed that we needed to see natural resources and human society as of permanent value, and detach our assessment of consumable value from these permanent values. The tragedy is that the creation of the notion of natural capital has done the reverse: it has enabled the free marketers to commodify the natural and social worlds and make them available for sale through a procedure known as shadow pricing and the creation of 'shadow markets' (Pearce, 1993).

Environmental economists have demonstrated their commitment to market solutions by focusing on a means of enabling the 'wealth beyond measure' that both they and Ekins seek to preserve, to be traded. Only this, they argue, can enable us to value it correctly, recognise its true importance, and then protect it. This process of thus creating 'shadow markets', where the ability of Brazilian rainforests to absorb carbon dioxide can be sold to European airlines, is fraught with technical and political difficulties (Sullivan, 2012). The creation of these shadow markets combines two of Polanyi's fictitious commodities – land and money – to create super-ficitious commodities in equally fictitious markets. It also creates a whole range of secondary markets and complex products that distort the process of trying to protect natural environments and natural resources (Clifton, 2009: 32–34).

In conclusion, it would appear that capitalism has proved itself highly effective in exploiting both factors of production, whether or not they are defined as 'capitals', and those who theorise about them. In fact the creative efforts of theorists with a pro-environment intention have been co-opted and used in the service of the very system which, according to many, they were seeking to radically amend. Rather than stretching both the theory and the practice of the existing model for the production of goods it may be necessary to suggest fundamental changes. Working with capitalists is like teaching a wolf table manners: he may learn to use a knife and fork, but there is no guarantee that he won't fancy you for dessert. From a bioregional perspective it is the predatory nature of capitalism that is the problem and one which needs to be addressed by questioning the ownership and sharing of resources, rather than just the nature of the use of commodities, fictitious or otherwise, in a process of production. (This discussion is taken forward in Chapter 8.)

4.2. Local economies and human scale

After 'capital' I would think that 'efficiency' has a good chance in the competition to be the most confused concept in the economist's lexicon. And of course the two are interrelated, because in lay and popular economic discussions, efficiency is frequently reduced merely to cheapness. Within a paradigm where profit maximisation is taken as the axiomatic objective of productive firms, this is unsurprising. It leads to the absurd situation where it may be efficient to over-exploit resources to the degree that we destroy our own life-support system. With such a serious threat becoming more realistic by the year, it is of vital importance that we redefine what we mean by efficiency. From an environmental point of view, and especially in the context of climate change, energy efficiency should trump financial efficiency in the process of production.

In this regard there is mixed news. A report to the Sustainable Development Commission offered evidence that the CO_2 intensity of production has declined by almost a quarter between 1980 and 2006. Increases in intensity were particularly marked for China, which dominates world production, but the global trend in carbon intensity is no longer declining and has even increased slightly since its low point in 2000. Those who would seek to create a green economy without any significant structural change set much store by 'decoupling' – that is, using improvements in design and efficiency to enable economic growth to continue but with a lower usage of energy. The SDC report is clear that this is not a viable option: it dismisses such hopes as a myth.

The reasons for this are illustrated clearly by Figure 4.2. The graphic illustrates the carbon intensities of production under a range of different scenarios and compares them with a scientifically agreed target for CO_2 emissions. Assuming a commitment to global equity and an increase in global population to 9 billion by 2050, the sorts of increases in energy efficiency required to maintain our current standard of living are inconceivable:

> If we were really serious about fairness and wanted the world's nine billion people all to enjoy an income comparable with European Union (EU) citizens today, the economy would need to grow 6 times between now and 2050, with incomes growing at an average rate of 3.6% a year. Achieving the IPCC's

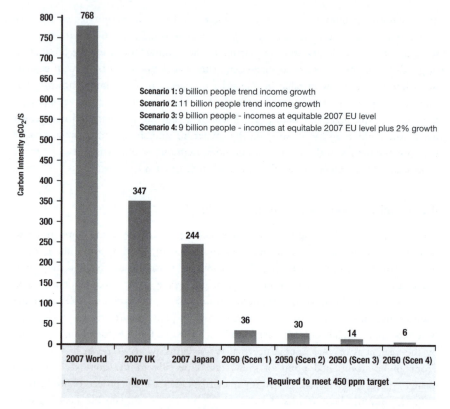

FIGURE 4.2 Carbon intensities of production now and required to meet 450ppm carbon target
Source: Jackson, 2009: Figure 17. Redrawn by Imogen Shaw from the original by
Tim Jackson.

emission target in this world [scenario] means pushing down the carbon
intensity of output by 9% every single year for the next forty or so years. By
2050, the average carbon intensity would need to be 55 times lower than it is
today at only $14gCO_2/\$$ (Figure [3], Scenario 3).

(Jackson, 2009: 55)

Energy efficiency is far from irrelevant to the conventionally managed business, since
its cost impacts strongly on the balance-sheet. However, the negotiation over value
and the need to reduce labour costs can often dominate over any concern about
energy costs. Hence major reorganisations of systems of production and distribution
can often be 'efficient', in conventional terms, even when they demand vast amounts
of energy. From his vantage-point at the National Coal Board, E. F. Schumacher was
shocked by the inefficiency he found in industrial production systems: 'The most
striking thing about modern industry is that it requires so much and accomplishes so
little. Modern industry seems to be inefficient to a degree that surpasses one's ordin-
ary powers of imagination. Its inefficiency therefore remains unnoticed' (1973: Ch. 8

part II). Schumacher identified an excessive focus on growth and economies of scale as the cause of this inefficiency. Here he is joined by green economist Milani, who argues that 'Small is not always necessarily better, but increasingly the most resource-efficient and productive technologies tend to work on a human scale ... The local scale allows direct accountability as well as general participation.' (Milani, 2000: 187–88) Schumacher's book title, which later became a mantra for the environmental movement, *Small is Beautiful*, misrepresents his position, which was rather that we should focus on appropriate scale when designing production systems (of which more in Chapter 10), rather than seeking smallness in some slavish or nostalgic manner.

The financial crisis has demonstrated the vulnerability that results from excessive scale. The slogan 'too big to fail' could be applied as well to our food distribution systems and energy networks, as to our major banks. That within a capitalist economy individual firms will seek to consolidate their power is not a new observation, but the undermining of true competition and innovation is increasingly evident in the global economy, where a tiny number of corporations dominate markets for music or steel production (Power and Hallencreutz, 2007; Nolan *et al.*, 2007; Hamilton, 2009). It seems natural that companies in any sector would wish to enhance their power by either creating cartels or taking over their competitors, and yet such behaviour strikes right at the heart of the market model of numerous competing players and free entry by others. On reflection, this model begins to seem rather inefficient, with firms making rapid switches between productive sectors and a constant churn of new entrants as older firms, which cannot compete effectively, are driven out of business. It is only the unrealistic assumptions about homogeneity of labour and products that can save it.

An example of gross inefficiency driven by the demands of scale – or of political economy[2] – is the shift from conventional docks to container ports which took place in preparation for the major expansion of trade that was one of the hallmarks of globalisation. This was motivated partly by technology, but also as a means of avoiding conflict over wages and conditions in the traditional ports, which were heavily unionised. Thus each old port had a container port constructed nearby – Immingham for Hull, Avonmouth for Bristol, and so on – involving a huge energy input. In conventional economic terms this reconstruction generated economic growth, as did the later renovation of port areas into arts and café quarters, but in terms of thermodynamic efficiency, it was a disaster.

The container illustrates two other aspects of our existing production systems that have to be re-examined in the face of the ecological crisis: standardisation and specialisation. Standardisation is a feature of modern economic life that affects sectors as diverse as agriculture and accounting. The Department for Business Innovation and Skills's website helpfully informs us that 'Standardisation is a prime means of diffusing innovation through the whole economy, ensuring that the bulk of firms do not lag too far behind the early adopters of new ideas', which leaves me with the question: 'What about if they were bad ideas?' There is very little research into the role and popularity of standardisation, and no apparent critique, so I am left to my own devices. The need for standardisation seems to be linked to the increasing diffusion of economic relationships. When we shopped locally the phrase *caveat emptor* was sufficient to guide our consumer behaviour: if a shopkeeper sold us something unacceptable then we would cease to use her shop. Economic relationships were based on personal information and trust. In the globalised economy we need the standards institutions as guardians of quality, a quality that can only be underwritten if there is also a uniformity between the productions being regulated.

There are signs of hope that the popularity of standardisation may be waning. The fisheries policy designed by the EU single market legislation resulted in UK consumers standardising on a very small range of fish – salmon, tuna, cod and haddock – which EU regulations require to be of a standard size. This policy is currently under review (see European Commission, 2011) with the presumption being that, while minimum sizes will stay, the process of discarding fish that are not specifically part of the crew's quota will be ended, meaning that those readers who eat fish may be about to make the acquaintance of some unfamiliar species.

In economic theory 'specialisation' is related to the division of labour and means the focus of the individual's work on one aspect of the production process. This, Adam Smith opined having visited a proto-industrial pin factory, was the more efficient way to produce goods; workers who focused on one tiny aspect of the production process could become extremely expert and therefore (financially) efficient (the social and personal consequences of this move from general to specialist work will be discussed further in Chapter 6). Global specialisation derives from that other leading political economist David Ricardo, whose theories of comparative advantage suggested that countries should focus on the production of whichever goods or services they could produce most efficiently with their endowments of skills and resources. Even if they were less efficient at the production of everything than their trading partner (which was the case with most trading partners of the nineteenth-century Britain where Ricardo wrote his theories), they would still be best placed to focus on one specialism and trade for the rest.

Interestingly, there was also specialisation under central-planning systems, with countries within the Comecon block being encouraged to become part of a shared system of production and some of the Central European countries losing the high-quality production they had previously enjoyed (Salvatore and Sgarbi, 1997). So although capitalism and communism are often presented as contrasting economic systems, they shared this central feature of productive organisation. The explanation is simple: specialisation best supports financial efficiency and economic growth. It is not so helpful in an era of environmental crisis when our focus needs to be on energy efficiency and we recognise that we need to contract, rather than expand, the size of our economy.

Specialisation can reduce the variety and psycho-social value of our consumption (as discussed in Chapter 7) but it can also leave us vulnerable. We rely for our necessities on a global trading system with extremely long supply chains: the vagaries of climate change suggests that this is increasingly insecure (as detailed in Chapter 9). A bioregional approach to the economy would suggest a system of regional specialisation to substitute for the global specialisation of today's economy. Specialisation would not mean that production of a certain good migrated to the area of the world where the labour was cheapest, but rather that areas would attract craftspeople with a certain specialism because the local climate or available materials suited their work. As already discussed, the primary role of the bioregion in a redesigned economy would be to represent the unit from within which people sought most of their goods and services; the basics of life would be provided from within the bioregion and hence each bioregion would offer a different kind of lifestyle. However, luxury goods would still be traded, and it would be here that specialisation would come to the fore in offering a range of high-quality, crafted goods that were valued and preserved. This is the opposite interpretation of specialisation from a system that is based around the domination of the production of identical goods by economies with low wages costs, a system where the goods are cheap, rapidly become obsolete and have limited value.

In this section we have explored how some of the central guiding concepts of the global economy – efficiency, specialisation, and standardisation – need to be re-examined in an era when we have come to realise the limited nature of our planetary systems, our resources and most importantly the energy we can use to support economic activity. So far, the discussion has been in a systemic framework: the following section takes a similar discussion to the level of the firm.

4.3. Co-operative theory of the firm

The example of the construction of container ports provides a stimulus for a deeper discussion of the nature of the capitalist firm, and its appropriateness in an era where rapid innovation and maximum (energy) efficiency are essential. Within the conventional theory of the profit-maximising firm a level of conflict between employees and managers is assumed as axiomatic. The separation of ownership and control (Berle and Means, 1932) and the problem of 'bounded rationality' (Simon, 1957) mean that there must be a compromise between conflicting objectives, and hence both sides must settle for what is defined as 'satisficing' rather than 'maximising' solutions. This is clearly a less than optimal outcome, and the continuous negotiation over the product also absorbs resources in a way that is efficient in an era when we recognise the strict planetary limits on these resources. Smith (2011) has questioned the basic assumption of conflict by studying the nature of these negotiations within a co-operative firm. Here, ownership and control are reunited, 'hence eliminating the problem of agency and, in theory at least, managerial conflict should be removed as the worker-owners share the same values and goals'. In co-operatives there is still negotiation, but this focuses on the conflict between social and economic goals. Sanchez Bajo and Roelants (2011) agree that the existence of 'presentee' owners in contrast to absentee shareholders can help to support the ability of an enterprise to perform its producer function.

The pressure on shareholder-owned firms to maximise returns can also work against innovation. New research from Cleveland, Ohio also indicates how the process of financialisation can cause investment to be diverted away from innovation and into speculation. Margaret Levenstein of the University of Michigan and her colleagues have studied the process of local investment and innovation in Cleveland in the 1920s, when it was at the cutting-edge of technological developments (Lamoreaux,

Levenstein and Sokoloff, 2004). The innovation networks broke down as a result of local investors sending their money to New York, where it fed the bubble that resulted in the stock market crash. They lost their money and the Cleveland local economy never recovered.

The development of the co-operative in the UK is frequently credited to one of the most insightful students of political economy in the early years of capitalism: Robert Owen. Owen was, famously, a gamekeeper turned poacher, a self-made man and factory owner who turned away from his effective methods of management and control and spent his latter years seeking the re-empowerment of the worker and the citizen. He also invested the majority of his considerable fortune in his experimental schemes to develop systems of work organisation and work process that could be socially benign as well as economically efficient. Owen's adherence to the labour theory of value convinced him that the extraction of rents by non-productive owners of capital distorted systems of exchange (Cato, 2006). He therefore argued for a system of pricing based directly on labour:

> Owen argued that the natural value of things made by men depends on the amount of labour incorporated in them, and that this labour is measurable in terms of a standard unit of 'labour time' … Labour, he contends, should supersede money as the standard for measuring the relative values of different commodities; and the exchanging of one thing for another should be done in terms of their relative values thus ascertained.
>
> *(Cole, 1954: 95)*

According to Polanyi, Owen derived his thinking from seventeenth-century Quaker theorist John Bellers, who organised his Friends to oppose the factory system as they had opposed slavery, through their Meeting for Sufferings. Polanyi takes up the theme:

> 'The labour of the poor being the mines of the rich', as Bellers said, why should they not be able to support themselves by exploiting those riches for their own benefit, leaving even something over? All that was needed was to organize them in a 'College' or corporation, where they could pool their effects. This was at the heart of all later socialist thought on the subject of poverty, whether it took the form of Owen's Village of Union, Fourier's Phalansteres, Proudhon's Banks of Exchange, Louis Blanc's Ateliers Nationaux, Lassalle's Nationale Werkstatten, or for that matter, Stalin's Five-Year Plans.
>
> *(Polanyi, 1944: 111)*

In 1819 Owen republished Bellers's plan for 'Colleges of Industry' within which skills and productive value were shared. He also adopted Bellers's idea for labour-notes, which were based on time and enabled the exchange, between artisans, of products of equal value measured in terms of effort. To facilitate such exchanges Owen established his National Equitable Labour Exchange in London in 1832, with another later appearing in Birmingham (Cato, 2008). In its own terms, Owen's

Exchange was not a success, but his ideas inspired the growth of the co-operative firm as well as the trade-union movement, which sought, respectively, to increase the power of the artisan and the labourer.

Although the co-operative movement still represents a significant proportion of our national economy, the debate over the ownership and control of industry is no longer at the forefront of national discussions. This is in stark contrast to the early years of the last century, when the Fabians, who argued for state control of industry, debated hotly with the guild socialists, who argued for worker control of individual workplaces through guild organisation and the syndicalists who favoured direct action and placed their faith in trade unionism. G. D. H. Cole, the historian of his period and Owen's biographer, contrasts the demand for industry-wide control or state ownership from the fledgling Labour Party, with the position of the guild socialists: 'the "workers control" they stood for was, above all else, control by the actual working group over the management of its own affairs within the framework of a wider control of policy formulated and executed as democratically as possible, and with the largest diffusion of responsibility and power' (Cole, 1960: 246–47).

Support for co-operative enterprise is not limited to the socialist wing of the political economy debate: for mainstream economists the extraction of the value of productive activity in profits is inefficient since it leads to rent-seeking (Hill and Myatt, 2010: 124). The landlord or shareholder who is able to live from rents has no incentive to contribute his labour, generating an inefficient use of the labour commodity. He may also lack the incentive to use his land productively. However, if an economic system is undermining the conditions for its own continuing existence it is surely inefficient in a much more fundamental sense. Marx's study of the labour theory of value bore fruit in his description of the central contradiction of capitalism: while a quantity of the value generated by any firm was paid to its employees, another share was always extracted to be paid in profits. This need not be spent in the economy but might either be saved or invested into the growth of the firm. Hence it would not imme-diately be re-spent on goods, leading to a mismatch between the spending power of those who created goods and their ability to buy those goods. Over time this would lead to an excess of production relative to purchase, and a periodic failure of aggre-gate demand and depression (Harvey, 2010; the way that demand is artificially sti-mulated to avoid the consequences of its failure is the subject of Chapter 7). Scholars in the eco-socialist school have updated this view of the capitalist crisis to generate what they label 'the second contradiction of capitalism' (O'Connor, 1988), in which capitalism expands to such an extent that it undermines its own 'productive condi-tions', degrading the environment and exhausting the inputs it needs to make pro-ducts and create profits by selling them. This brings us to consider whether the extraction of surplus value for the benefit of shareholders not only undermines the efficiency of firms but also undermines their role as part of a sustainable society.

While the discussion focuses around the justice or otherwise of the share of pro-ductive value by economists such as Owen (who held to the labour theory of value), the extraction of this surplus value turns out to be highly relevant to our considera-tion of a sustainable economy. Whether they are investors such as shareholders, or middlemen and merchants, the need to take value from the production and distribution cycle, what is now referred to as the 'supply chain', has an in-built tendency to impose greater pressure on resources. This was also recognised in the work of William Morris who, according to O'Sullivan (1990: 179), observed that 'by abolishing the production of surplus value, ... the new society was able to lessen the impact on the rest of nature, by a considerable amount'.

We began this section with a discussion of the advantages of the co-operative firm in terms of innovation and productive efficiency, before considering how this relates to the personal and community rewards that co-operative firms can bring in contrast to shareholder-owned businesses. But what can we conclude about their contribution to the growth of a sustainable economy? In terms of a sustainable approach to economic activity I think we have to take seriously the suggestion that the extraction of surplus value increases the ecological impact of the economy and may therefore be a luxury we can no longer afford.

4.4. Back to the land (ethic)

Unsurprisingly, the area of productive activity where most attention has thus far been given to a bioregional approach to production is in the agricultural sector. According to Pretty, the bioregional approach to agriculture would involve designing whole 'agroecosystems' according to sustainable design:

> For transitions towards sustainability, interactions need to be developed between agroecosystems and whole landscapes of other farms and non-farmed or wild habitats (for example wetlands, woods and riverine habitats), as well as social systems of food procurement. Mosaic landscapes with a variety of farmed and non-farmed habitats are known to be good for birds as well as farms.
>
> *(Pretty, 2007: 143)*

Pretty identifies the philosophy of permaculture as providing suitable guidance for the development of these agro-ecosystems: agriculture would respond to natural systems rather than conflicting with them. Techniques to support such integrated production-and-conservation systems of sustainable landscape design include: integrated pest and nutrient management, conservation tillage, agroforestry, aquaculture and wetlands, water harvesting, and the integration of livestock into whole-farm systems.

Permaculture is a way of looking at the world as a system and creating 'conciously designed landscapes which mimic the patterns and relationships found in nature, while yielding an abundance of food, fibre and energy for the provision of local needs' (Holmgren, 2002: xix). Its proponents consider it to be a design philosophy for a sustainable society: 'Permaculture thinking is also a holistic and systems-based approach to understanding and designing human-nature relations' (Barry, 2012: 82). Although permaculture arose in the sphere of agriculture, or what its proponents often prefer to call 'gardening', its insights have been generalised into a system of planetary stewardship or 'care for the earth'. According to Barry (2012: 94):

Permaculture uses the diversity, stability and resilience of natural ecosystems to provide a framework and guidance for people to develop their own sustainable solutions to the problems facing their world, on a local, national or global scale. It is based on the philosophy of co-operation with nature and caring for both planet and people. But it is not about any simplistic or prescriptive 'reading off' of how we should organise social systems from nature. It is about observing natural design principles and seeing if they 'work' for managing human–nature relations, not about applying such principles in some unreflective manner.

Permaculture follows a series of principles that its proponents claim arise from nature, such as 'use and value diversity', 'produce no waste', and 'use small and slow solutions'. It challenges the immediate rush to action, which is the response of many when first learning about the environmental crisis and cautions, instead, that we should engage in maximum contemplation and minimum action. According to the Permaculture Research Institute of Australia, 'The philosophy behind permaculture is one of working with, rather than against, nature; of protracted and thoughtful observation rather than protracted and thoughtless action; of looking at systems in all their functions, rather than asking only one yield of them; and allowing systems to demonstrate their own evolutions'.[3]

In separate but related work concerned with the human ecology approach to ecosystem management, Bardsley (2003) identifies human ecology as a distinct paradigm in terms of its approach to sustainability, this time in the context of agriculture. His contrast of the two paradigms is reproduced in Table 4.2. The focus of the human ecology paradigm is resource management, as opposed to resource exploitation. Bardsley argues that this approach, developed in the margin and in areas vulnerable to risk, should now be mainstreamed as a response to climate change. Thinking in this vein and applying the thinking of permaculture to production systems we arrive at an approach known as 'industrial ecology', a design system for production that minimises the throughput of materials and energy, and seeks to work

TABLE 4.2. Aspects of the neoclassical and human ecology paradigms

Dominant neoclassical paradigm	Alternative human ecology paradigm
Focus on the core	Focus on the periphery/margins
Maximise profitability	Maximise socio-ecological sustainability
Maximise production	Maximise diversity
Focus on top-down governance	Focus on bottom-up governance
Tendency to standardisation	Support diversification
Strengthen private institutions	Support alternative and public institutions
Develop scientific and technical innovations	Search through traditional methods and enhance these through innovation
Focus on individualism	Focus on community/co-operatives
Accumulation of power and enterprise amongst individuals and businesses	Dissemination of power and enterprise

harmoniously with natural systems, imposing minimally upon them. In this paradigm we have a more embedded approach to the 'circular flow', which contrasts strongly with the limited conception of the 'circular flow' of neoclassical economics (see Figure 4.3). The conception of the economy is as a limited system, within which all waste products must become useful inputs to the next production process, and design focuses on the achievement of 'closed loops' where neither materials nor energy is wasted:

As is the case for permaculture, industrial ecology seeks systematic change in the design of industrial systems:

> Design, here, does not mean the conventional topdown, solution-driven process that is always constrained by the pre-existing mental models of experts operating in worlds fragmented by narrow disciplinary professional niches. Design is, rather, a mindful set of actions taken to transform everyday activities from old, unsatisfying ways to a new set that moves the action in the intended direction.
>
> *(Ehrenfeld, 1997: 91)*

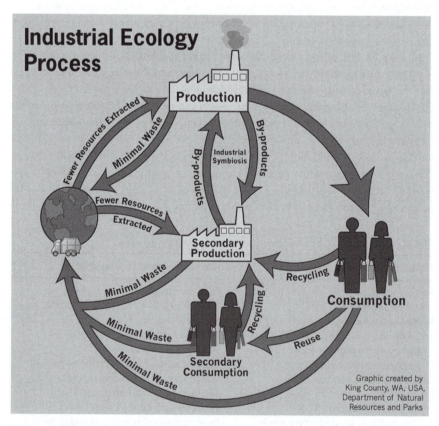

FIGURE 4.3 The production-consumption process as viewed by industrial ecology
Drawn by Wendy Gable Collins; my thanks to the International Society for Industrial Ecology for permission to reproduce this graphic free of charge.

Rather than a collection of technological fixes, industrial ecology seeks to embed industry within the ecosystem: design responds to natural limits and as such 'Industrial ecology offers a bridge between the specific innovations occurring in cleaner production and the attainment of an industrial system supplying human needs within the constraints of global and local carrying capacity' (Lowe and Evans, 1995: 52).

Ehrenfeld (1997: *passim*) lists the key principles to guide product development and design. First he requires that industrial producers 'Improve the metabolic pathways of industrial processes and materials use' by seeking to 'keep substances that upset natural processes out of the environment' and 'preventing the outputs from industrial activities from interfering significantly in normal natural processes'. Second, he recommends the creation of 'loop-closing industrial ecosystems' to replace the linear production systems of traditional industry, where feedstocks and energy are taken in at one end and wastes expelled at the other. The third change should be the dematerialisation of industrial output, by 'bringing demands for resources in balance with the capacity of the environment'. This is partly achieved by redefining what it is we feel we are producing for, shifting the nature of consumption (discussed further in Chapter 7) or moving toward the provision of a service (say hedge-cutting) rather than selling every tenant on an estate a hedge-cutter. Finally, Ehrenfeld recommends the 'systematizing patterns of energy use' by assessing the energy embodied in inputs to production processes and considering the whole life-cycle of the product, not just the phase that takes place in the individual factory.

This takes us to the more ambitious proposal (Lowe and Evans, 1995) that industrial systems should be designed to match ecosystems, their goal being 'to achieve a better match of industrial performance with ecological constraints'. This could in particular facilitate the closed loop production system, since 'The broadest application of this analogic approach is to describe manufacturing complexes as "industrial ecosystems". This idea suggests a web of interaction among companies such that the residuals of one facility become feedstock for another' (Lowe and Evans, 1995: 48). This provides a vision for the organisation of production within a bioregional economy whereby buildings produce more energy than they consume, and can sequester carbon dioxide, and where waste is eliminated as defunct products and the residuals from production processes can biodegrade into useful feedstocks to new productive processes (Porritt, 2005). Extending permacultural principles to industry and following through on the vision of industrial ecology would enable us not only to reverse the industrialisation of agriculture that has been so destructive to the environment during the past 50 years but also to take the ethic of sound land management and ecological care into the industrial sphere.

4.5. Conclusion

When systems of industrial production burst onto the British landscape in the eighteenth century they represented a break with a timeless pattern of social and economic life: it is this fundamental change in the relationship between people, their land and their systems of provisioning that has led to this process being termed a 'revolution'. In the 250 years since the advent of industrialism this system has spread geographically and across the productive sectors. It has brought extraordinary technological innovation paralleled by unimaginable improvements in lifestyle and longevity. While the yields of this system have been apparent and immediate, the costs have been more diffuse and have taken longer to express themselves.

I began this chapter by considering how the relationships between employer and employed, and between labourers and the resources they work with, changed as agricultural production gave way to industrial production. The complex social networks that typified production in rural communities that had changed little since feudal times were replaced by market exchanges. This process of disembedding of productive systems from social and environmental systems has, of course, accelerated rapidly during the process of globalisation. It has led to the failure of accountability for actions, to a disjuncture between producers and consumers, and to an alienation of people from their landscape. As outlined in the following chapter, a bioregional approach to production and provisioning would repair the damage caused by these changes.

In this chapter we have considered the creation and distribution of goods and services within a market system but taking the achievement of sustainability to be the most important guiding principle. However, it is important to question whether this market system is the most conducive to achieving sustainability, or is perhaps at all compatible with a sustainable future. Most of the discussion relating to the link between the market as a system for allocating goods and the achievement of an equal and sustainable society is reserved for Chapter 10. However, this question needs to be raised as a precursor to Chapter 5, where I move on to consider the same questions – questions relating to 'provisioning' – without feeling constrained by the strait-jacket of the market ideology. This may appear to be a utopian project, but I would rather concur with Polanyi in his suggestion that it is in fact the ideology of the free marketeer that is utopian, and dangerously so:

> the origins of the cataclysm [the Second World War] lay in the utopian endeavor of economic liberalism to set up a self-regulating market system. Such a thesis seems to invest that system with almost mythical faculties; it implies no less than that the balance of power, the gold standard, and the liberal state, these fundamentals of the civilization of the nineteenth century were, in the last resort, shaped in one common matrix, the self-regulating market.
>
> *(Polanyi, 1944: 31)*

While the precise forms of the institutions have changed since Polanyi wrote his masterpiece in 1944, his central point remains: that they all collaborated in the underpinning of a unified system with the market economy at its heart. Like Polanyi, I would challenge this totalitarian approach to economic life. In the following chapter we escape the bounds of the market system to imagine an economic life where provisioning is not dependent on the getting and spending of money.

5

PROVENANCE AND PROVISIONING

> The russet, crab and cottage red
> burn to the sun's hot brass,
> then drop like sweat from every branch
> and bubble in the grass.
> I, with as easy hunger, take
> entire my season's dole;
> welcome the ripe, the sweet, the sour,
> the hollow and the whole.
>
> From 'Apples' by Laurie Lee (1985)

In the previous chapter I discussed in some detail how production and exchange might be organised so that they were considerably less wasteful of resources and more supportive of human flourishing. This chapter expands and deepens that analysis through a discussion of an economy that is conceptualised entirely differently from the one we live within today, an economy that does not rely on the market as its central organising form. In Chapter 4 I identified various ways in which the market system of economic organisation is inherently unsustainable. In this chapter I flesh out the framework developed in Chapter 4 to bring to life the bioregional economy as an economy that is essentially human and sustainable *by design*. The analysis is conducted in a Polanyian framework, responding to his account of the great transformation that occurred when the societies of Western Europe shifted from the traditional pattern of subsistence and local embedding to one of global network, a process whose apotheosis is found in the globalised, 24/7, high-speed economy of the twenty-first century. To some this account may appear nostalgic, but I would wish it rather to be viewed as a proposal for a better future, informed by the past certainly, but also responding to the manifold technological and intellectual advances that the two centuries of fossil-fuelled economic growth have brought us.

The following section presents Polanyi's account of the great transformation and the conditions that made it possible. In Section 5.2 I explore the concept of self-provisioning and offer an account of how this process survived, in beleaguered pockets of resistance, the onward march of the market economy. Section 5.3 focuses on the most basic of our needs – that for food – and provides a case-study of how our approach to the provisioning of food is in reaction against the globalised system of production and distribution. Section 5.4 explores the concept of a 'sustainable livelihood': here there is a historical account of the system of commons that typified much of Western Europe before the advent of the market economy. In Section 5.5 I provide a case-study of one particular bioregion – the Somerset Levels – in terms of how its landscape, crops and products intermingle to create a unique productive ecosystem. Finally, in Section 5.6 I return to Polanyi's conditions and imagine how we might reverse them to enable the system of locally based, resource-secure, resilient economies that a sustainable society requires.

5.1. Coming down to earth

In the previous chapter I limited my discussion to the expected economic concepts like production and consumption; here I begin instead with the idea of an economy as being a system to meet human needs. Polanyi's work is valuable in questioning the priority placed on the market in most economic theory. His account of how we arrived at the situation where most of our needs are met by the market is instructive. Polanyi identifies three stages in the:

> subjection of the surface of the planet to the needs of an industrial society. The first stage was the commercialization of the soil, mobilizing the feudal revenue of the land. The second was the forcing up of the production of food and organic raw materials to serve the needs of a rapidly growing industrial population on a national scale. The third was the extension of such a system of surplus production to overseas and colonial territories. With this last step land and its produce were finally fitted into the scheme of a self-regulating world market.
>
> *(Polanyi, 1944: 188)*

Given that, as we have seen in the previous chapter, the market system needs to be re-evaluated in an era when our most pressing task as a human community is to ensure the sustainability of our society, we might raise questions about all three of these processes of transition. It is taken for granted by most contemporary economists that land can operate like any other resource; in other words that the process of the commodification of land – its bundling into parcels over which ownership rights can be asserted – and of its sale in a market are unproblematic. However, in societies separated from us in time and space this was very far from the case. Although it is difficult for us today, some two centuries after our ancestors moved from the land into the industrial towns and cities, to imagine life outside the market, this form of

economic organisation is, rather than the ubiquitous and inevitable rule of its imagining, in reality something of an aberration in economic history. Its role as the
central and controlling mechanism in economic life is a modern and short-lived one:
'Though the institution of the market was fairly common since the later Stone Age,
its role was no more than incidental to economic life' (Polanyi, 1944: 45).

In the context of Britain the narrative of how land that had once been owned in
common became subject to the property rights of the few is framed by the concept of
'enclosure'. Christopher Hill's account of the century of change that surrounded the
English Civil War provides a definition of enclosure derived from its earliest phase:

> 'Enclosure' meant that land held in scattered strips in the village open fields was
> consolidated into compact holdings, which the occupier might hedge about so
> as to protect them from other people's cattle. He was then free to experiment
> with rotation of crops, or to switch from arable to pasture. The great age of
> enclosure for sheep-farming had perhaps come to an end by the end of the
> seventeenth century; but enclosure and consolidation for improved arable
> farming, to feed the expanding industrial areas, was proceeding apace.
>
> *(Hill, 1961/2002: 18)*

Peer-review literature on the enclosures is sparse, with the accounts most often being
given by social historians rather than economists. This was not the case at the time of
second large-scale wave of enclosure, which occurred from the last decades of the
eighteenth century onwards in England, when it was a central theme in contemporary debates about political economy. The one side, for the 'improvers', argued
that the open-field system was inefficient and that commons represented resources
left idle. On the other side, for the 'people', were those who argued the rights of
natural justice for people to be allowed to maintain their ability to work to provide
for the livelihoods directly. Whether we take Thompson's (1963) account of the
enclosures as a means of forcing labourers into the growing industrial centres, or
whether we take Hill's view of pre-enclosure England as 'a backward economy' with
high levels of underemployment, this was certainly a cataclysm for England's peasants.
(What those whose livelihood was based on subsistence made of their 'under-
employment' during the winter months when they had time to sit by the fire and
mend socks is not recorded.)

From a Polanyian perspective this process precisely describes the transition from an
economy based on sustainable livelihoods, to one reliant on international trade. The
sheep who replaced the cottagers and commoners on England's fertile fields were the
basis of the country's wealth from the Middle Ages onwards. The story of the Great
Transformation is one of the struggle between these sheep, and the rich men's for-
tunes they carried on their backs, and the poor people who needed to use their
grazing land to grow their own food. Once deprived of this means of subsistence
they became the labourers, for whom 'under-employment' now became a meaningful category, and who required work to earn money to buy their bread. Following
the Enclosures, as Polanyi disparagingly comments:

> The creation of goods involved neither the reciprocating attitudes of mutual aid; nor the concern of the householder for those whose needs are left to his care; nor the craftsman's pride in the exercise of his trade; nor the satisfaction of public praise – nothing but the plain motive of gain so familiar to the man whose profession is buying and selling.
>
> *(Polanyi, 1944: 77)*

Polanyi's second stage of the transition to a market economy he calls the 'forcing up' of production of food and organic raw materials' in response to the movement of the population from the land and its rapid expansion in the industrial cities. What he has in mind here, I think, is the loss of balance between people and their land, which is a nexus of interacting pressures and conflicts rather than a simple cause-and-effect process. Malthus's renowned concern for the negative impact of population growth failed to identify the causes of the increase in population he observed. During this phase the political economy debate shifted away from the most productive use of land towards the relationship between land use and population, with those in favour of enclosure taking a Malthusian line that land 'improvement' would avoid the need for the 'preventive check' of famine (Ward, 2002). Those who defended subsistence agriculture argued that the relationship between land use, subsistence and population growth was more subtle.

In an economic system focused on profit, rising population represents a larger productive workforce and more consumers and hence greater market demand. While some environmentalists have traditionally taken what can be judged to be a neo-Malthusian stance on the population question, the more nuanced response to the debate is to recognise that the shift to the market broke the connection between people, their need for resources and the land they inhabited. In a peasant community, each new birth represents a mouth that needed feeding from a limited land resource; in contrast, in an economy where livelihoods are based around the labour-market, each birth represents a potential labourer whose time can be sold. Evidence of the extent of child labour in Victorian cities or in the megalopolises of the global South today is greeted with horror, and yet it is a rational response at the individual level to an economic system in which people have no right to land and need their children to guarantee their subsistence.

Polanyi's third point is linked to the second, since once the industrialised country's population was engaged in producing goods for trade rather than for its own subsistence, their basic needs for food and the raw materials to make clothing had to be met from the work and land of others; and in the colonial era and subsequently, this has meant through using the under-priced land and labour of countries of the global South. Extending Polanyi's insight into the present globalised economy we can characterise the system of global trade as a means of enabling the rich Western economies to rent land in the poorer countries, an exchange that cannot be fair while the former's currencies dominate the system of global trade. (For further discussion of this point see Cato, 2009a.)

The market system has dominated the Western economies for several centuries, and in the last century began a gradual ideological colonisation of the rest of the world. The social and economic situation we share today is a result of its power and a consequence of its design. For some, the gross inequalities and ecological pains are a price worth paying for the high levels of consumption that we enjoy today, and that they believe others will enjoy in the future. Those who take a less sanguine view might consider an alternative approach to provisioning based on self-reliant and small-scale units of production and distribution to be worth consideration. As Dobson makes clear, the use of the term 'self-reliance' rather than 'self-sufficiency' is an important distinction:

> Despite green politics often being identified with the self-sufficiency commune movement, it is most generally seen to be organized around principles of self-reliance rather than self-sufficiency. What is the difference? Self-sufficiency may be described as 'a state of absolute economic independence', while self-reliance is best understood as 'a state of relative independence'.
>
> (Dobson, 2007: 82; quoting Bunyard and Morgan-Grenville, 1987: 334)

The extent to which societies seek independence and the argument over the extent of the role for trade is discussed further in Chapter 9. The remainder of this chapter sketches a vision for an economy in which provisioning no longer relies on the global market but instead is based around self-reliant local communities. The content is a mixture of theory and practice. Because I am seeking to move my own patterns of provisioning towards my local bioregion, many of the examples given in this chapter are drawn from the area of Stroud, the innovative market town where I live.

While developing these ideas I have discussed them with a range of different audiences. What interests me is how receptive people are to this vision of a locally based economy that requires considerable commitment to hard work. The most frequent response is something along the lines of 'That sounds idyllic but it just isn't possible'. I challenge the idyll by pointing out that a considerably lower standard of material consumption is implied, together with much more manual work. The response is usually the same: 'Oh, I don't mind *that*'. The barriers to such a self-reliant approach to economic life appear to be intellectual: the market myth is a hegemonic one and people find it hard to imagine other worlds as possible. We may not enjoy hard work, but we are not so far distant from our peasant ancestors that we cannot understand the sense of satisfaction that comes from a day spent in the garden or on the allotment despite an awareness that it would involve considerable manual work.

As the following quotation from the fourteenth-century allegorical poem *The Vision Concerning Piers Plowman* demonstrates, the contempt of the working person for the 'bludger', whether mendicant or merchant, has a long history:

> All living labourers - that live by their hands
> And take the just wages - they honestly earn,
> And live in love and in law - for their lowly hearts
> Have the same absolution - that was sent to Piers.
> Beggars and bidders - are not in the bull,

> Unless the occasion be honest – that makes them to beg.
> He that beggeth or cadgeth – unless he have need
> Is as false as the fiend – and defraudeth the needy;
> He beguileth the giver – all against his will
> For if he wist he were not needy – he would give to another.[1]

We should also be aware of the risks of romanticising the hard daily toil of those who for centuries supported the peasant economies of Europe, as well as those who lead a similar life across the world today. Although the call for a 'rehabilitation of manual labour' (Fairlie, 2009) may become an inevitable one, we should remember that while Van Gogh's portrait of the potato eaters has often been interpreted as one of the nobility of the worker who earns his bread directly from the soil, the artist himself lived amongst the peasants of the Borinage as an act of solidarity with what he saw as a desperately oppressed class.[2]

5.2. A self-provisioning economy

To suggest that people might meet their own needs directly is an idea that struggles within the ideological hegemony of the market as the primary system for the provisioning of one's needs in the developed West. Although England was the first country to undergo the industrial revolution and the great transformation in economic relationships that it gave rise to, most of us can trace our family tree back to a time when our ancestors first left the land. To think about a self-provisioning economy is to imagine their provisioning strategies transposed into the technological and cultural realities of the twenty-first century.

In a way entirely appropriate to a book with such an earthy theme I need to begin the discussion in this section with some ground-clearing. In the previous chapter I stuck fairly rigorously to accepted economic concepts, such as efficiency, factors of production, consumer behaviour, market exchange, and so on. In this chapter I am intending to break the bounds of this conventional discourse and to help me I need some alternative concepts. First we are going to move away from the consideration of employment and labour and use instead a concept that combines and summarises both: the concept of livelihood. The Merriam-Webster online dictionary tells us that the word denotes 'means of support or subsistence' and that it has an older, now obsolete meaning relating to the quality or state of being lively. If suitably hyphenated the word can imply some rather energetic gangsters, but when preceded by the adjective 'right' it acquires a sense of exaltation associated with the Buddhist 'noble eightfold path' and a refusal therefore to engage in any activities that might harm others, in order to meet one's own needs. The Oxford online dictionary agrees that the word implies 'a means of securing the *necessities* of life' rather than focusing on consumption or the acquisition of wealth. It finds a derivation from the Middle English 'livelode', meaning a way of life, a combination of the words for 'life' and 'course'. This focus on life, and a lifetime perspective give a hint to the way in which we might contribute our individual skills to the benefit of the wider community, as well as to our own support, is a useful indication of the much deeper and more relational approach to meeting our needs that a bioregional economy would require.

My other chosen word is 'provisioning'. This requires some adjustment from the standard definition of the verb as meaning to 'supply with food, drink or equipment, especially for a journey'. Merriam-Webster's 'to supply with needed materials' is helpful in implying an approach based on sufficiency, as is their suggestion that the word probably arose in relation to preparing a ship for a journey. Ecofeminist economists such as Mellor (1997), have used this concept to support their conceptualisation of a sustainable economy, in contrast to one dominated by the objectives of the mythical 'rational economic man':

> Is it possible to devise an economic system that is ecologically sustainable? By 'economic' in this context I mean a system of provisioning for the *whole* human community that is sufficient to meet survival and quality of life needs, while being ecologically sustainable. A provisioning that would be, in both senses, a 'sustaining economy'.
>
> *(Mellor, 1997: 134)*

Although theorists of bioregionalism have made tremendous contributions in terms of visioning an alternative approach to our relationship with land, and to linking this to our ability to behave as what Dobson would call 'ecological citizens', their proposals in terms of political economy are far more vague, and in many cases nonexistent. In Chapter 8 I make some tentative forays into this arena; here my discussion is limited to considering how local communities might support the sustainable livelihoods of their citizens, as part of the sort of network of self-reliant local economies that would instantiate a bioregional economy.

Much of this activity is underway, and in the UK context it has been popularised under the brand of the Transition Towns, a movement of community-led response to climate change and Peak Oil that grew from its roots in Kinsale, Ireland to emerge in the south-western UK in 2006 and has since spread to other towns and cities in that country and beyond (North, 2009; North and Cato, 2012). Barry (2012) views 'the Transition movement as a form of prefigurative green politics', a form of green political action that draws on ideas from outside its usual 'normative hinterland'. The aim of the movement is to respond positively to the reduced energy framework that sustainability requires, and to find a means of preserving the optimal features of our current society (defined in terms of well-being) while following a path towards aggressive energy reductions, defined for each community according to an Energy Descent Action Plan (Hopkins, 2008).

At a more theoretical level, a related exercise has been carried out on behalf of the UK's Department for Business, Innovation and Skills. It involved the development of a range of different future scenarios based on the need to rapidly reduce energy consumption. The scenarios are based on a series of 2 x 2 matrices arising from two 'axes of uncertainty'. The x-axis 'describes the significant uncertainties in the global political and economic context in 2050', while the y-axis 'looks at the type of innovation which attracts investment' (Foresight, 2008: 11–12). On the x-axis are represented possible assumptions about the extent of co-operation between nations, while the y-axis marks out the continuum between investment in optimising existing systems or developing wholly innovative solutions.

This process results in four possible scenarios: Green Growth, Carbon Creativity, Resourceful Regions and Sunshine State. Two of the scenarios have commonalities with a bioregional future, although both are based on this relocalisation as a response to a failure of global solidarity, which is by no means the basic assumption of a more regionally based economic future. In the first, the Resourceful Regions, 'The key distinguishing feature is that English sub-regions have a high degree of autonomy, matching Scotland and Wales':

> The countryside is used more intensively than in the past, for food production, mining and other activities. Within built-up areas, retrofitting rather than new build is the preferred approach. Any new buildings are increasingly built in a local vernacular style, and there is considerable emphasis on urban green space to tackle overheating. People in this Britain like to think they are self-reliant, and are proud of being British, even though the country is closer to breaking up than any other time in the previous century. Their living conditions vary widely as regions have their own economic structures and differing levels of economic success. But acceptance of the situation is underpinned by strong regional identities and the effectiveness of most regional governments' moves to support vulnerable groups and public services such as public transport.
>
> *(Foresight, 2008: 14)*

In the Sunshine State scenario, 'Government has fostered an emphasis on localism to respond to energy problems', and there are other aspects of the imagined future that could find resonance with a bioregional approach: 'There are more local shopping streets and other community resources, partly because of planning decisions intended to promote local autonomy and partly because of municipal enterprise' (Foresight, 2008: 15).

I cite these examples not to support their vision of the future, which I think is limited by the nature of the underpinning assumptions, as well as the method used, but to indicate that government is considering the future design of economic systems that must result from rapid reductions in energy use. Policy focus has been most strongly on the Green Growth scenario, with profit-driven companies providing technological solutions, and to a lesser extent the more co-operative Carbon Creativity approach, but these are political choices. In a democracy, visioning the future is a job for all and these scenarios make clear that a bioregional future is a realistic possibility.

As Barry (2012: 88) notes, however, 'The report, while in many respects offering some welcome insights in terms of challenging the lock-in' to centralised systems of energy production, does not deal with 'lock-in' to patterns of development, land-use or lifestyles that require and demand high carbon energy use'. More useful here is the Sustainable Development Commission report *Prosperity without Growth*, which specifically identifies 'alternative hedonism', a new approach to provisioning, which the report's authors consider reflects 'a nascent disaffection with consumerism'. The dissatisfaction arises from the work-and-spend treadmill that reduces the quality of personal relationships, what Kate Soper called in her evidence to the Commission (Soper, 2008) 'fatigue with the clutter and waste of modern life' (Jackson, 2009: 12). Attempts to enable these transitions towards local sufficiency economies are severely limited, and are inevitably constrained by the ideological and geopolitical domination of the globalisation model of provisioning. My own local community of Stroud has produced a report exploring the potential for meeting our own needs for food from the local land (Macmillan and Cockcroft, 2008), but there is little evidence that local policy-makers see this as a key priority, much less an aspect of their regeneration rather than their climate change strategy.[3]

Barry (2012: 107) identifies the Transition Towns as 'pioneers' or 'foot soldiers' of the new sustainable economy and society who 'challenge the dominant cultural and economic narrative':

> Objectives such as food and energy self-reliance and security, which are central to the Transition vision, resonate with a fairly traditional pioneer mentality' of people venturing into new lands and without the infrastructure of society, or a national or globalised economy, and who had to support and fend for themselves. The transition vision of a local economy progressively decoupling from the long supply chains of energy, materials and commodities of the globalised economy does herald a clearly more self-reliant economic and social vision. In the absence of political leadership the activities of community groups such as those who carry the label Transition Towns are significant.

In critiques of green political economy much is made of the comfortable, middle-class roots of its progenitors and their marginal position in society and in political debate. However, at least in the context of the UK, we can see statistical evidence that the 'pioneering' of lifestyles with some element of self-provisioning is growing apace. In the case of England, a survey in 2011 showed that there were 152,442 allotment plots in production and a waiting list of a further 86,787 wanting to join those already producing their own fruit and vegetables (Campbell and Campbell, 2011). In the following section I focus on food as an iconic and resonant example of 'consumption'.

5.3. What's eating us?

The market system's primary claim to supremacy is based on the concept of allocative efficiency: we teach our students that the self-interested decisions of millions of individuals will, thanks to the miracles of the invisible hand, achieve the best possible allocation of the available (scarce) goods. While this claim tends to be made only in terms of the narrowly defined Pareto optimum – that is, a situation in which it is not possible to improve somebody else's position without making another person worse off (Feldstein, 1999) – it is none the less a fairly strong claim. Yet it seems to be assaulted daily by evidence that the market system is resulting in grossly inefficient allocations: a yawning gulf separates the market model and the real world.

The most shameful example is glaringly obvious every day in the global allocation of food. Due to a combination of climate-related weather events, wars and speculation in the global food market, 2008 was a particularly bad year in terms of global food security. According to the World Food Programme, the number of under-nourished people in the world increased to 963 million, a rise of 115 million from 2006. Meanwhile, the countries of the West have seen a boom in obesity and diseases related to over-consumption, particularly diabetes. The World Health Organization (WHO) estimates that obesity accounts for some 7–8% of the 'total disease burden' in its European region (WHO, 2008: 1). It tells us that, across the world, the prevalence of obesity nearly doubled between 1980 and 2008 and that in the European region half the population were overweight, with around one in five being obese. A massive global study of diabetes, which included 2.7 million participants, found that nearly 10% of the sample group had the disease. The incidence of diabetes is very uneven, with very low prevalence in sub-Saharan Africa, east and south-east Asia and no increase over this period in Asia or Eastern Europe. Amongst the rich countries the fastest increases were in North America.

The data are clear: many people in the world do not have enough to eat, a significant proportion die from hunger, and a significant proportion die from over-consumption. So while the global market can offer rich Western consumers strawberries in January, it cannot claim to be achieving a just allocation of food. Since Pareto optimality does not concern itself with issues of equity, then it might be an efficient allocation according to economic theory, but if a theory considers a distribution system efficient when it causes death and suffering on such a wide scale, surely we should question the theory and come up with a better one. If the market is now global, then under-nourishment of one-sixth of the world's population is an indictment of a distribution system based on the market model (World Food Programme, 2009).

Food is the most fundamental way in which we interact with our environment. Although the economic system set free of its physical connections has enabled our consumption of unseasonal fruits and vegetables that have travelled thousands of miles, it cannot remove our need to consume parts of our environment in order to survive. This, the most basic level, defines the nature of consumption within any economic system; in the bioregional system of provisioning it is made central. Although scientific analysis of food suggests that genetically modified (GM) foods are no different from non-GM and that a potato grown in Bolivia may provide us with the same chemical content as a potato grown in Tetbury, in reality we are, in a very real sense, what we eat, and what we eat is, under most systems of agriculture, constituted of the soil where it was grown. In Chapter 2 I explored the way geology might be used to define bioregions. What it certainly can do is tell us about the rock that underlies our homes and gardens, and which has, over time, become both the building materials for our homes and the structure of the soil. If we grow food in our soil, the proportions of trace elements the food contains are related to the structure of that soil. If we use local water supplies, the water has filtered through these rocks and also contains a different proportion of minerals of different types depending on the nature of those rocks. The proof of this lies not in the pudding but in the teeth we use to eat the pudding. Our teeth form very early in life and absorb elements as they do so – such as oxygen and strontium – that occur naturally in different isotopes. By assessing the relative proportions of these isotopes that were absorbed in the diet, archaeologists are able to determine where people lived during their early years (Natural Environment Research Council, 2010). You literally are what you eat – as well as what you drink and what you breathe.

By the standards of comparative societies past and present the consumption of the wealthy Westerner is bizarre. Like our consumption patterns in general it is driven by variety and titillation rather than healthy appetites (Thorpe, 2009). The American Psychiatric Association has been imaginative in its pursuit of diagnoses for a range of 'eating disorders', including 'purging disorder' and 'avoidant/restrictive food intake disorder'. A US alternative medical guru Steve Bratman has identified a disorder 'orthorexia nervosa', which he defines as 'an unhealthy obsession with eating healthy foods'.[4] The first apparently scientific exploration of this disorder identified the use by sufferers of 'attribute characteristics' that show the 'feelings' towards food. These include the word 'artificial' being applied to industrially produced products and the word 'healthy' being applied to biological produce. While there is certainly something wrong here, it seems questionable whether it is the use of these labels. Perhaps orthorexia nervosa, or at least the symptoms of consumption-related stress that it is evidence of, indicates a breakdown in the relationship between our physical selves and the natural environment we need to consume. We engage in this fetishistic consumption, I would argue, because we have lost any sense of connection with how and where our food is produced. Labels such as 'wholefood' or 'organic' suggest foods that we can trust without knowing their provenance directly.

A healthier, or at least more enjoyable, response to this dislocation is the rise in popularity of the farmers' market. As well as the concept of 'provenance', the literature discussing the farmers' market is framed in terms of 'embeddedness', whether this is social (knowledge of vendors), spatial (support for local production) or environmental (organic production or concern for food miles) (Feagan and Morris, 2009). This suggests a continuing motivation amongst consumers towards the closely related systems of provisioning that typified pre-market economies and that the bioregional economy seeks to revive.

So it seems only appropriate to indulge myself by both localising and personalising the discussion. My own county of Gloucestershire is one of the UK's several proud apple counties. My home town of Stroud has its own apple, the Lodgemore Non Pareil, and the nearby village of Taynton is the proud possessor of varieties of apple, pear and walnut. The Gloucestershire love of apples is an example of what the French would call an attachment to *terroir*, the sense of pride in your local place and its specialities that could be taken as constitutive of a bioregional approach to provisioning. The contrast with a globalised market approach to provisioning is instructive. While the market economy needs global uniformity and standardisation, the bioregional economy revels in difference and local distinctiveness. The word 'terroir' comes, of course, from the word *terre* meaning land, and it is this attachment to land – your local land, as expressed in the particular products it is suited to producing – that lies at the heart of the ability of a bioregional economy to enable a process of environmental re-embedding.[5]

Although this discussion arises from rural and specifically peasant communities there is no reason why it should not be extended to an urban context. Although industrial workers had left the land this did not mean that they abandoned self-provisioning, as is testified in the UK by the allotments movement. The drinking of tea and 'small beer' was a response to the lethal quality of drinking water in the early industrial cities, and local food specialities responded to specific working conditions and long hours. An example is the eating of tripe in England's mill towns. This unprepossessing product of cows' guts was cheap to buy, could be cooked when time permitted and then eaten cold and, perhaps most importantly, would slip down a throat made dry by a day in the mill, where the air was always filled with cotton fibres (Maconie, 2007).

I began this discussion with food because it is an aspect of our consumption that we can never wholly disconnect from our natural environment. However, other aspects of our material life offer their own opportunities for re-embedding and re-identificiation with our local soil. Photo 5.1 is a picture of a mug that I bought at a craft fair in Stroud. What attracted me to it was not its beauty but the fact that it had been made using local clay. The potter who sold it to me was intrigued to find out what Stroud clay might be like, so she abandoned her plastic bag of shop-bought clay and sallied forth into her back garden to dig a pit. What she found beneath the top-soil was clay of a beautiful red colour and smooth consistency. After considerable work purifying the clay she made it into just one mug, and this was the mug I bought. To me it has a value far beyond the 'bare price' I paid for it. I feel similarly about my 'bioregional hat', also illustrated (Photo 5.2). This was made by my basket-making teacher Sheila Wynter, from rushes gathered in the River Avon near Tewkesbury. The hat smells of the West Country and allows me to take a small part of home with me during my summer travels. These are just two illustrations of how consumption based on local products enables the sort of re-embedding with the local natural environment that ecological citizenship requires.

Our need for shelter can also express a local culture and has always responded to locally available materials. The appeal of this approach to building was demonstrated by the popularity of Ben Law's Woodland House (Photo 5.3), which was awarded the prize as the most popular house on the UK television show Grand Designs (Willi, 2011). Built from sweet chestnut wood cut in his own Prickly Nut Wood it uses the roundwood method of construction that best retains the natural shapes of the tree within the finished house. The roof is made from individually split shingles, while the clay for the render was dredged from the local pond. The house is, clearly, beautiful, but its beauty is enhanced by the way it seems to emerge from its local setting.

More generally, we have seen a growing commitment to vernacular architecture, which represents the architecture that was possible before the era of fossil fuels. Our present building methods rely on the hugely energy-intensive brick, which is frequently transported over large distances. Building with wood, by contrast, offers the ability to sequester carbon for the lifetime of the building. In my own bioregion the natural building material is Cotswold stone, which now attracts premium prices and defines conservation areas across the region. In the Costwold Stone Belt, as Trueman

PHOTO 5.1 Mug made from local Stroud clay
Source: Author's photograph.

PHOTO 5.2 Hat made by Sheila Wynter from Gloucestershire rushes
Source: Author's photograph.

PHOTO 5.3 Ben Law's woodland house
Photograph by Ben Law www.ben-law.co.uk

observed some 70 years ago, 'A single build of brick here becomes an eyesore' (Trueman, 1938: 21). William Cobbett, who travelled through the area on one of his rural rides, would have begged to differ. As he reports on his journey between Malmesbury and Worcestershire: 'The subsoil here is a yellowish, ugly stone. The houses are all built with this; and, it being ugly, the stone is made *white* by a wash of some sort or other' (Cobbett, 1830/1985: 376).

It is easy for those who take comfort in the ubiquity and omnipotence of the global market system to dismiss the growth of farmers' markets or the huge popularity of sustainable construction as quaint aberrations or fits of nostalgia. However, I believe it is possible to interpret them differently: as examples of a growing reaction of people against the essentially dissatisfying world that the market economy offers. The response to the creation of 'labour' as a fictitious commodity arose first – in the form of civil unrest, labour organisation and the demand for democratic representation. The response to the creation of a market for the fictitious commodity of 'land' has been slower, largely because its negative consequences were exported to the colonised areas of the world. As the limits of that strategy become clear, and the limits of the earth are transgressed, the environmental movement is the political expression of a human response to this economic failure. The more direct economic expression, akin to the growth of labour power, is the rise in the power of the food producer. The rise of supermarket activism and guerrilla gardening, not to mention the demand for land rights expressed through the work of organisations such as The Land is Ours and Reclaim the Fields, may be seen as the first hints of this movement finding means of political expression.

5.4. Sustainable livelihoods

The concept of a sustainable livelihood is well recognised in the field of development studies:

> Measuring rural livelihoods and environmental dependence is not straightforward ... there is not an established right way to systematically collect data that convey their importance. Such resources, harvested in non-cultivated habitats ranging from natural forests to rangelands and rivers, often contribute significantly to households' current consumption, provide safety-nets or pathways out of poverty ... Environmental income often consists of many different and sometimes irregularly collected resources: the forest fruits picked during herding, the medicinal plants collected when grandfather was sick, last month's particularly rich fish catch, and so on. A myriad of resources gathered from multiple sources makes environmental income much harder to recall and quantify than a single annual corn or sorghum harvest.
>
> *(Wunder* et al., *2011: 1)*

This is the opening paragraph of a book that attempts to put a monetary value on the subsistence activities of poor people in 'developing' countries. Such activities are often devalued and overlooked as communities are engulfed by the market system and yet they represent a means of dignified self-reliance as well as a way of achieving a livelihood, often in symbiosis with nature.

As Polanyi makes clear, such a lifestyle was also typical of those who lived in our own land, and it vanished only shortly before living memory, with some hints remaining in the vegetable growing and clothes-making of our grandparents' generation. The reason for its disappearance was the loss of common rights to land and its use, which accompanied the rise of the market – and in particular the labour market. The political economy of that process will be discussed further in Chapter 8; in this chapter we will merely focus some attention on piecing together the way our ancestors created sustainable livelihoods before the advent of the market system. Here I am deeply indebted to the painstaking work of Jeanette Neeson, whose historical analysis of the system of common land usage and its demise is relied on heavily in this section. The award of the Swedish Bank Prize for Economics to Elinor Ostrom has brought more attention to the study of forms of resource sharing that do not rely on strictly enforced property rights. In English history, this was the nature of the land system until the early modern period, and it was a system that revolved around the use of commons.

Snyder describes the common as 'a territory which is not suitable for crops' and lies 'between the extremes of deep wilderness and the private plots of the farmstead' (1990: 32). Yet commons were not, as suggested by critics, wild spaces where the fittest fought for the right to over-graze, but rather were large proportions of land (Neeson, 1989, estimates up to 30% of British rural land) whose use was controlled by a complex system of social and economic norms. Perhaps more importantly – from the perspective of this book – they represented a form of subsistence in which meeting your needs from the local environment was explicit:

The commons is a curious and elegant social institution within which human beings once lived free political lives while weaving through natural systems. The commons is a level of organization of human society that includes the nonhuman. The level above the local commons is the bioregion. Understanding the commons and its role within the larger regional culture is one more step toward integrating ecology with economy.

(Snyder, 1990: 40)

Neeson's close, historical study of some British commons indicates just how much they were able to provide, and offered far more than the 'trifling fruits of overstocked and ill-kempt lands', which were dismissed by those who sought 'improvement' (Humphries, 1990). Obviously there was grazing and the possibility to gather firewood and other materials that were used for fires – furze (gorse) and bracken (fern). The commoners also took hazel loppings to make hurdles for penning sheep, and fern was also used for animal bedding and, once burnt, its ash was used to make soap. In addition:

Reed was plentiful and valued most as thatch for roofs and also to cover the stacks, ricks and clamps for all kinds of crops and vegetables. Rushes – bulrushes – were equally plentiful, waterproof, and woven into baskets, mats, hats, chair seats and toys … they were also good for bedding, as a netting in the plastering of walls, and wrapping for soft milk cheeses. They made cheap, bright rushlights too.

(Neeson, 1989: 166)

The list of foraging crops, especially nuts, berries and fungi is equally long, as were the possibilities for foraging salad crops and herbs. It is clear from these accounts that the communing lifestyle offered two other characteristics crucial to a bioregional approach to provisioning: seasonality and shared experience.

Humphries (1990: 31) has attempted to place an economic valuation of what was offered by this access to common land:

Summarizing, then, for a family in the fortunate position of being able to keep a cow, by and large on common land, and assuming the opportunity cost of the labor involved, though not negligible, was minimized by the employment of underemployed family members and offset by the value of by-products such as skim milk and manure, then the annual income from the cow was often more than half the adult male laborer's wage and an average-priced cow would pay for itself in about a year. If after enclosure the family retained some access to a cowkeep, their rent was adjusted accordingly, and if food had to be grown on an enclosed plot of arable, the opportunity cost[6] in terms of wages forgone was undoubtedly raised. This cut profits in half. But for the majority of families even this reduced rate of return was unavailable, as all possibility of cowkeeping was eliminated with enclosure.

Development economists have identified the inability to place a monetary value on the products of subsistence work as a threat to this form of livelihood: unless it can be priced, it will be counted at nothing and dismissed, just as the commoners of early modern Europe were dismissed, before their land was taken and made 'efficient'. Wunder *et al.* propose a range of techniques to enable monetary valuation including barter values, contingent valuation and embedded time methods. However, as they admit in their title, this style of life is, quite literally, priceless. We face a similar problem today in assessing the value of the food grown on allotments and other forms of household production. If we were able to price the work undertaken outside the market by our grandparents, and the work done today without payment, it would cast a different light on the perennial question of economic growth.

The remainder of this section focuses on one particular aspect of our environment that has been the focus of some of these valuation techniques, but here is used to represent something eternal as well as priceless: our woodlands. In his *Earthcare Manual* Patrick Whitefield (2004: 299) notes that 'Any discussion of productive woodland in Britain must be seen in the context of our consumption of timber. At present we import 90% of what we consume, so if we're talking about sustainability it's premature to look at domestic production until we've firmly grasped the nettle of reducing consumption'. Whitefield cautions against exaggerating the unique role of trees in supporting a healthy biosphere: 'Peat bogs, for example, keep much more CO_2 out of the atmosphere than any plantations of trees which might replace them, and in some cases grassland ecosystems can be more diverse than a woodland which might succeed them' (Whitefield, 2004: 299). He concludes that woodlands are especially valuable because they are capable of offering sustainable yields of a whole range of useful products without this affecting their ability to play a positive role within a healthy ecosystem.

Figures 5.1 and 5.2 reproduce data from Whitefield (2004) concerning the ecological and economic potential of woodlands. They can absorb pollution, sequester carbon, support microclimates, regulate water systems, underpin soil formation, and provide habitats for a diverse range of creatures. Without threatening this role, it is possible to harvest a wide range of products from living forests. These are illustrated in Figure 5.2 and include food, fodder, timber and biofuel. A range of other opportunities to generate livelihoods are also illustrated in the figure including recreation and aesthetic enjoyment. The way in which working with materials drawn from nature can support a different kind of relationship with the natural world is explored in the following chapter, but here I will just briefly draw attention to the way in which woodlanders seek out woods that suit their purpose, and how this requires an intimate knowledge of the different trees. To a wood-worker, wood is no longer just wood, since different trees are suitable for different uses. Hazel is ideal for coppicing (cutting to promote additional growth of poles at ground level) because it will grow again from the stool (the remaining stump). Alder is a water-loving wood that grows close to rivers; it is thus resistant to rot and hence useful in the making of wooden clogs. Cricket bats use *Salix Alba Caerulea* (Cricket Bat Willow) because it also holds water and so is flexible. Sycamore is ideal for bowls and rolling pins because it has a smooth grain and does not impart any flavour to the food. Beech is a favourite for

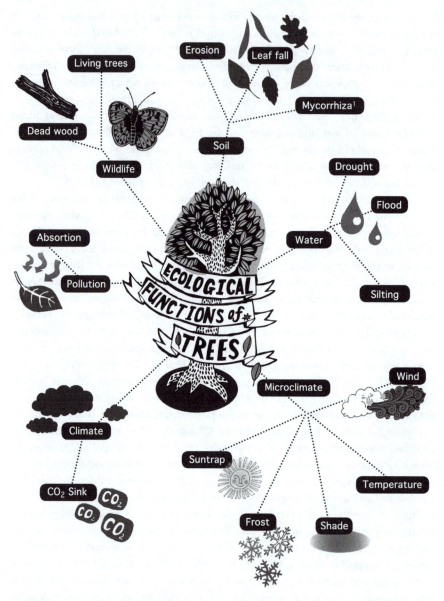

FIGURE 5.1 Ecological functions of woodlands
Source: Redrawn by Imogen Shaw from the original in Patrick Whitefield's *Earth Care Manual*.

furniture, because it grows tall and straight and without frequent knots, but ash is also useful for furniture because it is very good to work when green and this can be used to add to the firmness of joints. This represents a layman's introduction to the way of the woodlander, but gives a hint at the depth and subtlety of the relationship with natural products that a subsistence lifestyle entails.

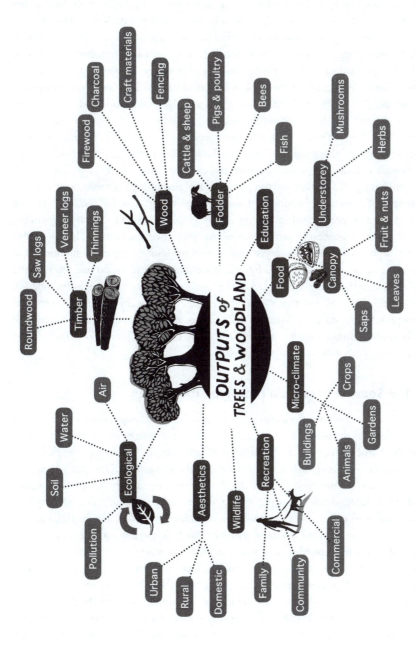

FIGURE 5.2 Provisioning potential of woodlands
Source: Redrawn by Imogen Shaw from the original in Patrick Whitefield's *Earth Care Manual*.

Bell's account of rural East Anglia on the brink of the Second World War offers an account of such a woodworker and what we might call his phenomenological understanding – that is, the knowledge of somebody who has worked with the land, rather than observing those who have done so. His work in the woods is marked by the annual cycle, since wood cannot be cut when the sap is rising and can achieve different effects depending on the season. His work was fitted to the season: 'The father at this time of year [new year] used to be given a hedge to cut by his master, and he used to make it up into little faggots especially for the brick oven, called batlins. They used to bake once in three weeks' (Bell, 1939/2009: 15). His deep knowledge of the woodland was a learned skill that ensured his close relationship with the landscape: 'A stack of hurdles stands brand-new and bright in the sun. They are made of ash, rived and riveted, with here and there slivers of the green bark still on them. They last longer than willow hurdles, though willow look stouter because the bars are wider' (Bell, 1939/2009: 23).

In concluding this section on the potential for enabling sustainable livelihoods in the context of a developed economy I am struck by the polarised approach to human well-being that is propagated in the apparently globalised world. It is always striking how solutions to economic problems that are promoted enthusiastically for poorer societies, such as co-operatives or sustainable rural livelihoods, are never mentioned in the context of our own society. Why is it, for example, that we do not think of the so-called underclass in the UK or US as the 'landless poor' as they might be called in Brazil or India? To suggest that this might become a politically pertinent question is not mere whimsy since, as Barry (2012) makes abundantly clear, the 'politics of actually existing unsustainability' is likely to rapidly become a politics of crisis, and the most pressing crisis will be a crisis of provisioning.

5.5. The Somerset Levels: a prototype bioregion

To make specific this vision of a bioregionally based provisioning system, in this section I offer a detailed discussion of one area of the UK that might be considered a bioregion: the Somerset Levels.[7] In the absence of any geographical or hydrological sense of how our native bioregions might be defined, I return again to Trueman's geological divisions of the British Isles. One of the 20 regions into which he divides England and Wales is labelled 'the Bristol District and the Somerset plain'. The geographical map (Figure 5.3) offers one suggestion for defining bioregions, but in this case the natural boundaries of the Quantock and Mendip hills suggest another, enclosing as they do the area recognised locally as of particular character and distinctiveness.

As described above, a bioregion can be identified by topographical features, watersheds, typical species, dominant crops and the crafts, products, and cultures they give rise to. It is thus co-defined by ecological and human systems. In the UK context, the drained wetlands that make up the Somerset Levels can be identified as a unique biome that might form the heart of a bioregion. The Somerset Levels and Moors is an area of 64,000 ha. lying to the south-west of Bristol and in the heart of the West Country of the UK. It is the most significant grass wetland in England, a coastal barrier of 'Levels' (marine clays lying on average only 6m. above sea level) and

'Moors' which can be as much as 6m. below peak tide levels and therefore prone to frequent flooding (Hume, 2008). The area is thus a specialised ecological system, which has grown up in parallel with human communities.

It is an interesting example of an area's landscape being the result of centuries of human intervention; it was the use of a system of ditches (known locally as 'rhynes') that allowed the draining of the land for year-round agriculture. The typical species is the willow, which has been harvested since the Bronze Age and is managed by pollarding – that is, the harvesting of shoots. The pollarded willow is used for thatching spars, hurdles and firewood. Willow for basket-making is produced from the same species grown as a shrub and is known as 'withies'; the craft of using willow to make utensils and works of art dates back to the time of the Celts. Willow is used today to make hurdles, crab and lobster pots, eel-traps, coracles and baskets; willow wood is also used to make cricket bats. The rush is a similarly versatile crop that has been harvested in the Somerset Levels since prehistoric times. The true bulrush (*Scirpus lacustris*, as opposed to the false bulrush or reedmace – *Typha lattifolia* – which is often mistaken for it), grows in water and is harvested in the summer, traditionally between the hay and corn harvests. Rush has a wide range of uses, including the seating of chairs and making of hats. (Bagias, 2003, provides a beautifully illustrated account of this region and its craftspeople.)

It should be clear from this discussion that the landform and landscape have associated species, which then determine the products and crafts that make up the traditional economy of a bioregion. Although today most baskets sold in the UK have

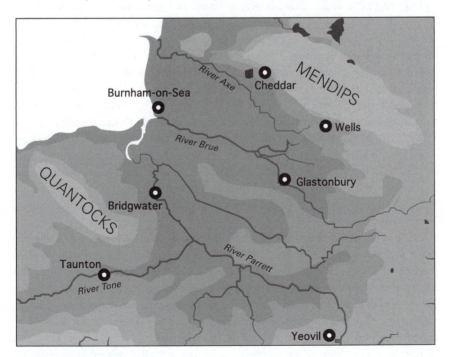

FIGURE 5.3 Map of the Somerset Levels
Source: Original artwork by Imogen Shaw.

TABLE 5.1 Typical features of the Somerset Levels bioregion

Characteristic	Expression	Comment
Topography	Low-lying moorland surrounded by two ranges of hills	Poor arable land – mainly used for grazing
Watershed	Floodplains of the Severn, Parrett, Axe and Brue	Reclaimed wetland still at risk of flooding
Plant species	Water-loving trees such as willow and alder, and plants such as rush and reed	*Salix* thrive in moist habitats and are fast-growing (three years to harvest)
Animal species	Wetland birds such as heron, crane, egret, bittern, snipe, lapwing and predator species; otter, marsh frogs	Drained wetland provided grazing for cows. Hence dairy industry and land for orchards
Crafts	Basket-making, rush-seating	Now residual due to global trade and lower wage-rates in producer countries
Products	Willow and rushwork products, cider, cheese	Skills being lost; production for tourists
Culture	Distinct Zummerzet dialect/accent	Now spoken mainly by the elderly
Festivals	Wassailing (a pagan festival to ensure good apple harvest); scything festival	Obsolete or extinct festivals like these are now enjoying a revival

been made in China, and even the fibres for thatching are often imported from there, within the past century Somerset was a centre of basket crafts, and much of the willow produced in the UK for residual craftspeople is still produced there. This is the heart of a bioregional approach to provisioning: an area whose climatic and geographical features support a particular natural and/or man-made product. This must be the key to an economy that is embedded within the ecosystem in which people borrow for their needs from the local natural environment. It also inevitably leads to craft specialisms, with experts in the making of baskets or chairs developing their own community of practice and sharing innovations in technique and materials.

Table 5.1 begins to link the different features of the Somerset Levels bioregion. The topographical and watershed features are very closely linked in this case, since the flat landscape gave rise to a unique wetland ecosystem, which then became home to particular water-loving species. In the case of plant species, these then led to traditional crafts, which are still present but largely for niche markets and as part of heritage tourism.

The preceding discussion of one proto-bioregional economy makes clear the key threat to provisioning on such a local model: the sorts of natural and manufactured products that a specific local environment will support are likely to be uniform. The implications of this for our cultural approach to consumption are discussed in Chapter 7, but we should be clear that the aim for each bioregion is self-reliance, not full self-sufficiency. This consideration also underscores the importance of the process of determining bioregions and of ensuring that their boundaries are wide enough so that all basic needs can be met within them – a discussion I take forward in Chapter 10. Of course the assumption is that, within these bioregions, specialisation will take place, and a different process of defining needs and how to meet them will prevail from the consumer's casual stroll around the supermarket.

5.6. Conclusion: abundance without exploitation

The focus of this book, and of any economic analysis that takes climate change seriously, must be on energy. The contest over the definition of a 'green economy' rests on a deeper conflict over the belief or otherwise in our ability to find a power-supply for capitalism that is carbon-free. On the one hand we have the proponents of further growth and wider globalisation, who base their faith on an as-yet-undiscovered source of carbon-free electricity, or more simply on human ingenuity guaranteeing our ability to find such a source. On the other we have those who consider that there are natural limits to the size of the economy and that therefore an economic system designed to grow is in urgent need of structural change.

It must be clear by now that my own view is that the process of globalisation is wasteful of energy and inherently unsatisfying: it must be challenged. Such a challenge requires no less than that we question the market economy itself as a system of provisioning. We need to reverse the 'great transformation' that pulled our ancestors away from the land, from which they met their own needs, and into industrial cities where they sold their labour for money that they then used to buy what the market made available. This chapter has given examples of what this might mean, and in fact does mean, in practice. But how might we theorise the path of transition that is necessary to enable us to reinhabit our local land? We can begin this by recalling the three conditions Polanyi identified as facilitating the move away from the land and considering how these might be reversed.

First among Polanyi's conditions for the creation of a market economy is the assignment of land, and all the resources the earth provides, into a market system of distribution. This Polanyi refers to as the commercialisation of the soil and the designation of land as a commodity, and which he considers can only ever be a 'fictitious commodity'. Historically the commercialisation of the soil took the form of using enclosure laws to abolish the system of social regulation of land use common in Europe at the time of the industrial revolution. In the parts of the world that were colonised it meant the debasement of spiritually grounded notions of stewardship or relationship, which I have alluded to in Chapter 3.

So how might we begin to reverse our commercial attitude towards the land and replace it with a more relational and respectful attitude? The notion of 'stewardship' is a useful one, and one that is perhaps still apparent in the nature of land ownership in the UK. Despite – or perhaps because of – the origin of the marketisation of land in England, the elaborate system of property rights to land typical of the settlement of the great plains of the US, where land was stolen from native peoples partly because of their refusal to accept that their mother could be owned (Zinn, 1980), or the later expropriation of the land of the native peoples of Australia, where land was simply defined as *terra nullius* (Duffy, 2008), land in England is still considered to have been given into the stewardship of the sovereign by God. This gives us an opportunity to redefine how land is perceived outside the market context. If the sovereign is, essentially, the steward of all the land of England, then that stewardship duty could simply be passed to a body more representative of the people of England in 2012. It might be the duty of such a Land Stewardship Council to determine the uses of land, respecting the land itself and the other creatures with whom we share it.

Just as all those who formally 'own' land in England still do so at the behest of the sovereign – a position that has remained unchanged since 1066 – land could be reallocated away from uses designed to achieve maximum profits and towards uses designed to achieve the creation of resilient local communities within a framework of sustainability. Such major land reforms are taking place across the world today, most notably in Bolivia and Brazil. The UK could follow this example but set the achievement of sustainability as the pre-eminent goal of such a reform and pass on responsibility for its achievement to the bioregions of the UK.

Land is the key to achieving sustainability not only because it provides the means for supporting livelihoods without recourse to wasteful global supply chains, but also because well-designed land management offers the opportunity for massively increasing the potential for carbon sequestration. Although the requisitioning and reallocation of the landed estates of England (Wales and Scotland may in fact take more readily to this proposal) may seem an extreme proposal, it should be remembered that the need to move rapidly onto a path towards sustainability is an urgent one. The market system has proved itself incapable of rising to this challenge, with rates of food security in the UK showing little sign of improvement and planning policy being directed in favour of profit-driven development rather than sustainability (Cato, 2011b). A reconsideration of how land is owned and used, and a redirection of its use towards socially and environmentally beneficial ends, is urgently required. The archaic nature of English land ownership merely facilitates this process and gives the UK an advantage in taking the first step to reverse the transformation to a market economy.

This links us to Polanyi's second stage of the great transformation: the disconnect between people and their land in terms of their strategies for provisioning. Polanyi describes the way in which the commercialisation of land created a force pushing people off the land and into the industrial cities, where population rates increased rapidly. This is a complex feedback loop where population, demand for food, and internal migration join together in a process that has continued to this day. What was lost was the ability of the people of England to subsist from their own local soil. In a world where the majority now live in cities, re-establishing the connection between people and land is a challenging stage for the return to a land-based economy. However, the power of the proposal for a bioregional economy is that it re-establishes the connection between people living in an area and their local land, and it revives the sense of accountability that was lost with the movement to the cities and the shift from local provisioning. As we have seen above, there is already a movement underway to relearn the skills of production of food and shelter, but this process needs to be accelerated. Clearly, land reform is one important contribution to this process; other policy means of supporting self-reliant local economies are discussed in Chapter 10.

This discussion has already prefigured to some extent the response to Polanyi's third point: that once the majority of the nation's people were employed in the production of manufactured goods they were forced to import their food, thus making use of the land resources of others, initially the peoples of colonised lands. What he describes is the beginning of the process of globalisation, which removed from the English, in his view, the means of providing for their own subsistence. Polanyi's is an historical account, but this process is proceeding apace across the world today, as peasant farmers are displaced in the process of what has been termed 'the Great Land Grab' (Hall, 2011; De Schutter, 2011). Then, as now, this represented the expropriation of the resources of others by means of the superior power of those in the industrialised West. This will be discussed further in Chapter 9, but for now I should stress once again the power of the concept of the bioregion in the context of this discussion.

Because land is fixed, in a geographical as well as an economic sense, considering the local land to be the preserve of local people, and clearly defining their provisioning rights as primary, can be applied equally in all parts of the world. So often the attempt to find solutions to environmental problems, which are unquestionably global problems, founder on cultural differences and conflicts of interest. But the ethic of the bioregional economy, and ethic of local responsibility and land care, would be equally relevant in Finland or Indonesia. It is a basic expression of the human reliance on the soil, and it was the most destructive consequence of the great transformation to alienate us from this understanding.

6

WORK AS CRAFT

Good citizenship, found in play, is lost in work.

Richard Sennett, *The Craftsman*, p. 274

We have now explored the inadequacies of the existing model of economic production and considered ideas for a more locally embedded alternative. In this chapter we move on to consider the actual business of work. Many of the early critics of capitalism, and of the classical economists, identified the change in the nature of work as a key aspect of that system of economic organisation, and one that had the potential to be socially damaging. Marx, for example, was critical of the way that the alienating organisation of work under capitalism was psychologically destructive, as well as undermining to social relationships. As we will see later, the English utopian socialists sympathised with this critique, suggesting a need to reject the picture of work as inevitable drudgery, as theorised by the classical economists Smith and Ricardo, and to restore the dignity and spiritual value to work. This is one task of this chapter: to re-vision work in the context of a bioregional economy.

But what of the environmental consequences of the managerialised workplace or factory? How does the global system of production and distribution of goods affect our view of our place in the world? In this chapter I explore the disconnection that arises from the separation of work from the local natural environment, and examine the way that craftwork might permit a re-embedding that is necessary if we are to become ecological citizens living productive lives within sustainable and convivial communities. And I hope to make a deeper argument that, while it may be far from the worldview of academics, it none the less has much to offer them. I will argue that work can help to bring us to a more secure form of knowledge, that it is precisely the engagement with the material world through craftwork that allows us to escape from the fruitless dispute between different epistemological positions, what Ingold (2010: 95) calls the 'endless shuttling back and forth between the mind and the material world'.

In my constant fear of being labelled a Luddite I should make clear at the outset that I am not by any means suggesting that all work should become craftwork, or that we should abandon complex goods that require specialised knowledge and production processes; rather, I offer a more sociological account of the impact of the work system as structured under globalised capitalism on our social and environmental relationships. As the previous chapter made clear, it is the proposal of a bioregional economy that much of what we consume to meet our fundamental needs is locally produced, and this will mean a massive increase in productive labour, some of it in skilled craftwork. I also argued in Chapter 4 that we might ask questions about how the factories that remain would be organised, reappraising in the process what the co-operative form of enterprise might have to offer. I recognise this as a limitation of this book, which is already very ambitious in its scope. It is a future task for me and for other green economists to describe more closely how the productive facilities and systems of today's economy can be transitioned to fulfil functions that are useful within a bioregional provisioning framework, a process of industrial conversion that will form part of our response to the large-scale reduction in energy use that climate change demands.

This chapter focuses rather on the social and environmental consequences of an industrialised model where decisions about what is made, and how it is made, are controlled by those who own capital. The process by which globally based capital came to control the productive economy is outlined in Section 6.1, which also offers, by way of comparison, a consideration of the life of the craft worker, as epitomised by George Eliot's hero Adam Bede. Section 6.2 explores the relationship between the kind of work that is undertaken and our relationship with the natural world: here I argue that the process of dislocation from our environment has arisen partly as a result of our dislocation from physical work. Section 6.3 details the way in which workers were trained for craftwork in earlier times – through apprenticeship – and explores the social impact of such a system of training. Section 6.4 offers a case-study of craftwork in one sector: that of woodland crafts. Finally, in Section 6.5, by way of conclusion I broaden the discussion from the individual's relationship with nature to the way that work has impacted on our human society.

6.1. Adam Smith vs. Adam Bede

Advocates of a market view of the economy and proponents of further and faster globalisation tend to seek inspiration from the work of Adam Smith, who is taken to be the founding father of market economics. Smith's work *The Wealth of Nations*, was published in 1776, on the cusp of the industrial revolution and before its technological advance had had the chance to impact significantly on social and economic structures. The economist who better represents the theory that has come to dominate our modern world is David Ricardo, whose most renowned work *Principles of Political Economy and Taxation* was published some 40 years after that of Smith, and whose work set the parameters for the world of laissez-faire capitalism and export-led growth that we inhabit today.

The most famous story in *The Wealth of Nations* is that of the pin factory, the archetype for the division of labour that was used to subdivide minutely tasks within workplaces in order to achieve efficiency; and yet even Smith, who lauded this system of production as efficient, accepted that the division of labour would reduce workers' intelligence (Spencer, 2009). Linking back to the discussion in Chapter 4, we need to be cautious in allowing that the pin factory was an efficient way of organising the production of pins. It is almost certain that it enabled more pins to be made for less money, and therefore reduced the price of pins for those wishing to buy them, as well as increasing the profits for the person who owned the pin factory. Everything that happened outside the pin factory was excluded from consideration and would be defined as an 'externality' by the inheritors and refiners of Smith's theories. This includes the reduction in workers' intelligence, the lowering of their sense of well-being, and other negative psycho-social consequences that might arise.

The redefinition of work, by those who were not in a position to have to undertake it, made it clear that it was not to be a pleasant experience. According to Spencer (2009: 97):

> The classical economists were in broad agreement that work was 'toil and trouble' (Smith, 1976: vol. 1, 47). It was taken for granted that people would suffer pain in meeting their basic material needs. Work was never an end in itself, only ever a means to an end. There was an acceptance that those who worked (i.e. wage-labourers) would seek to avoid work and to indulge in leisure, and it was recognised that incentives as well as sanctions would be needed to encourage the workforce to work hard.

By contrast Fourier, the French utopian thinker, was critical of the way that Smith depicted work as a 'unversal bad', which he saw as creating a myth that undercut the attempts of social reformers to improve the quality of work. He considered that the repetitive nature of factory-based work deprived people of their need for contrast and variety, one of twelve God-given passions that characterised human nature, which he appealingly referred to as 'the Butterfly' (Spencer, 2009). Fourier argued that, if organised communally, and so that workers enjoyed variety and autonomy and were properly rewarded, work could be 'a servant of the passions and thus a route to self-expression and self-realisation' (Spencer, 2009: 100).

A more rounded and humanist view of the nature of work, and one quite at odds with the economistic conception of Smith and Ricardo, is offered by George Eliot in her portrait of the carpenter Adam Bede. The eponymous hero of her novel is a journeyman carpenter in rural England some two centuries ago. The novel explores the frustrations and satisfactions of productive, emotional and spiritual life through the experiences of its central character. The novel opens with a description of Jonathan Burge's 'roomy workshop' where Adam works:

> The afternoon sun was warm on the five workmen there, busy upon doors and window-frames and wainscoting. A scent of pine-wood from a tent-like pile of

planks outside the open door mingled itself with the scent of the elder-bushes which were spreading their summer snow close to the open window opposite; the slanting sunbeams shone through the transparent shavings that flew before the steady plane, and lit up the fine grain of the oak panelling which stood propped against the wall.

Adam's world is the village of Hayslope in the rural district of Loamshire. This is contrasted with the much harsher existence of the people who live in Stonyshire, a nearby industrial district. Eliot uses the novel to contrast the social consequences of the different kinds of work: the embedded life in Hayslope builds community and underpins conviviality whereas the workers of Snowfield, a small industrial town, suffer social distress of various kinds. It does not seem too far-fetched to read in the novel Eliot's view of the challenge to community posed by the shift from craft-based to industrial work (Creeger, 1956).

Adam Bede is much more of a craftsman in the spirit of the nineteenth-century Arts and Crafts movement than a labourer as portrayed by the classical economists. This movement was a peculiarly English response to the loss of skill in craft that resulted from the spread of the factory system and mass production. Growing up in the 1880s it rapidly spawned a range of institutions including the Art Workers' Guild (1884), the Arts and Crafts Exhibition Society (1887), the Central School of Arts and Crafts in London, and the publication *The Studio* (Crook, 2009). The movement reacted against the loss of beauty when objects were made without individual care as well as the loss of quality in production.

According to the theorists of arts and crafts, mass production threatened not only the quality of goods but also the spiritual life of those whose labour was denigrated in their production. The writings of John Ruskin and William Morris make clear the particular value to be accorded to 'manufacture' in its original sense of hand-wrought goods, rather than the artificial value of mercantile trade: 'Political economy has misunderstood the value of exchange as opposed to manufacture and not recognised the specific social value and utility of production' (May, 2010: 192). John Ruskin was deeply disapproving of the exclusive focus on financial efficiency that characterised the organisation of work under capitalism: 'Ruskin sees a false economy in the production of goods in the cheapest manner, denying as it does the individual worker's ability fully to invest their soul in the product on which they are working' (May, 2010: 192). Ruskin distinguishes between work that produces life and work that produces death, a distinction that finds its most pithy exposition in his famous slogan, 'There is no wealth but life'. He proposed an intellectual distinction between wealth and 'illth', a prefiguring of the concept of 'uneconomic growth' of ecological economist Herman Daly (1999).

Ruskin's associate William Morris suggested that the work conditions inherent in capitalism, especially the loss of control, were almost immoral: 'Thus worthy work carries with it the hope of pleasure in rest, the hope of the pleasure in our using what it makes and the hope of pleasure in our daily creative skill. All other work but this is worthless; it is slaves' work – mere toiling to live, that we may live to toil' (Morris, 1885 /1973: 88). The separation of people into intellectual and manual occupations under capitalism, Ruskin argued, culminated only in 'morbid thinkers' and 'miserable workers' (cited in Thompson 1976: 37). By contrast he sought to rehabilitate the artisan, who was being eliminated in his nineteenth-century society by the advent of systems of mass production.

This dedication to craftwork as an important part of the social as well as the economic framework recurs periodically in radical thinking. The ethos of the Arts and Crafts movement saw a revival in the inter-war period, again focused on the workshop (Saler, 1999). As Crook (2009) makes clear, this involved a clear attempt to rehabilitate the social role of the artisan:

> The ideal of workshop production, facilitating as it did the social and creative unity of craft production, intersected with other ideals cherished by the movement. One was the ideal of rural living, whose simplicity, intimacy and naturalness was favorably contrasted with the artificiality and complexity of urban life ... The other was socialism, or rather a particular variant of socialism 'guild socialism'. In contrast to the pro-industry policies espoused by the Labour Party and trade unions, guild socialism remained committed to the ideal of the workshop.
>
> *(Crook, 2009: 27)*

The workshop was a place of social interaction and for the sharing of skill and insight into production: it 'bound together pedagogy, humanity and creativity'. As we saw in the quotation from *Adam Bede* above, the idea of the workshop is central to this conceptualisation of work as part of a social human community. The workshop is a space for the development of skill, the mentoring of younger workers by the older: it was an important social as well as economic setting.

Green economists are the contemporary expression of this tradition, with their accentuation of the philosophical and sometimes spiritual values associated with privileging work as a social, humanising process and not merely an instrumental necessity. Robertson (1985) develops a concept he calls 'ownwork' only part of which is in the formal economy. In his explanation of how 'ownwork' might differ from wage labour he quotes Khalil Gibran's words in *The Prophet*, 'You work that you may keep pace with the earth and the soul of the earth. For to be idle is to become a stranger unto the seasons, and to step out of life's procession that marches in majesty towards the infinite' (Robertson, 1990: 65). This quotation speaks of a time when work was connected to the local environment, and thus to the seasons; when work was part of the process of our embedding with the natural world, rather than an unpleasant necessity that required the exploitation of natural resources.

Schumacher also discussed at length the social role of work and the psycho-social consequences of a dislocating, factory-based work environment. Schumacher argued that industrialised work was:

> Mechanical, artificial, divorced from nature, utilizing only the smallest part of man's potential capabilities, it sentences the great majority of workers to spending

their lives in a way which contains no worthy challenge, no stimulus to self-per-
fection, no chance of development, no element of Beauty, Truth, or Goodness.

(Schumacher, 1979: 27)

His own theory of good work makes a link to the Buddhist concept of 'right livelihood', which is a means of achieving subsistence without causing offence to one's
own values, to other people or to one's environment.

This work stands in implicit critique of the new Ricardian paradigm, which
reached its apotheosis in the final decades of the last century and came to be labelled
the 'international division of labour': China had become the new workshop of the
world, with India providing the services that required computer expertise or the
knowledge of the English language (Perrons, 1981; Wilkinson *et al.*, 2001; Batra,
2007). Other countries developed particular areas where they had an absolute
advantage, but most of the world's economies have been forced into a ruthless
competition to pick up the scraps, a process that saw them reducing social and
environmental standards and called by critics the 'race to the bottom' (Chan, 2003)
and installing favourable corporate tax regimes, so that they gained a reduced amount
of revenue from production taking place within their territorial boundaries
(Christensen and Murphy, 2004).

This new regime had no place for locally specific skills or production that
responded to a nation's resource endowments or cultural specialisms. Globalisation
meant that resources could travel the world at little cost, and so a Mexican sombrero
might as well be woven in China as in Oaxaca. The skills that generations of workers
had passed down, whether in handcrafts or industrial processes, no longer had any
economic value and so were lost. 'Labour' had become a process of offering oneself
as the generic production unit Smith and Ricardo had imagined, at the lowest cost,
to whomever controlled the productive capital. In this context:

> The residual pride of the producer in the product or service in which his or her
> labour is embodied, a labour already fragmented by specialisation and capita-
> listic machine production, now becomes a melancholic nostalgia for medieval
> craftsmanship rather than a realistic attitude to work or professional ambition.
>
> *(Toprowski, 2009: 153)*

As we saw in the previous chapter, a bioregional approach to economics would
consider the question of work more widely than merely in terms of a market economy: issues of provisioning and livelihood are also of importance. In green political
economy the discussion of work is not separate from the question of subsistence.
According to Barry (1999: 182):

> Where green politics differs from other political theories such as liberalism or
> socialism is that whereas the latter view the link between production and
> consumption in terms of ensuring full employment in the formal economy, the
> green view is to encourage an ideal of self-provisioning, both individually and

collectively, within the informal economy, as much as possible, and restructuring the 'formal' productive sphere so as to enhance the internal goods of work.

The attempt to consider the social importance of 'work' rather than the narrowly economic advantages of efficient labour resound through the centuries as the voice of the authentic human need for meaningful and creative employment. At present the Ricardians are in the ascendancy and arguments about the quality of work tend to focus around the importance of a work–life balance, which implicitly accepts the classical economists' view of work as separate from life and as inherently odious. The following section offers an alternative view of the role of work in human lives: as an activity that is constitutive of the human being as a unique form of self-conscious animal life.

6.2. The body of the artisan and the spirit of place

This section draws extensively on work by Pamela Smith and her tracing of the development of a new understanding of physical work in the early modern period in northern Europe. It builds on the idea that work is a process of mediation between human beings and the natural world (White, 1996). Smith explores the relationship between people and the environment expressed through their work and how this became what she defines as an 'artisanal epistemology'. This epistemology arose as a result of the artisans' need to understand the natural materials that they used during their processes of creation: 'When artisans looked to nature, they were interested, not surprisingly, in its powers of generation and transformation, for they themselves worked with the materials of nature and struggled to manipulate and control them in order to produce objects' (Smith, 2004: 16). Through this process they came to regard nature as the source of secure knowledge: 'Nature increasingly came to be regarded as an authority to which to make appeal when other traditional sources of authority either failed or were not available' (Smith, 2004: 9) This knowledge arose through their direct experience of natural materials: 'certain knowledge can be extracted by engaging with nature, and ... this engagement takes place through a bodily encounter with matter' (Smith, 2004: 59).

Smith identifies this arising of a new sense of self-respect and philosophical insight amongst men and women who had been, up until this period, found in the lower social classes, and suffering from a disdain for craftwork 'as deforming to mind and body' (Smith, 2004: 7), which had been created by the slave culture of Greek society and had persisted in the classically influenced culture of the West. The new self-confidence of the Medieval artisan found inspiration in the philosophy of Paracelsus. Philippus Aureolus Theophrastus Bombastus von Hohenheim was a philosopher as extraordinary as his moniker: a scientist and alchemist, he lived at a time when those two fields of study were not in conflict, and made contributions to many contemporary fields of learning. He had an exalted view of the role of the craftsman, whose duty was to 'reform ... fallen nature' (Smith, 2004: 84), a spiritual task that was akin to the process of creation in microcosm. For Paracelsus:

knowledge of nature was gained, not through a process of reasoning, but by a union of the divine powers of the mind and the body with the divine spirit in matter. He called the process of this union 'experience'. In explaining this concept, Paracelsus drew on the terminology of theory and practice but inverted the traditional understanding of these terms in a remarkable way. Paracelsus defined scientia, not as a body of knowledge formed into a discipline by its logical structure, but as the divine power in natural things that the physician must 'overhear' and with which he must achieve union in order to gain knowledge of medicines.

(Smith, 2004: 87)

This gives us our first inkling of the way that work could, to the pre-capitalist mind, have a spiritual character. In stark contrast to the repetitive work of the production unit of industrial capitalism, the Medieval craftsman saw in his work a contribution to the reflection of divine order in the earthly realm: 'The art of the craftsman "reformed" nature by creating noble objects from the dross of fallen nature. The work of artisans, like the practices of agriculture and medicine, worked to redeem the body and life of humans after the Fall' (Smith, 2004: 84).

I have discussed Smith's account of the artisanal epistemology at length because it provides the basis for reconceptualising work as a means of effecting the re-embedding of people with their environment that both ecofeminist and green economists believe is a necessary requirement for the human community to find a non-threatening relationship with nature and with the others with whom they share their environment. For this process to be effective it is essential that work is seen as an embodied and embedded process, as in the following account of the subjective experience of the process of glass-blowing:

The stretch-out occurred in two phases. First, she lost awareness of her body making contact with the hot glass and became all-absorbed into the physical material as the end in itself ... The philosopher Merleau-Ponty describes what she experienced as 'being as a thing' ... If I may put this yet another way, we are now absorbed in something, no longer self-aware, even of our bodily self. We have become the thing on which we are working.

(Sennett, 2008: 174)

In his novel *Anna Karenina* Tolstoy (1877/2012: 306) describes a similar process in a different setting in Chapters 4 and 5 of Book 3, where Levin chooses to join his peasants to mow a hay meadow. Shame-faced at first in anticipation of the peasants' sceptical response to the master playing peasant for a day, and anxious lest he is physically unable to mow adequately and for a whole day, Levin loses himself in the shared experience of physical labour and undergoes a transcendant experience:

Another row, and yet another row, followed – long rows and short rows, with good grass and with poor grass. Levin lost all sense of time, and could not have told whether it was late or early now. A change began to come over his work, which gave him immense satisfaction. In the midst of his toil there were moments during which he forgot what he was doing, and it came all easy to him, and at those same moments his row was almost as smooth and well cut as Tit's. But so soon as he recollected what he was doing, and began trying to do better, he was at once conscious of all the difficulty of his task, and the row was badly mown.

These quotations suggest that work-as-craft provides a unique opportunity to find a connection with natural materials and, by extension, with the natural world from which they are derived. As discussed in the previous chapter, craftsmen also need an intimate knowledge of the natural world from which they derive their materials. Thus work-as-craft also provides the opportunity to relate deeply to other species, whether plant or animal, who provide its raw materials. Because nature's patterns of tree growth or bark formation are filled with infinite variety the process of transforming these into usable or beautiful objects is a responsive and creative one.

As the scene from *Anna Karenina* demonstrates, work also has a special role in rehabilitating our relationships with members of our own species. As we have already seen, the guild socialists considered that a revival of craftwork was capable of revitalising human relationships:

> Morris saw labor as central to the process through which humanity might rediscover fellowship and reverse the alienation of life under capitalism ... Morris also realized that labor was a process through which humanity might rekindle a harmonious relationship with the rest of the natural world.
>
> *(Hale, 2003: 280)*

In this era of ecological rather than social crisis, we might extend this argument to suggest that, through its requirement on the craftswoman to engage physically with the natural world, craftwork using locally sourced materials provides a unique opportunity for environmental re-embedding.

By way of example we might consider the work of the Buckinghamshire Bodgers, celebrated by Stuart King.[1] The local geology and climate of Buckinghamshire are ideal for the growth of beech trees, long favoured by furniture makers because of the tendency of their saplings to grow densely and for the mature trees then to grow straight upwards in search of light. This gives them a long, straight grain that is ideal for the manufacture of tables and chairs. Bodgers worked – and still work – in woodlands using the natural power offered by a hazel branch, which is turned into useful work via the appropriate technology of a pole-lathe. Their work is slow and therefore inefficient, by the standards of the modern global economy. But it grows naturally from the local environment, which it neither challenges nor threatens. These seem to me qualities of this work that are worthy of consideration as a prototype for work in a sustainable society. The way that woodland workers relate to their materials is discussed further in Section 6.5.

The artisanal epistemology described by Smith assigns a supreme role to the craftsman that justifies the Medieval view of the craft as a 'mystery'. It also links to the role identified for the economist in Chapter 3 as one of responding to natural systems, of eschewing the traditional technological approach of domination and imposition, and in seeking rather, as suggested by the philosophy of permaculture, to discern the movement of natural systems and fit one's production into them. This sets those who *make* right at the heart of the process of creating a sustainable economy: 'Practitioners, I contend, are wanderers, wayfarers, whose skill lies in their ability to find the grain of the world's becoming and to follow its course while bending it to their evolving purpose' (Ingold, 2010: 92). The work of some of these makers is celebrated in Table 6.1, which presents John Seymour's list of forgotten crafts. Some of these are forgotten, but many are currently being revived either in the form of a 'hobby' or by dedicated craftspeople, such as those we will meet in the following section.

Table 6.1. John Seymour's forgotten crafts

Woodland crafts. Coppicers, hurdle makers, rake makers, fork makers, besom makers, handle makers, hoop makers, ladder makers, crib makers, broaches and peg makers, clog sole cutters, bodgers, charcoal burners, oak basket makers, trug makers, stick and staff makers, field gate makers, willow basket makers, net makers.

Building crafts. Stone masons, joiners, roofers, floor layers, wallers, thatchers, slaters, lime burners, paint makers, glass blowers, glaziers, stained glass artists, mud brick makers, tile makers, chimney sweeps, plumbers, decorators, bridge builders, French polishers, sign writers.

Field crafts. Hedge layers, dry stone wallers, stile makers, well diggers, peat cutters, gardeners, horticulturists, vintners, arborists, tree surgeons, foresters, farmers, shepherds, shearers, bee keepers, millers, fishermen, orchardists, veterinarians.

Workshop crafts. Chair makers, iron founders, blacksmiths, wheelwrights, coopers, coppersmiths, tinsmiths, wood turners, coach builders, boat builders, sail makers, rope makers, wainwrights, block makers, leather tanners, harness makers, saddlers, horse collar makers, boot and shoe makers, cobblers, clog makers, knife makers, cutters, millstone dressers, potters, printers, typographers, calligraphers, bookbinders, paper makers, furniture makers, jewellers, mechanics, boiler makers, boiler men, soap makers, gunsmith, sword smith, brush maker, candle maker, artist, sculptor, firework maker, cycle builder, bone carver, musical instrument maker, clay pipe maker, tool maker.

Textile crafts. Spinner, weaver, dyer, silk grower, tailor, seamstress, milliner, hatter, lace maker, button maker, mat and rug maker, crochet worker, tatting and macramé worker, knitter, quilter, smock worker, embroiderer, leather worker, felt maker.

Domestic crafts. Fish smoker, bacon curer, butter maker, cheese maker, brewer, cider maker, wine maker, distiller, herbalist, ice cream maker, butcher, fishmonger, pie maker, pickle maker, baker, barrister and coffee roaster, homeopath, reflexologist, osteopath, naturopath, storyteller, teacher naturalist, historian, jester, actor, administrator, philosopher, labourer, poet, writer, midwife, publican, bookseller, librarian and idiot – there is no unemployment in this traditional model!

(Seymour, 1984)

6.3. The role of the guild and the apprentice

In the wake of the outbreak of social unrest in Britain's cities in the summer of 2011 there were renewed suggestions that society is suffering from a chronic malaise, and a key culprit identified is often the broken family, and particularly the absent father. But perhaps we are putting too much pressure on this small unit; perhaps we are underestimating the extent to which the task of socialising young people occurs in the workplace as much as in the home. Certainly, this was a central role of the guild in pre-industrial times, and the apprenticeship involved much more for the young man or woman whose parents bought it than just learning the skills associated with a certain trade. The movement from autonomous work, whether as peasant or craftsman, and towards 'wage slavery' is marked by the movement from the craft guild to the trade union. The first was focused on control of the quantity of the product; the second merely on the price for which one could sell oneself and the conditions within which the sale would take place.

The medieval guild system is not the subject of much study amongst contemporary economists, but it was proposed as an alternative to state organisation of industry by the English 'utopian socialists', whose strand of socialism was ultimately defeated by the Fabian statist variety in the period leading up to the First World War (Penty, 1906; Hobson, 1914). In many respects, the guild socialists were ahead of their time, for they displayed an ideological concern for nature and what we might now call 'the environment' that seems almost contemporary. This was paralleled with a concern for the waste of resources that takes place in a capitalist production system, where resources are used to produce what can be sold for a profit rather than what will increase human well-being. Central to this understanding was the concept of 'sufficiency', meaning the avoidance of wasteful production (Cole, 1930). This had first emerged in the work of William Morris, who decried the manufacture of articles of 'folly and luxury, the demand for which is the outcome of the existence of the rich non-producing classes' and which 'I will for ever refuse to call wealth: they are not wealth, but waste' (Morris, 1885/1973: 91). The seminal work of the movement, *Restoration of the Gild System* by Penty, praised the social arrangements of the middle ages for their simplicity: 'To medieval social arrangements we shall return, not only because we shall never be able to regain complete control over the economic forces in society except through the agency of restored Guilds, but because it is imperative to return to a simpler state of society' (quoted in Thompson, 1996: 31).

In pre-industrial European society, productive trades were closely controlled by craft guilds: 'The relations of master, journeyman and apprentice; the terms of the craft; the number of apprentices; the wages of the workers were all regulated by the custom and rule of the guild and the town' (Polanyi, 1944: 73). As I have described elsewhere (Cato, 2006: Ch. 7), guilds played an important social role, as well as providing a moral framework within which skilled work, and the sale of its products, could take place. Guilds provided a system for the sharing of skills through apprenticeship, and for the structuring of life in the Medieval cities of Europe.

As the power of the church to control economic life declined, a conflict arose between the craftsman and the merchant. According to Sennett (2008: 117), 'The good craftsman is a poor salesman, absorbed in doing something well, unable to explain the value of what he or she is doing'. I have discovered much the same attitude among present-day craft workers, who find it difficult to price their wares and find the question of how long it took them to make a certain piece both insulting and unanswerable. The guilds mediated the relationship between creative workers and those who need what they produced, with the objective of protecting livelihoods and the standard of the craft. Merchants, by contrast, sought to maximise the value of arbitrage they could extract. During the conflict between the values of craft and the values of trade, the guilds enforced restrictions on the sorts of practices that characterise a market system.

Three offences within English Common Law – engrossing, regrating and forestalling – were introduced to support the work of guilds in regulating markets, and repealed in the late eighteenth century as capitalist markets came to dominate the political economy (Britnell, 1987). Engrossing was a medieval version of cornering the market: buying up such large supplies that you could determine the price and hence exploit consumers. According to later market theory this need not be controlled by law, since the large number of producers in the perfect market will ensure that prices only reach reasonable levels – any higher and new producers will enter the market. Forestalling meant controlling your local market by preventing others from selling there – more like a cartel where individual markets are controlled by particular suppliers, who between them control the whole trade. Regrating meant reselling at a higher price, thereby increasing the final price to the consumer by guaranteeing a cut for a series of middlemen.

The verdict of contemporary academics on the role of the guilds is one of restrictive practice, but this assumes a framework of market competition that simply does not apply in the context of medieval Europe where the guilds thrived (Richardson, 2001). It also projects into the distant past a market focus on efficiency and production, ignoring the way in which in pre-industrial times economic relationships were socially embedded. In a locally embedded economy the producer and consumer are part of the same community: if the producer's wages are reduced by greater 'efficiency' he will have less to spend on his neighbouring producer's wares. This local accountability prevents the 'race to the bottom' of the global economy and it was strictly enforced by the guilds. The guild was linked to the social health of the cities, with each guild being responsible for defence of a part of the town or city wall in case of attack. Guilds also maintained the health of the Christian community, celebrating their patron saint and performing his or her story at the annual mystery plays.

The most obvious social role of the guild was in what would now be called training, but which then involved a relationship between apprentice and master that was much wider than the mere acquisition of the skills of the craft itself. Such an approach to 'training' engaged the young person physiologically and psychologically in the community of their fellow makers: 'The pervasive character of the epistemology of handwork arose largely out of the experience of training by apprenticeship and its basis in the bodily techniques of observation, imitation, repetition, and active doing' (Sennett, 2008: 28) Medieval apprenticeships were not easy; all 'began in manual labour', with young people having to earn the right to learn the more skilled aspects of the craft. The process of learning was primarily by imitation, but a particular form of imitation:

> For an artisan, imitation could denote both copying and the bodily techniques of a master, as well as reproducing the appearance and processes of nature. But it also constituted a bodily form of cognition and was connected to a view that matter and nature are alive and exist in synergy with the human body.
>
> *(Smith, 2004: 95)*

This was a predominantly relational way of becoming a skilled and productive member of society. The learning process itself required a humility and a commitment that is unlike that required for intellectual education. As Sennett explains:

> The apprentice is often expected to absorb the master's lesson by osmosis; the master's demonstration shows an act successfully performed, and the apprentice has to figure out what turned the key in the lock. Learning by demonstration puts the burden on the apprentice.
>
> *(Sennett, 2008: 181)*

Acquiring the skill was a lengthy and demanding process that in itself transformed the apprentice: 'ten thousand hours is a common touchstone for how long is takes to become an expert ... The seven years of apprentice work in a medieval goldsmithy represents just under five hours of bench work each day; which accords with what is known of the workshops' (Sennett, 2008: 172). If it is not too crass, I would like to suggest that this indicates the flaw with modern ideas of 'mentoring', where a person who is without skill and has no justification to expect respect other than their age, attempts to indicate to a younger person how they ought to behave. How different the relationship would be if the young person could begin to grasp the superior skill of the older, and over time, as they understood the craft better, that respect could only grow.

In stark contrast to this model of respect for skill, the harsh situation facing our remaining skilled craftspeople is clear when you consider how the global market forces them into competition with destitute labourers, and even children, in some of the poorest societies in the world. As a response, some woodworkers in Herefordshire are creating their own association to justify prices that might support a livelihood. Recalling the medieval commitment to the 'just price' they are rehabilitating the term, as in the following form of words they use when selling their wares:

> Before industrialisation, prices were fixed by guilds which protected the livelihoods of craftspeople. The 'just price' reflected their skill, the time invested and their needs. We are reviving this custom, which we see as analogous with the system of fair trade. If you earn more than the average wage – and therefore more than we do – please pay the just price. We also list a 'bare price' which is a realistic comparison with mass-produced and imported goods. We will not sell for less than the bare price because this also prevents craftspeople from undercutting each other. We are prepared to negotiate between these two prices on the basis of your ability to pay.

In an economistic worldview, the work of our surviving craftspeople is anachronistic, over-priced and valueless. It is a residual form of workthat has become obsolete now that we can employ those with similar skills in other countries to undertake work for less reward. Just as the negative consequences of factory work, like pollution, are defined as 'external' to a socially and environmentally disembedded economy, so the positive consequences of a work system based on relationships, skill and self-respect are considered external to a discussion of how an efficient economy would be structured. The serious impacts of the current work system on both society and the environment are thus unrecorded and unconsidered.

6.4. The Woodlanders

In this section we are going to move from *techne* to *episteme*: we are going to instantiate the discussion in a real example of a craft environment – the woodland – and take forward the focus on woodlands as livelihoods undertaken in the previous chapter to consider them also as sites of skilled work, and places where deep and important relationships between men and women and their environment can take place, mediated through the process of craft.

Wood is one of our oldest resources, our relationship with it dating back to pre-history. 'The art of coppicing goes back at least 6,000 years in Britain to the Sweet Track in the Somerset Levels, a Neolithic wooden walking track over a mile long running across wet or flooded peat … Poles of ash, oak and lime were cut down, transported to the Levels and pegged together in the winter or early spring of 3807 or 3806 BC. A series of trestles, driven into the wet peat, supported an oak walkway of split trunks' (Deakin, 2007: 366). As well as being a natural method for sequestering carbon, wood offers a bewildering variety of uses and associated crafts. Most obviously, large timber has always been used for the construction of buildings, initially in its natural 'roundwood' form, but later being shaped with tools such as adzes and later by use of mechanical mills to create squared timber. Wood has also provided the fuel to warm the majority of human dwellings since our ancestors discovered how to control fire, as well as offering the opportunity to cook food, and thus make a wider range of plants available for nutrition. Just as our ancestors learned to domesticate cattle and sheep so they learned, through observation of the ways of trees, how to maximise their yield of useful products with minimal effort. The process of copsework is such an example of the management of natural woodland for human purposes: a symbiosis of human and arboreal species. As listed by John Seymour and reproduced in Table 6.1, woodlands have fed a huge variety of skilled craftspeople and met a wide range of our needs in processes of sustainable production and consumption.

Meeting a need by exercising craft on a natural material is a process of relationship, and the evidence of that relationship persists through time as demonstrated in Ingold's (2010: 98–99) description of the *charpente* or workshop in the French Alps:

> Its floor, walls and roof-beams have been hewn from timber, just as have the planks on which he now works. You can see in the beams traces of the movements of the axe that cut them, following the grain that reveals the pro-venance of every beam from a tree once growing in the forest.

Deakin describes the need for craftwork to respond to the products of the natural environ-ment, and therefore continue to 'fit' within them even after having been transformed:

> The proportions of each room, and of the house as a whole, were pre-dicated on the natural proportions of the trees available. Suffolk houses like mine tend to be about eighteen feet wide, because that is about the average limit of the straight run of the trunk of the youngish oak suitable in girth for making a major crossbeam of eight inches by seven. The bigger barns tend to twenty-one feet wide, with slightly bigger timbers. Uprights too are of tree height, the idea being to select trees or coppice poles of about the right cross-section, so they can be squared with an adze with the minimum of work.
>
> (Deakin, 2007: 7)

Working with wood also requires intimate knowledge of the material, or rather materials, since each wood has its own properties, and indeed each tree is different depending on the environmental conditions that formed it. Wood is also a seasonal material, having completely different qualities depending on the season during which it is cut. The woodworker requires 'deep knowledge of the behavior of materials, for example, that by which carpenters of his day knew how to choose, cut, and prepare wood panels, so that even after centuries very little warping or twisting takes place' (Smith, 2004: 86). The consequences of misunderstanding your material could be minor – the splitting of a piece or the warping of a component so that it became unusable, for example – or spectacular, as in the example of the twisted spire of Chesterfield church, the result of insufficiently seasoned roof timber, which warped under the weight of the roofing lead.[2]

In my own auto-ethnography of woodwork, which must bring as much hilarity to the genuine craftspeople as it brings joy to me, I have begun to understand how woodlands appears to those whose partners they are in the production of wooden goods. I think of this as 'a walk in the woods with Mr Clisset' in tribute to the Herefordshire maker, whose typical chairs are illustrated in Photo 6.1.[3] After some time spent working with wood, the trees start to suggest themselves in the form of different pieces of furniture. Particular arrangements of branches can be found, or even encouraged during growth, that will lend themselves to the production of a high chair or a music-stand: the process of craft enables this intimate relationship between the maker and the natural process of tree growth.

In his discussion of the relationship between landscape, performance and memory, Pearson develops further the way in which a close relationship with the local environment can be developed through human work. He draws on the work of Ingold, for whom 'Taskscape is to labour what landscape is to land':

> In emphasizing the role of human agency, Ingold characterises landscape as *taskscape*: inhabitants know their environs not as spectators but as participants.

PHOTO 6.1 Clissett chairs
Source: With thanks to Terry Rowell for this photograph of his beautiful Clissett chairs, which he has provided for reproduction free of charge.

> Landscape is taskscape in its embodied, or congealed, form: just as landscape is
> an array of related features, so taskscape is an array of related activities.
>
> *(Pearson, 2006)*

According to Ingold a task is a 'constitutive act of dwelling … a practical operation
carried out by a skilled agent in an environment that only gets meaning from its
position within an array of related activities' (Ingold, 2000: 195). Our experience of
our landscape becomes real through our interaction with it in our work. This is a
mutual relationship, and one of tension rather than passivity.

   To be a successful craftworker is not to be supine in relationship with one's materials,
but rather to learn, through the many hours of practice that a skilled craft demands, how
to work in harmony with those materials. The acquisition of craft skills is thus a relationship between the worker and the material: to be successful you must learn to respect
the resistance of the material, but also the nature and extent of your own persistence.
Van Gogh is quoted as having said that 'nature always resists the craftsman', a point
developed further by Richard Sennett, who emphasises that any skilled craftsman will
come up against problems in working with his materials. Sennett explores the process
by which this 'resistance' can be overcome, a process that requires empathy between
maker and materials and a process that he analyses as having three stages:

> By contrast empathic problem-solving requires: (1) a leap of imagination; (2)
> patience to accept 'the temporary suspension of the desire for closure'; and (3)
> the ability to 'identify with the resistance'. 'The skills of working well with
> resistance are, in sum, those of reconfiguring the problem into other terms,
> readjusting one's behaviour if the problem lasts longer than expected, and
> identifying with the problem's most unforgiving element.
>
> *(Sennett, 2008: 221–22)*

Other authors have elaborated on this question of the relationship between the craft
worker and his materials. As Ingold correctly identifies, in seeking to split a log the
woodsman follows the grain already in the timber: 'It is a question', write Deleuze
and Guattari, 'of surrendering to the wood, and following where it leads' (2004: 451;
quoted in Ingold, 2010: 92). This seems to me a perfect metaphor for developing a
more harmonious relationship with nature, and therefore the ideal learning experience for an ecological citizen. This 'textility' sought by Ingold (2010), a way of
interacting with natural materials in a responsive relationship rather than one of
domination, can be found in the work of the wildwood makers, whose work is
celebrated in Photos 6.2 and 6.3.

6.5. Conclusion: a community built of craftspeople

The central argument of this bioregional investigation of work is that how we produce has a fundamental impact on ourselves as workers, on the society we build
together and on our relationship with the environment from which our resources are

PHOTO 6.2 A rocking-chair in yew and cherry by Gudrun Leitz. For more information visit
the website: www.greenwoodwork.co.uk.
Source: Photo by Gudrun Leitz, reproduced with permission.

drawn and on which our livelihoods all ultimately depend. In this concluding section
I am going to explore in more detail how the actual activity of working impacts on
the sort of society we build together.

In his sociological study of modernity called *Risk Society*, Ulrich Beck writes of the
first question that people ask each other in social situations: 'What do you do?' This, I

PHOTO 6.3 Craft in the woodland: a group present their work after a week spent at Clissett Wood
Source: Photo by Gudrun Leitz, reproduced with permission.

think, betrays his German origins as well as, perhaps, his age. In the globalised world people are not defined in terms of their work, and they are not characterised by their skills. As we will see in the following chapter, they are much more likely to be defined in terms of their consumption than their production: this, I would argue, is a system of identification that is socially as well as environmentally pernicious. Whereas mutual respect for skilled work builds a community, the competitive process of status attainment via positional goods works against the cohesiveness of communities.

Ingold argues against what he calls a 'hylomorphic model of creation', by which he means that our work involves the imposition of a form determined by our will on the material world. Like Smith, he identifies this way of seeing our interaction with the material world as being derived from an Aristotelian worldview, based on an understanding of creation as the bringing together of form (*morphe*) and matter (*hyle*). By contrast he argues that 'the forms of things arise within fields of force and flows of material. It is by intervening in these force-fields and following the lines of flow that practitioners make things. In this view, making is a practice of weaving, in which practitioners bind their own pathways or lines of becoming into the texture of material flows comprising the lifeworld' (Ingold, 2010: 91).

In his sociological analysis of craftwork, Sennett explores the connections between the structure of work organisation and the nature of the work undertaken within them. He draws a parallel between the embodied nature of craftwork, the need to learn motor co-ordination and control within one's own body, and the similar process of building communities between people: 'Is there some bodily basis for working cooperatively? What might experiences of physical coordination suggest about social cooperation? This is a question that can be made concrete in exploring how the two hands coordinate and cooperate with each other' (Sennett, 2008: 161). Extending this analogy, Sennett suggests that co-operative work patterns benefit from the contrasting skills and differing abilities of their members, much as the different digits of the hand have their individual roles and make unique contributions to a piece of craftwork:

> The digits of the hand are of unequal strength and flexibility, impeding equal coordination. When hand skills develop to a high level, the inequalities can be compensated; fingers and thumbs will do work that other digits cannot perform themselves. The colloquial English usage of 'lending a hand' or the 'helping hand' reflect such visceral experience. The compensatory work of the hand suggests – perhaps it is no more than a suggestion – that fraternal cooperation does not depend on sharing equally a skill.
>
> *(Sennett, 2008: 162)*

Sennett's account of a workplace – where different skills are respected and valued, and what may appear a weakness in a competitive workplace can become a strength – is validated by researchers in the field of co-operative studies (Sanchez Bajo and Roelants, 2011).

The cohesion that typified pre-modern communities was not achieved by chance: it was rather built on the highly developed system of craftwork that was destroyed by the specialisation of skill and the division of labour from Adam Smith's pin factory onwards. The craftspeople who fought the advent of the machine, and the deskilling it inevitably brought in its wake, were not defending their rates of pay or even the variety of their work experience; they were seeking to protect a way of life where autonomy, skilfulness and social learning were constitutive both of the workplace and the wider society. Central to this type of work, and binding craftsmen together within the craft, and working together to strengthen society more widely, was the guild. Guilds are much misunderstood institutions, and, like many of the social and economic organisations that pre-dated capitalism, they have not been portrayed sympathetically by later scholars, or even attracted much attention.

The ideology of work under capitalism is one of division: division of labour into its different types of skill, division of people between tasks, division of specialisms between different national economies. But labour is also divided from the natural world and its species. The process of acquiring raw materials is separated from the process of transforming those materials into useful products. The consequence of these multiple and interacting divisions is to divide us from ourselves (a process characterised by Marx as alienation), to divide us from one another, and to divide us from the other species with whom we share the planet. For green economists the dislocation between ourselves and our planet is a key cause of the ecological crisis; to repair this dislocation we need to re-vision work as a process of unification rather than division. The Ricardian work system that has come to dominate the world economy over the past two centuries is destructive to the process of building a sustainable society: it separates people from each other and it creates in the work situation another site where people are separated from nature. Skilled craftwork achieves the opposite: it binds people together in their work and thus provides the basis for stronger social relationships. And perhaps even more importantly from an environmental perspective, it offers a unique mechanism by which we can begin the urgent process of re-embedding ourselves in the natural world.

7

WHAT ABOUT MY IPAD?[1]

Getting and spending, we lay waste our powers

William Wordsworth, from *The world is too much with us*

The premise of this book is that we need rapidly to achieve reductions of some 90% in our consumption of energy if we are to avoid a climate-change catastrophe. The bioregional economy has been proposed as an alternative model of provisioning to the global market, and previous chapters have begun to sketch out how such an economy might function. It has become clear already that the quality and quantity of 'consumption' within such an economy would be wholly different from that which the globalised economy offers. This chapter addresses consumption, its link to personal identity and the way demand is manipulated and controlled not in the interests of society but in the interests of companies that produce the goods and services that we consume.[2] While much attention has been paid to the potential of climate change to undermine our systems of provisioning for basic resources, much less attention has been paid to the way in which, as members of a human community, our social identity is equally important to our survival. For many people, their identity is built on energy-intensive patterns of consumption. How can they adjust to a world with far less energy available? How can we manage this transition? What aspects of a bioregional economy might provide substitutes for the identities offered by the globalised economy?

One of the first broadly economic responses amongst concerned environmentalists to the message that over-consumption was problematic was to undertake lifestyle change. This might involve, at the first stage, using energy-efficient light-bulbs and recycling more waste, and later switching to lower-energy systems of transport or improving the insulation level of the home. However, the impossible next step within an economic system that is premised on growth is to suggest the need not for more consumption, no matter how greenly inclined, but rather for less consumption. Dobson critiques the potential of the green lifestyle strategy to effect political change because of this limitation:

it does nothing to confront the central green point that unlimited production and consumption – no matter how environmentally friendly – is impossible to sustain in a limited system. The problem here is not so much to get people to consume soundly but to get them – or at least those living in profligate societies – to consume less.

(Dobson, 2007: 121)

The focus of this chapter is on the subtle interplay between the human need for a social identity and the design principle of a capitalist economy to grow. The work of Thorstein Veblen, the institutional economist, in anatomising the nature of consumption as a means of establishing social status, underpins much of the discussion in this chapter and it forms the focus for Section 7.1. Section 7.2 moves on to provide evidence of the central role that consumption plays in the identity of members of industrial societies and the threat to their survival posed by the failure of such an identity. Sections 7.3 explores how an economic system that is designed to grow must be supported by the creation of demand on both the production and the consumption sides of the economy and how that identity is inherently unsatisfying. Section 7.4 sketches out how a bioregional economy could offer an attitude to consumption based on a recognition of abundance and on embedded relationships with the local natural environment and our fellow creatures, and Section 7.5 briefly concludes.

7.1. The pecuniary standard of living

Veblen's book *The Theory of the Leisure Class* was first published in 1899 and was notable at the time for eschewing the modelling and mathematics of the 'marginal revolution' in academic economics and focusing rather on a socio-cultural explanation for consumption behaviour. Consumption, Veblen posited, was not motivated by a desire to subsist but rather as a means of establishing social status:

> The end of acquisition and accumulation is conventionally held to be the consumption of the goods accumulated ... But it is only when taken in a sense far removed from its naïve meaning that consumption of goods can be said to afford the incentive from which accumulation invariably proceeds. The motive that lies at the root of ownership is emulation.
>
> *(Veblen, 1899/1994: 17)*

Veblen's notion of 'pecuniary emulation' challenges the conventional economic account of a struggle for subsistence within an over-arching framework of scarcity: in more marginal economies subsistence is a motivation, but it is rapidly replaced by a desire to advertise our ability to consume and hence to establish our superiority. One means of establishing superiority is to indicate one's ability to subsist without labour, what Veblen calls 'conspicuous leisure', and to denigrate the work, especially the manual work, of others. The concept of 'leisure' in this context 'does not connote indolence or quiescence. What it connotes is non-productive consumption of time' (Veblen, 1899/1994: 28). At the turn of the twentieth century, establishing status was achieved through advertising one's lack of need to engage in work, and especially in manual labour; through one's ability to accumulate power that enabled one to acquire goods produced through the labour of others, and the more labour they had obviously required to be made, and the more pointless and unnecessary they were in supporting subsistence, the more one's status was established (perhaps Fabergé eggs are the apotheosis of such consumption); and finally, through one's ability to engage in the 'devout observances' that typified the leisure class, predominantly sport.

While Veblen offers a brilliant exposition of the role of consumption in the period, his book was written at a time when both mass production and political mass mobilisation were in their infancy. As will be discussed later in this chapter, the ability to create desires for goods through psychological manipulation, and to broaden the pool of those who could have access to them, has been the story of the last century of capitalism. The extravagant lifestyle thus created in the Western world is now being propagated in the countries that have moved more recently into the industrialised market economy. Within the logic of the existing economic model this is consistent, but its costs in ecological terms are unsustainable. Later in the chapter (in Section 7.3) we will also explore how this lifestyle, which, when Veblen described it, was the preserve of the few, has since become the aspiration of whole populations. In a sense this has invalidated its role, since demonstrating one's superior affluence through patterns of consumption becomes pointless if those one is advertising to enjoy a similar standard of life. In this situation, hierarchy must be established through niche or maverick patterns of consumption, or through deliberately accelerated changes in fashion that enable a competitive process of consumption through constant change.

The purpose of this first section is to revive and reinforce Veblen's conception of consumption as related to the establishment of status rather than the meeting of need. This is an encouraging insight, since it suggests that our task in ensuring that patterns of consumption fit within planetary limits does not necessitate the seemingly impossible aim of focusing directly on the objects of desire with which people surround themselves – the multiplicity of electronic gadgets and fashionable home furnishings that they have come to regard as their birthright – but rather in shifting the basis on which social status is established.

In work that takes inspiration from Veblen, Hodgson (2003) explores the role of habit formation in the field of consumption behaviour. He argues that the standard model of the utility-maximising agent omits the important element of our economic behaviour that arises from learned behaviour.

> Habits themselves are formed through repetition of action or thought. They are influenced by prior activity and have durable, self-sustaining qualities. Through their habits, individuals carry the marks of their own unique history [.] habit does not mean behaviour. It is a propensity to behave in particular ways in a particular class of situations.
>
> *(Hodgson, 2003: 164)*

Habits represent a way of adapting to social constraints, codes for making choices to avoid the time-consuming process of considering all our options each time. Both through laziness and to avoid social censure, 'We acquire habits of thought and behaviour that dovetail with those of the culture as a whole' (Hodgson, 2003: 169). In brief, our consumption decisions take place within social institutions and on the basis of habitual conditioning. Encouragingly, in view of the threat posed by present habits of consumption, an institutionalist view would suggest that such habits can be changed: people do develop new preferences:

> beliefs may change, not simply as a result of receiving information, but also because habitual mechanisms of interpretation may alter. In contrast to the pervasive idea of the given individual, the individual is formed and reconstituted in an ongoing process. Institutions matter in both cases. But in the habit-based conception, they can also lead eventually to new habits and new preferences or beliefs.
>
> *(Hodgson, 2003: 171)*

The emphasis on consumption taking place within the context of social institutions and being responsive to changes in the norms of those institutions as well as in response to changed information suggests an important role for cultural leaders, as well as educators and politicians, in setting the parameters within which consumption can form part of life in a sustainable society. This is a distinct cause from the behaviour change that is now so fashionable, requiring genuine engagement and leadership, rather than subtle attempts to manipulate behaviour through incentives.

Although mainstream economic analysis generally eschews the role of psychological factors, at least at the academic, theoretical level, the limited number of studies that exist indicate that responses to changes in consumption levels are far from rational (Rabin, 1998: 13). Crucially, our satisfaction or otherwise with the material level of our lives is highly sensitive to changes but has less to do with the absolute level of material consumption. The habitual nature of our assumptions about consumption means that we are challenged by rapid changes in the availability of material goods. However, after the adjustment has been made we are likely to be as content with the changed level of life we experience without whichever good or service once seemed so critical to our well-being.

So in addressing the issue of consumption we have established in this first section that consumption is a form of social behaviour, responsive to and established within a cultural frame of reference. Our consumption is based on patterns we acquire within society and can be changed without much long-term cost to ourselves. Our reasons for consumption relate more to our desire to be admired and respected by our peers than to our own innate greed or addiction to consumption for its own sake.

7.2. Shopping for an identity

The underlying argument of this chapter is that consumption takes place within a cultural framework and mediates our sense of our selves within social systems. Veblen's theorisation suggests that this has been true for more than 100 years, but social changes during the past century have accentuated the importance of consumption (rather than production) in establishing who we are. The process of globalisation of the economy has broken down traditional national boundaries and the liberation of women has to some extent removed traditional gender-based identities. This has increased our sense of the riskiness of the society we live in (Beck, 1992). Globalisation has also deskilled and homogenised the nature of our work, so we can no longer base our sense of self on a particular productive skill or expertise (Giddens, 1991).

In response, argues Bauman, modern citizens must establish identities for themselves via their consumption (2005a). The oppression that was once exerted via the work ethic has been replaced by the equally oppressive consumption ethic, and this is particularly destructive to those without sufficient money to buy the goods that establish a superior identity. For Bauman, establishing an identity through consumption is an unsatisfying and also a transient activity:

> They wander through the shopping-mall winding passages, guided by a semi-conscious hope of finding an identity badge or token that will bring their selves up to date – and also by a semi-conscious apprehension that they might not notice the crucial point at which what were badges of pride become transformed into badges of shame. For their motivation never to dry up, it is enough for the shopping mall manager to follow the principle … that the last bit on offer does not fit the rest of the identity jigsaw-puzzle, so that the assembly has to be repeatedly started again from scratch. If identity jigsaw-puzzles are available solely in the commodity form, and cannot be found outside shopping malls, the future of the market is assured.
>
> (Bauman, 2005b: 17)

The establishment of an identity based on consumption is a dynamic process: while we can locate ourselves as hippies or yuppies and buy the appropriate products to establish ourselves as such, the link between hierarchy, consumption and status requires, at least for most consumer-based identities, the acquisition of not only more goods, but goods that advertise ourselves as having a superior place in the hierarchy. Consumption is thus used as a means of establishing identity in a relative sense, by purchasing goods that inherently establish our superiority because they are exclusive and particularly sought after by others, sometimes referred to as 'positional goods' (Hirsch, 1976). In order effectively to establish ourselves as superior to others we need to acquire goods that are not only expensive but difficult to come by. But can we consider these goods to be scarce in the conventional economic sense?

The idea of scarcity is central to conventional economic theory: without scarcity there can be no price and hence no market (Robbins, 1962). Yet repeatedly amongst the writings of those who focus on human motivations, rather than abstract theory, the question arises as to how much this idea of scarcity is perceived, rather than real. A distinction is drawn between absolute scarcity, and the relative scarcity that arises as a result of the gap between our inherent sense of need and what we can acquire. Sahlins (1972) raised this issue in his discussion of neolithic societies as the first affluent societies since they had adopted what he called the 'Zen road to affluence', by identifying their material needs as minimal and then easily meeting them, allowing plenty of time free for leisure, community-building, and artistic and spiritual pursuits.

For Panayotakis (2011), scarcity has been invented and is maintained by a capitalist economic system in order to create the right incentives to facilitate its smooth functioning and the extraction of labour and profit. He argues that this is grossly inefficient and inappropriate, directing ingenuity, energy and innovation towards the stimulation of consumption desires rather than towards addressing the ecological crisis: 'this system is not just wasteful, it is downright dangerous, since it turns the very technological potential that could increase human well-being and enrich human life into a series of grave threats to humanity and the planet alike' (Panayotakis, 2011: 149). The link between this critique and that of Veblen is the shared understanding that the desire to consume within a capitalist economy is a driver of demand necessary to guarantee the effective functioning of the economy itself. Thus hierarchical and expansionist consumer ideologies are vigorously encouraged.

Remembering Bauman, we should note how some of those who have fewer resources at their disposal sometimes respond with great creativity to the need to secure their position in a consumption-based hierarchy. Ponsford (2011: 541) studied a group of young single mothers in Bristol and argues that 'young mothers invest in consumer culture and the appearance of their children as a means of publicly displaying competent parenting ability and deflecting the negative value and pejorative judgement they feel is associated with youthful motherhood and poverty.' The valuation of mothering is based largely on consumption so that being a good mother entails being a good consumer (Freedman and Lustig, 2004; Power, 2005). The response to this by young mothers with limited resources provides evidence of the way in which consumer culture has hollowed out other means of establishing a social identity; their response is both creative, and disempowered.

While for me, and for most of the readers of this book, an identity derived to a significant extent from consumption decisions is a pervasive reality, it is of fairly recent origin in terms of human history. For members of traditional societies their lives were played out against a background that included both natural and supernatural forces, with which they interacted on a daily basis: 'The cosmos, in short, was a place of *belonging*. A member of this cosmos was not an alienated observer of it but a direct participant in its drama. Her personal destiny was bound up with its destiny, and this relationship gave meaning to his life' (Morris Berman quoted in Sale, 1991: 10). Such an understanding has more in common with the sense of self experienced by our medieval ancestors than it does with our own ideas about transient physical existence followed by biophysical extinction, which for most people also means metaphysical extinction. By contrast, 'For medieval people, reality consisted in the supernatural realm while the material world was transient and insubstantial' (Sale, 1991: 47).

This sense of oneself forming part of a wider spiritual universe persisted in the Western world right up to the early modern period, when the foregrounding of a scientific understanding diminished the deeper understanding of self. In Lewis Mumford's terms, the sense of spiritual purpose was replaced by a 'purposeless materialism':

There is a disproportionate emphasis on the physical means of living: people sacrifice time and present enjoyments in order that they acquire a greater abundance of physical means; for there is supposed to be a close relation between well-being and the number of bathtubs, motor cars, and similar machine-made products that one may possess.

(Mumford, 1934/1963: 273)

The consumption standard to which the consumers of the globalised economy aspire was established in the USA during the post-war years. This was a considered part of the US strategy of establishing the superiority of its way of life, which was based on the twin pillars of free-market capitalism and representative democracy. According to de Botton (2004) presidential candidate Richard Nixon made much play of the standard of living of the average American family during a visit to Moscow to open an exhibition 'showcasing his country's technological and material achievements' (2004: 33). At that time the level of material comfort enjoyed by US citizens was the envy of the world and it was also used as evidence of the superiority of the capitalist economic system: 'When Franklin D. Roosevelt was asked what book he could give to the Soviets to teach them about the advantages of American society, he pointed to the Sears catalogue' (de Botton, 2004: 40). As de Grazia tartly observes, the US operated as 'an imperium with the outlook of an emporium' (de Grazia, 2005).

Material consumption and standard of life became the battle-ground on which the struggle over the dominant politico-economic model of the twentieth century was played out. While technological superiority in the production of weapons of war formed part of a symbolic struggle, the most advanced of these weapons were never used. Rather, the USA used its advantage in terms of plentiful natural resources, technological knowledge and available labour to conquer the 'red peril', not through waging a hot war, or through achieving higher levels of education or social equality or mental health, but through producing consumer goods and advertising the lifestyle of the American household to countries that resisted the capitalist model. Hence, while attempts to prevent the import of Levis into the Soviet Union appeared farcical, this was the frontline of the Cold War and the ideological battle of the twenty-first century. Since the USA declared its victory and the eternal superiority of the system of US capitalism (Fukuyama, 1992) we have space to address both the validity of its model and the cost of its victory.

7.3. I seem to find the happiness I seek

In seeking the origin of a culture in which citizens identify themselves through their consumption, we should look back, I think, to the last great capitalist catastrophe: the Great Depression. This helps to challenge the environmentalists' demonisation of the pushers of demand and offer an explanation as to why people might use manufactured social dissatisfaction within an economic system that cannot survive with inadequate aggregate demand. While the fiscal solution to the economic troubles of the 1930s may have been Keynesian, the cultural solutions were, at least indirectly, Freudian.

In a famous passage in the *General Theory* Keynes describes how different cultures have dealt with the problem of insufficient demand:

> Ancient Egypt was doubly fortunate, and doubtless owed to this its fabled wealth, in that it possessed two activities, namely, pyramid-building as well as the search for the precious metals, the fruits of which, since they could not serve the needs of man by being consumed, did not stale with abundance. The Middle Ages built cathedrals and sang dirges.
>
> *(Keynes, 1936: bk. 3, ch. 10, sect. 6)*

Although Keynes is credited with solving the problem of the Great Depression through his theory of the multiplier effect of demand stimulation through public investment, as with the Tenessee River Authority in the USA, others have argued that in reality it was the switch to a wartime economy that put the capitalist economy back on an even keel (Galbraith, 1958/1970; Romer, 1992). This was effectively a strategy of making enormously big holes across Europe and then spending around another decade gradually filling them in; this is obviously to make no comment on the loss of life and livelihood that was the price of this strategy.

Keynes's argument was for injection of demand by public authorities, but the private sector had already begun its strategy of increasing demand before the stock-market crash and subsequent Depression. Although I should say at the outset that I do not believe that changing the sorts of light-bulb we use can save us from ecological catastrophe, it may be that understanding the behaviour of the Phoebus cartel of light-bulb manufacturers just might. The group was made up of all the leading manufacturers of the day, including General Electric, Osram and Philips (Monopolies Commission, 1951). At a meeting in Geneva in 1924 the Phoebus group decided to enforce a maximum life-time of the light-bulb at 1,000 hours, eschewing the superior design already achieved by Edison around the turn of the century. A long-lasting life-bulb reduced their profits and so innovation was restricted. The oldest light-bulb in the world is still in place and casting light over the Livermore Fire Station in California: it is 110 years old.

The strategy of creating demand through the deliberate design of obsolescent or poorly made goods flourished in the years following the war. It was parodied in a 1951 film by Alexander Mackendrick called *The Man in the White Suit* (Street, 2008: 81). In the film Alec Guinness played Sidney Stratton, a research chemist working in the textile industry. Stratton undertakes expensive research to discover a miracle fibre that is not subject to the depredations of dirt or wear: he uses his material to make a luminous white suit. His moment of glory is short-lived, however, since both managers and unions recognise the dangers posed by a suit that does not need to be replaced: Stratton is sacked and pursued both metaphorically and actually by both sides in the age-old capital-labour battle. Eventually he discovers that his suit is vulnerable to sunlight, but he remains undeterred, and we leave him in the final scene striding purposefully off to another research laboratory where his attempts to create genuinely sustainable products will doubtless be greeted with horror.

In the early days of the enthusiasm for creating demand, its proponents were quite explicit about the various techniques that they used. King Camp Gillette, inventor of the disposable razor, argued that:

> We have the paradox of idle men, only too anxious for work, and idle plants in perfect conditions for production, at the same time that people are starving and frozen. The reason is overproduction. It seems a bit absurd that when we have overproduced we should go without. One would think that over-production would warrant a furious holiday and a riot of feasting a display of the superfluous goods lying about. On the contrary, overproduction produces want.
>
> *(quoted in Slade, 2006: 10)*

A McGraw-Hill executive writing in *Advertising Age* in 1955 was even more explicit:

> As a nation we are already so rich that consumers are under no pressure of immediate necessity to buy a very large share – perhaps as much as 40 per cent – of what is produce, and the pressure will get progressively less in the years ahead. But if consumers exercise their option not to buy a large share of what is produced, a great depression is not far behind.
>
> *(quoted in Packard, 1957/1981: 23)*

Karl Prentiss, another advertising executive, wrote in *True Magazine* in 1958:

> Our whole economy is based on planned obsolescence and everybody who can read without moving his lips should know it by now. We make good products, we induce people to buy them, and then next year we deliberately introduce something that will make those products old fashioned, out of date, obsolete. We do that for the soundest reason: to make money.
>
> *(quoted in Slade, 2006: 153).*

Techniques to reduce the life of products included death-dating, the practice of ensuring that products will break after a short period, which began with radios in that same year and led to furious arguments between engineers, aiming to build the best possible device, and executives, whose eyes were fixed firmly on the balance-sheets. The increase in range of scope of technologically sophisticated products has vastly increased the possibilities for generating demand through artificially limiting the life of goods. The star performer in this arena is certainly the mobile phone: by 2002 over 130 million still-working portable phones were disposed of in the USA alone. Cell phones have now achieved the dubious distinction of having the shortest life cycle of any electronic consumer product and their life span is still declining (Slade, 2006: 263).

These strategies were successful in increasing the need to buy products, but were initially greeted with hostility by those purchasing goods they might reasonably have considered shoddy. Attention now turned to the need to create further demand by manipulating the consumption rather than the production side of the economy. In this atmosphere of joyful innovation for the common good the advertising industry was born as a saviour, if not of mankind, then at least of the capitalist system on which it found itself reliant. The adman's target was the thrifty housewife with her wartime motto of make-do-and-mend; such careful and attentive consumers were a threat to the flourishing of the economy. Ewen (2001) describes the early develop-ment of the US advertising industry in the 1920s and the pride that was shown in the ability of the US consumer to buy without considering quality too deeply, a fault that was identified in newly arrived immigrants from Sweden and Germany, who studied products in detail before buying them.

In 1957 Vance Packard's book *The Hidden Persuaders* blew the whistle on how scientific developments in psychology were being used to manipulate US citizens to undertake mass consumption. What he called the 'depth approach' to advertising was based on insights from social psychology. It was, as he described it, 'impelled by the difficulties the marketers kept encountering in trying to persuade people to buy all the products their companies could fabricate' (Packard, 1957/1981: 17). The role of Edward Ber-nays, Freud's nephew, was seen as central to this broader use of psychological insights (Tye, 2002), which he first described in his uncritical book on propaganda (1928). In his own words he describes how he had no qualms in using such methods:

> If we understand the mechanism and motives of the group mind, is it now possible to control and regiment the masses according to our will without their knowing it[?] … Mass psychology is as yet far from being an exact science and the mysteries of human motivation are by no means all revealed. But at least theory and practice have combined with sufficient success to permit us to know that in certain cases we can effect some change in public opinion … by operating a certain mechanism.
>
> *(quoted in Ewen, 2001: 83–84)*

Packard expressed horror at what he called the marketing to 'eight hidden needs', which he identified as emotional security, reassurance of worth, ego-gratification, creative outlets, love objects, a sense of power, a sense of roots, and immortality. Although his work is now more than 50 years old, the routes advertising finds to exploit our psychological needs appear to be similar today. This use of scientific methods to uncover our inner needs and then to design products to meet them resulted in what Packard referred to as 'the packaged soul'.

Consumerism in this sense of a spiral of the creation of desire, its temporary satis-faction, before new desires are aroused, was created in the USA, and was perhaps its most potent post-war export (Stearns, 2006). The citizens of Austerity Britain Round: The 1950s, were attracted by the allure of the glamour that they saw first on the 'silver screen' in Hollywood movies, and were later trained to expect this as their own aspiration (Grundle, 2009). According to de Grazia (2005), shifting the thrifty European publics towards an attitude of mass consumption was a sub-text of the Marshall Plan. The initial reluctance on the part of the British to enjoy shopping or wear lipstick is well expressed by J. B. Priestley, who referred to this process as 'Admass': 'the whole system of an increasing productivity, plus inflation, plus a rising standard of material living, plus high-pressure advertising and salesmanship, plus mass communications, plus cultural democracy and the creation of the mass mind, the mass man' (Priestley and Hawkes, 1955). The exposure of this as a deliberate ploy to increase sales (by writers such as Packard) was sudden and shocking:

> The post-World War II vision of a prosperous world, in which genuine human needs were to be met by a strong, efficient and growing economy, was shattered. Packard alleged that, instead of serving human needs, the big corporations were manipulating our very wants and desires, using everything from subliminal messages to the exploitation of sexual images.
>
> *(Hodgson, 2003)*

While the techniques used to encourage consumption were new, the understanding that capitalism as a system required pointless consumption was not. Alan de Botton (2004: 76) quotes Hume's essay *Of Luxury* (1752) in which he extolls the economic virtue of pointless luxuries: 'In a nation where there is no demand for superfluities, men sink into indolence, lose all enjoyment of life, and are useless to the public, which cannot maintain or support its fleets and armies.' This was the dawn of the discipline of economics, which coincided with the growth of the economic system of capitalism and the need to justify the inequalities of wealth and power that it brought with it. Prior to this period the poor and hard-working had been considered to be the creators of wealth, but this view was changed by the new ideology, which praised consumers rather than producers. It was demand that drove the new economy. Of course such arguments ring differently in an era when we have become more aware of the environmental consequences of that demand, but we are left with the manufactured aspirations of consumers whose economic duty has, for more than half a century, been to respond to the advertisers' injunctions to consume and consume again.

The consequence of this originally well-motived attempt to create habits of constant material aspiration in populations has been an addiction to consumption with its concomitant therapeutic literature (de Graaf, Wann and Naylor, 2001) and similarly named works addressing the epidemic of Affluenza by psychologists Oliver James in the UK (James, 2007) and Clive Hamilton in Australia (Hamilton and Denniss, 2005). These works use psychological theories to demonstrate how consumerism is deliberately mobilised by psychological drivers, needs, triggers and techniques (for individual self-affirmation, self-esteem, or belonging). They also show how, after a threshold, it does not make us happy, and how one needs to understand excessive consumption as something requiring a therapeutic approach, to focus on its effects on the individual, as well as a political perspective, given consumerism is a collective practice with collective impacts (Keat, 1994).

In the context of ecological crisis that forms the backdrop for the proposal of a bioregional economy the fact that consumerism is psychologically unsatisfying is crucial: 'consumerism is founded on the distortion of *real/natural human needs* and on the creation and proliferation of "false desires"' (Stavrakakis, 2006: 86). Campbell (1987) has argued that consumerism produces 'self-illusionary hedonism', which is virtual satisfaction: it is the fantasy rather than the product itself that the consumer receives. According to van Koppen, 'Campbell's theory sheds light on typical consumerist patterns such as shopping for fun, the abundant use of symbolic promises in advertising, and the functionality of fashion' (2007: 370). So the consumption of resources that threatens ecological balance is not enhancing our quality of life.

My writing of this chapter coincided with the death of Steve Jobs, who had a claim to be the master of this means of selling through distorted desire. According to Baggiani (2011):

> Jobs's success was built firmly on the idea that in another sense, you should not give consumers what they want because they don't know what they want. No one thought they wanted the first desktop Mac, iPod, iPhone or iPad before they existed. Jobs repeatedly created things that people came to want more than anything else only by not trying to give them what they already wanted. This challenges the idea that consumer culture inevitably means pandering to the conventional, to the lowest common denominator. Markets are not necessarily conservative: truly great innovations can become popular.
>
> *www.guardian.co.uk/technology/2011/oct/06/steve-jobs-changed-capitalism*

A companion piece by Jonathan Jones focuses on the 'soft-machine aesthetic' that Apple pioneered, making what had seemed geeky and cold appear friendly and cool: 'instead of chillin you out' they 'glow like fireplaces and nuzzle like digital pets' (Jones, 2011). Jones admits that he writes articles on an impractical machine that does not facilitate the process of typing because he is 'captivated by the beauty of this piece of technology'. Jones goes so far as to imply that the way an Apple computer slowly glows into life suggests that it is coming alive.

The attempt to create a physical affection, dependence even, on what is essentially a machine, has taken the distortion of consumption desire to new depths, as exemplified by the quotation credited to Jobs that 'You know you have created a great product when you want to lick it'.[3] The inevitable dissatisfaction that results from attempting to establish a personal relationship with a machine is iconic of the way that creating an impossible demand guarantees a future market, as identified by Abram, who describes how a relationship with industrial products diminishes us, while a relationship with natural products fulfils:

> In contrast, the mass-produced artifacts of civilization, from milk cartons to washing machines to computers, draw our senses into a dance that endlessly reiterates itself without variation. To the sensing body these artifacts are, like all phenomena, animate and even alive, but their life is profoundly constrained by

the specific "functions" for which they were built. Once our bodies master these functions, the machine-made objects commonly teach our sense nothing further; they are unable to surprise us, and so we must continually acquire new built objects, new technologies, the latest model of this or that if we wish to stimulate ourselves.

(Abram, 1996: 64)

7.4. An embarrassment of riches

In this chapter I have done my best to avoid the conventional environmentalist's parody of the manipulative capitalist producer, urging unwanted products on a docile citizenry merely in order to swell his profits. While this is a tempting portrayal, it does not help to explain how we have reached a point where our economy cannot flourish unless, in Tim Jackson's memorable phrase, 'We are being persuaded to spend money we don't have, on things we don't need, to create impressions that won't last, on people we don't care about'. The systemic nature of the relationship between desire for material possessions, aggregate economic demand, built-in obsolescence and unsustainable production means that we need to address this issue holistically: individual lifestyle choices will not be enough. In this concluding section I will argue that a bioregional economy could represent an alternative paradigm that would address all four aspects of this complex nexus simultaneously.

First, the issue of inadequate demand. This lies at the heart of the capitalist system of economic organisation and it is the failure of demand, mediated through the credit–debt cycle, that creates the so-called business cycle. In the 1930s Keynes transformed our understanding of political economy by arguing that fiscal and monetary policy could be used to stimulate aggregate demand, thus enabling us to grow our way out of recession. This was a brilliant insight, and an even more impressive political victory, but it cannot help us now, since we have already exceeded planetary limits and the ecological crisis demands that we find ways of creating a just and stable economy without artificial stimulation of demand. The ubiquitous refrain of the urgent need to return to economic growth as the solution to the economic crisis raises the question of why policy-makers are prepared to go to such extraordinary lengths to create demand rather than questioning the structural nature of an economic system that cannot survive its fulfilment. In the words of the Slovak social critic Slovaj Zizek: 'Why is it easier to imagine the end of the world than to imagine the end of capitalism?'[4] However we answer that question we need to be clear that the techniques for creating demand, which seemed entirely rational as a response to capitalism's last great implosion, cannot be used this time around.

The focus of this chapter is not only on our personal decisions about consumption, but how these are influenced by wider social forces. What can a bioregional economy offer as a substitute for the addictively desired iStuff that the twenty-first-century economy makes so freely available? How can we propagate a new ethic of consumption? Can we ever make thrift as sexy as an iPhone, and is there any other way of keeping our consumption within sustainable limits? When this seems like an impossible task there are three guiding lights: viewing consumption as an addiction and finding appropriate methods to address it; a belief that much consumption behaviour is based on habitual responses, and that habits can be changed; and that culture is plastic and the pain associated with changes in culture is fairly quickly overcome so long as the shift is socially sanctioned and shared within a community.

First I think we should be clear that the intention of the creation of consumption-related demand that has been described in this chapter is not to provide satisfaction; quite the reverse. If consumers were satisfied, then the economy as currently structured would be threatened, hence the need for a permanent creation of desires, a burgeoning of dissatisfaction within a world where consumption itself becomes exhausting. This reality is characterised in his highly polemical style by Uruguayan sociologist Eduardo Galeano:

> The invisible violence of the market: diversity is the energy of profitability, and uniformity rules. Mass production on a gigantic scale imposes its obligatory patterns of consumption everywhere. More devastating than any single-party dictatorship is the tyranny of enforced uniformity. It imposes on the entire world a way of life that reproduces human beings as if they were photocopies of the consummate consumer.
>
> *(Galeano, 1998: 252)*

Galeano's emphasis on uniformity is also significant: this economy dominated by global corporations impedes our ability to create meaningful identities, since brands and products are so similar that we can only express ourselves in our purchasing through buying the latest – that is, through buying more.

What the bioregional economy can offer in exchange for iStuff is a strongly embedded local identity to replace the global consumer identity; a stronger sense of connection between people, and between people and their local land; and a greater sense of sufficiency and security. If, as suggested by Panayotakis (2011), it is part of the rationale of a capitalist economy to engender a sense of scarcity, then the bioregional economy would replace this with an awareness, perhaps even a reverence, for nature's abundance. There would be no need to deprive us of a sense of satisfaction: rather, our awareness of the risk of provisioning failure could be replaced by a shared sense of security in the ability of our local natural environment to provide.

Recalling Abram's suggestion of the greater satisfaction derived from the variability and connection offered by natural products, we can also imagine a world where the frantic need to obtain the novel and the latest gadget could be eased by a satisfaction derived from a well-made – perhaps self-made – article that betokens skill and perhaps reinforces our relationship with the person who made it and the place from which the raw materials were obtained. While this is not a solution to our need for complex and particularly electronic goods, for which a larger market is likely to be required for the achievement of energy efficiency, such goods will need to be susceptible to mending and reuse, meaning that while we may not know the person who initially produced them, it is likely to be somebody we know who maintains and mends them (this point is discussed further as an approach based on 'trade sub-sidiarity' in Chapter 9).

In the early years of mass production Ruskin identified similar benefits from consumption based on quality rather than quantity. According to Craig (2006: 293), his lectures to working men suggested that they should practice 'good consumption', which was to be achieved by 'learning to read the "powers" of natural resources and the "virtues" of workers and consumers'. This is a relational approach to consumption within a framework of respect for the natural world and human (and perhaps non-human?) species. Such a virtues-based, embedded and relational approach seems appropriate to the bioregional economy. Although, as Craig also argues, such a shift is not possible on the personal level alone:

> Apart from the social spaces of a great many practices of good consumption (e.g. fair trade), it is difficult to see how the imaginative vision of an ethics of economic life can gain any purchase on the sweep of a global economy that mirrors far too closely the theoretical premises of classical political economy and its inability to address the aims of distributive justice and human development.
>
> *(Craig, 2006: 353)*

Jackson (2009: 159) identifies a discomfort amongst policy-makers at the idea that 'they have a role in influencing people's values and aspirations', a difficulty linked to the prevailing theoretical understanding of citizens as individualist consumers, with their consumer choice as constitutive of their individual freedom. Thinking back to the origin of advertising and its close alliance with PR we could reconsider the work of Edward Bernays, whose primary focus was the political sphere and whose intention was explicitly to 'engineer consent' and to sideline the requirements for argumentation and conflict typical of healthy democratic systems. Here we see the dichotomy of the politicians' reluctance to engage the public in a serious debate about the ecological implications of continued mass consumerism, while they simultaneously rely on the techniques of the PR industry that 'crystallised public opinion' (again Bernays's terminology) in acquiescence of a life whose central aim was material consumption.

The politicians' difficulty with influencing public behaviour seems to operate only in one direction: in influencing behaviour in a way that challenges the pro-growth, pro-business hegemony which is so dominant in the culture of Western developed economies. It is also relatively short-lived, since officially sanctioned 'Buy British' campaigns were a common feature of British political life until the 1980s. A prominent example is the Buy British Campaign of 1931 (Constantine, 1987), an attempt to address a balance-of-payments crisis while maintaining a political commitment to free trade. Such campaigns usually founder on the harsh politico-economic realities of global competition with lower-wage economies, but they indicate the willingness of politicians to influence the consumption decisions of the individual. Jackson concludes:

> the idea that it is legitimate for the state to intervene in changing the social logic of consumerism is far less problematic than is often portrayed. A critical

task is to identify (and correct) those aspects of this complex social structure which provide perverse incentives in favour of a materialistic individualism and undermine the potential for a shared prosperity.

(Jackson, 2011: 160)

While the insights of Freud can be used by private business to create insatiable and unsatisfied desires, and thus undermine both social cohesion and psychological well-being, in a democratic society where citizen autonomy is respected it would not be acceptable for policy-makers to use such techniques to achieve the opposite end. However, they could certainly limit the scope of such manipulative advertising. The Swedish Radio and Television Act (1996) has operated as a constraint on that industry in Sweden and, in spite of their queasiness about legislating to control advertising, Europe's politicians have never operated a free market in this area. They have repeatedly resisted attempts to allow direct-to-consumer advertising for pharmaceutical drugs, for example, in spite of continuous pressure from the industry. Many Organization for Economic Co-operation and Development (OECD) countries have also implemented bans on the advertisement of tobacco (Saffer and Chaloupka, 2000) and alcohol (Saffer and Dhaval, 2002). The latter represents an attempt to prevent the encouragement of individual behaviour that is self-destructive, but how much more important it is for governments to control the generalised consumption norm that is bringing in its wake such serious ecological and psycho–social devastation? I am not arguing here for a positive campaign for hair-shirts but rather for legislation restricting advertising to the role assigned to it within the economic theory of the market: that of communicating simply information about new products and their attractions. It is psychological mis-selling that should be banished.

Concepts such as 'prosperity without growth' and the need to focus on well-being and human flourishing suggest the beginnings of a positive message about consumption in the low-energy economy. We need to take seriously the call to outline a new ethic of consumption built around satisfaction rather than dissatisfaction, and local relationships rather than global competition. The beginnings of such an ethic are found in Sahlins's idea of the 'Zen road to affluence' and in constraining our idea of what we actually need rather than focusing exclusively on how we force the economy to produce for what a growth-driven system defines as our infinite desires. 'Barefoot economist' Manfred Max-Neef has made some useful progress in this direction as part of his project to develop a human-scale development theory (Max-Neef, 2003). He argues that, 'in conventional economics we have two links: wants and goods. In Human Scale Development Theory we have three links: needs, satisfiers and goods. For instance, there is the need for Understanding, whose satisfier is literature and whose good is the book'. Max-Neef requires us to take a step back from the market model of desires and goods to satisfy them, and requires us to question what satisfaction we are actually seeking and how this might be achieved, very often without the need to make a purchase. This process of redefinition would be the first step towards establishing the new ethic of consumption.

More practically, we can already find evidence of innovation away from providing marketable commodities and towards meeting needs, one example being the fully serviced home. If the company who builds a block of flats is responsible for their maintenance throughout their lifetime then it has an intrinsic incentive to ensure their energy efficiency, in contrast to an electricity company which remains profitable by selling as much energy as possible. Similarly, the water and sewerage supplies to the home can only be charged at the point of entry and exit; hence the absence of an incentive to ensure the circulation of grey water through homes. A service-management company would gain through reducing the level of new water demanded, and the volume of waste water leaving the home. Rather than choosing the design of the light-bulb, the secret to genuinely green consumption might be building the home to maximise natural light, and organising the tenancy of homes to create the right incentives for designers and constructors to follow this route.

Habits may be hard to break, but they can be changed and the legions of therapists are moving onto this turf (Rust, 2008). They will not succeed, however, unless supported by wider social institutions, and these cannot act to reduce aggregate demand unless we change our economic system to one that can survive while simultaneously growing smaller. Hence the political economy proposals for different decisions about the ownership and management of resources made in the final part of this book must run in parallel with policies to address the epidemic of consumption.

Throughout this chapter I have argued that consumption is about identity, and that identity-formation is a relational process. We might think of the human need for identity within community as one of needing to 'know your place'. In modern human communities this has come to mean knowing your place within a hierarchy, in a system based on power, a power you generally express through the acquisition of money and its use in a process of competitive consumption. In a bioregional economy identity would also be about knowing your place, but in the real sense of experiencing your local environment through your consumption of local foods and products made from natural materials. In such an economy we would all need to have a role in production, and so we would all come to understand at least one aspect of the natural world very intimately. Our relationships with each other would be mediated through our varying skills and knowledge of the resources and species we jointly depend on for our livelihoods.

The bioregional economy is primarily a local economy, and so our identities would be based more strongly on local products and environments and less on the disconnected global identities, which are costly in energy and resources, and also seem to bring little true satisfaction. In redefining identity as relational I believe we could substitute strong and pro-ecological identities for the destructive identities of the global shopping-mall. Instead of going shopping we might 'affirm human kinship with the multiple forms of the surrounding terrain' and aspire to what Abram (1996: 121) describes as 'the respectful, mutual relations that must be practiced in relation to other animals, plants, and the land itself, in order to ensure one's own health and to preserve the well-being of the human community' (Abram, 1996: 121).

7.5. Conclusion

The value of Veblen's socio-economic analysis of consumption is that it enables us to ask what that consumption is designed to achieve; whereas more mainstream economic accounts do not. Their picture of a utility-maximising individual cannot encompass the social function of consumption in terms of establishing status, while their vague definition of 'utility' cannot explain why the purchase of goods adds or does not add to human well-being. Veblen engages in a lengthy debate over the value of a different sort of spoon: do we choose one made of silver, steel or aluminium on the basis of serviceability? Why do we consider a silver spoon more beautiful than an aluminium one? His conclusion is that our choices are based clearly on an attempt to establish status:

> The case of the spoons is typical. The superior gratification derived from the use and contemplation of costly and supposedly beautiful products is, commonly, in great measure a gratification of our sense of costliness masquerading under the name of beauty ... The requirement of conspicuous wastefulness is not commonly present, consciously, in our canons of taste, but it is none the less present as a constraining norm selectively shaping and sustaining our sense of what is beautiful, and guiding our discrimination with respect to what may legitimately be approved as beautiful and what may not.
>
> *(Veblen, 1899/1994: 78–79)*

Within a capitalist economy the obscure object of desire is that which can most definitively demonstrate our wealth, since the system of social status within a capitalist economy is focused on money.

However, the choice of status is plastic, as is all human culture. In West Coast Pacific cultures the potlatch – a ceremonial gift-giving ceremony – was the ultimate ritual of status: giving rather than holding consumption goods was the way to acquire status. In communist societies manual labour, physical strength, and commitment to the communist ideal were prized and, although its appeal lost out in the competition with the West when consumer goods were offered, it provided a mythological basis for hierarchy in the Soviet Union for nearly 70 years. We should not underestimate the significance of shifting from one code of social status to another: as for other animals, for humans too our place in a social structure is essential to our well-being, in fact to our survival. Our challenge now is to replace the consumption-based hierarchy with one based on meeting our needs in the least impactful way possible.

Part III
Policies for a bioregional economy

8

SHARING OUR COMMON WEALTH

> Wealth is social welfare, collectively conceived, and not a measure of individual accumulation.
>
> (John Ruskin, cited in May 2010: 191).

It follows naturally, from what I have argued in Chapter 5, that in a provisioning economy our reliance on the resources of the local environment becomes much more apparent. As far as the UK is concerned, our strategy for acquiring even our most basic resources depends on vast global markets framed by international institutions over which we have only very tenuous democratic control. Yet that system will be radically changed as a consequence of the depletion of oil supplies and other non-renewable resources, and by policies designed to respond to climate change. In this chapter, beginning in Section 8.1, I explore this provisioning strategy and assess to what extent it can be compared with renting areas of land overseas, a strategy which, I argue, has arisen naturally from our colonial history. The theories of political economy that supported our colonial expansion, as well as the transformation to our own domestic economy, will be superseded as we move towards a sustainable future. The purpose of this chapter is to explore what the implications are particularly for how we conceive of the ownership of resources.

In Section 8.2 I develop an obvious point that is none the less often over-looked: that the requirement to end economic growth, which green economists suggest is essential for sustainability, will make the issue of equity – an issue that can be sidelined in a growing economy – much more pressing. I explore the relationship between sustainability and equity in the UK and, in general terms, in the global economy. A bioregional approach, I suggest, implies viewing the resources of the bioregion as 'common wealth'. In Section 8.3 I consider the allocation of the crucial resource from the perspective of a bioregional, provisioning economy:

land. I consider the implications of seeing land as a commonwealth, and I report on attempts to share it more fairly through policies of land reform and land taxation. In Section 8.4 I consider how we might develop techniques of participatory planning of local resources and offer a proposal for how we might share our bioregional commons, while Section 8.5 concludes by considering how far we should extend our notion of 'common wealth' to include other species.

8.1. The lowland clearances and the duty of England

The discussion of the work of Polanyi, which has informed several of the earlier chapters, suggests that our present method for gaining subsistence is a geographical and historical aberration. The most prevalent system of livelihood for humankind has been for small communities to meet their needs directly from land available locally. While the systems of political economy that governed the distribution of resources thus produced have varied – Polanyi notes the redistribution method based on the power of the chief that was and still is popular in some areas of Africa, while in the UK he identifies the feudal system as the dominant model – the basic link between communities and their resources is maintained.

The reason Polanyi focuses his analysis of the 'transformation' from such a system of provisioning on the UK is that he observes it as the origin of the economic model that began the historic shift away from such a provisioning strategy and towards globalised production and distribution systems. He claims that 'Market society was born in England' (1944: 32) and that 'The Industrial Revolution was an English event. Market economy, free trade, and the gold standard were English inventions'. In placing my study so clearly within my own democratic territory I am merely following Polanyi's prescription that 'whatever the scenery and the temperature of the final episodes, the long-run factors which wrecked that civilization should be studied in the birthplace of the Industrial Revolution, England'.

Our central role in such a global system of economic relationships finds its contemporary expression in the power of the City of London. On Ramsay's account The City grew powerful in the seventeenth and eighteenth centuries by providing the finance and insurance services for burgeoning global trade; until by the early twentieth century it could be seen as the metaphorical 'heart of the empire'.[1] The provision of both services and debt finance to leverage global expansion is just the most recent expression of this role (Talani, 2011). The 'imbalance' between the financial sector and the real economy that has recently been of concern is not a new phenomenon but an expression of the way that Britain grew rich as a trading nation and used its expertise in the creation of money through both promissory notes and credit notes to facilitate that trade (Mellor, 2010; Large, 2010: ch. 8). The innovation that made the UK the most powerful nation in the world in the eighteenth and nineteenth centuries was preceded by financial innovations that made the investment in global trade possible. From the perspective of a bioregionalist one might argue that, in Britain, our dislocation from the local environment in the sense of accessing our basic resources dates back hundreds of years.

Table 8.1 provides evidence of the historical evolution of our self-provisioning as a nation-state, presenting the proportion of our food that was produced within our own territory from the period shortly before the Industrial Revolution until the present. It is not, I think, an accident that the periods of our minimum reliance on our own production coincide with those times when we were most dominant in geopolitical terms. The colonial era certainly expanded the range of foodstuffs available, and coffee, sugar and tea in particular added greatly to the Englishman's personal satisfaction, to the extent that he would have been willing to spend 10% or more of his income on sugar and tea alone by 1800 (Hersh and Voth, 2009).

Once we had found a method for controlling global trade and profiting from it, the pressure to produce goods and services within our own territory waned. In fact, as we will see in the following chapter, British economists specifically argued that such a strategy was misguided, partly as a result of their own experience but, perhaps more importantly, to persuade other nations to join a trading system within which Britain was already dominant.[2] The spread of the market model, as an economic reality and a mythological force, was essential to the extension of the Great Powers of eighteenth- and nineteenth-century Europe. Adam Smith provided the myth of 'the bartering savage' (Polanyi, 1944: 46) while Galton provided the parallel myth of the racial superiority of the caucasian (1869) and 'Ricardo had erected it into an axiom that the most fertile land was settled first' (Polanyi, 1944: 192), suggesting that what was taken from the indigenous peoples of colonised lands could have been only marginal lands. John Locke gave the jusification for enclosing land, writing that putting a fence around land and improving it through agriculture gave settlers a right to owning the land, much to the astonishment of native Americans such as the Massassoit of the Wampanoag (Large, 2010: Ch. 10). Between them these mental constructs provided intellectual cover for the adventures of the far from noble savages who travelled the world seeking fame, resources and profit from the late fifteenth century onwards. This caused a fundamental change in our attitude to geopolitics: the central role of foreign policy was now ensuring access to resources rather than protecting the nation's borders. As Polanyi

TABLE 8.1 Indicative UK self-sufficiency rates in different historical periods

Time period	Percentage of food produced domestically
Pre-1750	c. 100
1750–1830s	90–100[a]
1870s	c. 60
1914	c. 40
1930s	30–40
1950s	40–50
1980s	60–70
2000	60

Source: Defra (2006), Food Security and the UK: An Evidence an Analysis Paper: statistics.defra.gov.uk/esg/reports/foodsecurity/foodsecurity.pdf
Notes: Defra note that these proportions relate to 'temperate produce'.
[a] Except in years of poor harvests.

has it, 'no people could forget that unless they owned their food and raw material sources themselves or were certain of military access to them, neither sound currency nor unassailable credit would rescue them from helplessness' (Polanyi, 1944: 199).

This domination, based around an extending empire backed up by financial and military power, enabled Britain not only to import large quantities of food but also to increase the variety and luxury of diets, at least of the growing middle class (Hersh and Voth, 2009). Although imperialism is no longer an acceptable ideology, and the process of political decolonisation has been one of the achievements of the past half century, we do not seem to have reached the point of questioning whether it is acceptable to import products grown on the lands of others, when they themselves do not have enough to eat. Although the focus of historians of decolonisation tends to be on political emancipation Polanyi concludes otherwise: 'The revolt against imperialism was mainly an attempt on the part of the exotic peoples to achieve the political status necessary to shelter themselves from the social dislocation caused by European trade policies' (Polanyi, 1944: 192).

I begin with this historical overview because I am seeking to challenge the justice of a system that enables those in the wealthy West to enjoy flowers grown on land and using water that would once have produced subsistence crops for Kenyan peasants. While the fair trade movement has questioned the prices we pay for such products, it has not challenged our right to use the land of others to satisfy our desires. This issue will be discussed further in the following chapter, where the trade system is examined in detail; for the purposes of this chapter the central issue is about who has the right to use that land, whether in Kenya or in Britain. These questions were raised with great vigour during the period of the Enclosures and the Clearances, when British peasants and commoners were driven off their land by over 10,000 Acts of Parliament (Large, 2010). The establishment of exclusive property rights at home was the counterbalance to the appropriation of land overseas. It was a philosophical as much as an economic shift, a move away from land as communally owned and socially governed towards a legalistic conception of land as a commodity like any other, what Polanyi refers to as the creation of a 'fictitious commodity'.

As discussed in Chapter 5, land gave people the means to meet their own needs directly by use of their own labour: this was what the movement for enclosure challenged and this was why it was so vigorously opposed:

> Enclosures have appropriately been called a revolution of the rich against the poor. The lords and nobles were upsetting the social order, breaking down ancient law and custom, sometimes by means of violence, often by pressure and intimidation. They were literally robbing the poor of their share in the common, tearing down the houses which, by the hitherto unbreakable force of custom, the poor had long regarded as theirs and their heirs.
>
> *(Polanyi, 1944: 37)*

The political arguments in favour of enclosure were couched in economic terms of 'efficiency' of land use and again supported by Ricardo with his law of rent, which often rose significantly after land was enclosed (Fairlie, 2009). On the one side were the self-styled 'improvers', chief among them Arthur Young, who relied heavily on 'scientific' projections but who was also capable of rhetoric: 'The advantages of enclosing to every class of the people are now so well understood and combated at present but by a few old women who dislike it for no other reason but a love of singularity and a hatred of novelty' (quoted by Humpries, 1990: 22). On the other side were those, such as contemporary writer Richard Bacon, whose argument parallels those made by green economists today about the way in which conventional measures of economic activity, such as gross domestic product (GDP) (Anderson, 1991), grossly underestimate the value of direct provisioning from land:

> Suppose for argument's sake, 20 five-acre farms, cultivated by spade husbandry, together were more productive than a single 100-farm using machinery. This did not mean that the landowners would get more rent from them – far from it. As each 5-acre farm might support a farmer and his family, the surplus available for tenants to pay in rent would be small. The single tenant farmer, hiring labourers when he needed them, might have a lower yield, from his hundred acres, but he would have a larger net profit – and it was from net profit that rent was derived. That was why landlords preferred consolidation.
>
> *(Inglis, 1971: 386)*

Where the commons survived they did so because local people fought for them, as in South London, where open land such as Putney Heath and Wandsworth, Plumstead and Wimbledon Commons were preserved for leisure uses, although traditional forage rights often disappeared (Bradley, 2009). A similar story is told by Grantham (1997) of common land in the Oxfordshire rural town of Chipping Norton.

The dismantling of the commons was disastrous for commoners but crucial for the growth of the industrial market system, which they were required to staff. It brought about a range of unforeseen social and demographic consequences. Neeson's (1989) account makes clear the link between the ending of subsistence and the population explosion, which Malthus and other political economists later bemoaned. She also chronicles how the move from commoner to labourer undermined the resilience and self-reliance of British citizens. The purpose of this discussion is not to hark back to some lost utopia, but rather to remember that, before the market, there were other ways of sharing resources within and between communities and to draw attention to the way in which economic theory, rather than empirical economics, has been used to argue for the continuing ownership of land by the few at the expense of the many.

What are known in academic circles as 'common property institutions' have attracted greater attention since their leading proponent, Elinor Ostrom, was awarded the Swedish Bank Prize for Economics in 2009. The citation acknowledged:

> Elinor Ostrom has challenged the conventional wisdom that common property is poorly managed and should be either regulated by central authorities or privatized. Based on numerous studies of user-managed fish stocks, pastures,

woods, lakes, and groundwater basins, Ostrom concludes that the outcomes are, more often than not, better than predicted by standard theories. She observes that resource users frequently develop sophisticated mechanisms for decision-making and rule enforcement to handle conflicts of interest, and she characterizes the rules that promote successful outcomes.

www.nobelprize.org/nobel_prizes/economics/laureates/2009/press.pdf

Two of the features identified by Ostrom as being necessary for the successful management of commons are a limited scale and clear boundary delineating what is to be managed (Ostrom, 1990; Wade, 1988; Agarwal, 2001; Large, 2010): both are features necessary for bioregional economies, though they were undermined by the process of globalisation.

In the context of this discussion the bioregional economy has two important features to recommend it. First, it attempts to make a fair sharing of the earth's resources feasible and meaningful. The sheer scale of the global marketplace invalidates the achievement of equity, as well as stretching our sense of moral responsibility beyond breaking point. When considering the starving children of Burma or Bolivia we feel our lack of power to make a difference precisely because we cannot trace the complex relationship between our over-consumption and their deprivation. Our comprehension that this connection exists is intuitive and strong, but we cannot find statistical evidence or argue a rational line from one to the other. In a bioregional economy the resources of our bioregion would be ours to share as a community. Those of every other bioregion, whether in Angola or Aberdeen, would be outside our purview. This immediately feels like a rapid and shocking shrinkage in what we will have access to. As discussed in the following chapter it does not mean that trade is impossible, but such trade will be seriously curtailed, as will the variety of goods we can routinely make use of. We will be cutting our coat according to our cloth rather than living at the expense of the rest of the world and enjoying a standard of living bought through illegitimate military and currency power.

Second, and perhaps more importantly, the bioregional economy has the significant moral and democratic advantage of making a direct link between the area whose resources you, as a community, control and the area from which you elect political representatives. Political economy means that any response to issues surrounding energy or resource allocation only make sense if you have responsibility for the resources in the area where you also vote. This is the politico-economic impact of the bioregional model and it will invalidate much of the hand-wringing and protestations of powerlessness in the face of global forces that are the routine response to questions surrounding global inequity. But while we will be choosing representatives to make decisions about trade regimes and the framework for limiting carbon emissions, decisions about how we share our resources within our own bioregion can be more participatory than that. The advantage of reducing the level at which resources are owned and shared enables the introduction of more democratic methods for their allocation, and one proposal for how this might be achieved is made in Section 8.5.

8.2. Sustainability and equity

In this section I trace the relationship between sustainability and equity, arguing that once the boundary of the economy is closed, as I have made clear already the ecological crisis implies that it must be, then the question of how we allocate what remains inside the boundary gains an added salience. First, I begin with evidence that, while the globalised capitalist economy is effective in terms of generating growth, it is not effective in allocating the product of that growth equitably. In fact, growth has been associated historically, and is associated today in the world's fastest growing economies, with increasing levels of inequality. The relationship between globalisation and inequality ceased to be controversial when Swedish Bank Prizewinner Joseph Stiglitz made the connection in his 2002 book. More recently the OECD has joined him: Secretary-General Angel Gurría expressed concern about the impact of inequality on the stability of the social contract in a report focusing on inequality (OECD, 2011). He made this comment in launching the report, which provides stark evidence of the rapid recent increase in inequality within nations North and South, and between nations.

The inequality following in the wake of globalisation has also been evident within the economies that are driving the process (see Figure 8.1). Even before the economic crisis of 2008, the UK was experiencing rapidly accelerating inequality. In his analysis of the anti-poverty policies of the Labour governments from 1997 onwards, Driver (2008: 165) is clear about the limited nature of their success:

> Trends in income inequality under Labour can be compared with the Conservative years using the Gini coefficient. During the 1980s, as we saw earlier,

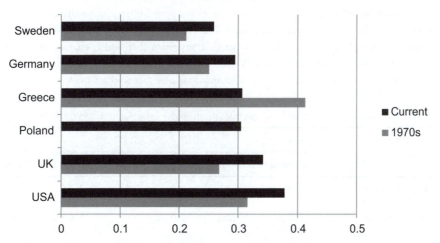

FIGURE 8.1 Gini coefficients for OECD countries, mid-1970s and current compared
Note: No coefficient is available for Poland for the earlier period.
The Gini coefficient compares the actual distribution of incomes in a country with a perfectly equal distribution to create a ratio that can range between 0 and 1, where 0 represents complete equality and 1 complete inequality.
Source: Author's graphic based on data from the OECD statistics database: http://stats.oecd.org/Index.aspx?QueryId=26068

the Gini coefficient rose from 0.25 to 0.34. A further peak was reached of 0.35 under Labour in 2000–2001. It then fell slightly during Labour's second term, only to start back up as Labour entered its third term. Overall, income inequality in Britain appears to have remained much the same across most measures after 10 years of Labour in government.

The overall picture is one where the better-off amongst the poor – and particularly those who are in work – have seen their relative position improve, but this has been bought at the cost of the poorest of the poor. In addition, because of unrestrained salary growth at the top end of the distribution, overall inequality rates barely changed.

The last three years of the third Labour government saw significant increases in inequality, which by 2009 had reached its highest level since comparable data were first collected in 1961. Incomes ceased to grow in all groups except the very highest and during the past decade incomes have grown fastest in the highest-income group and slowest in the lowest-income group (Brewer *et al.*, 2009). Table 8.2 indicates the shifts in income during the period of New Labour government. The initial improvement in the position of the poorest, which was largely a result of active labour-market policies and particularly the introduction of the Working Families Tax Credit, was reversed in the third term, raising questions about the efficacy of that policy (Godwin and Lawson, 2009).

The limited concern shown by politicians for these rising rates of inequality are a natural consequence of the central role that growth plays in the economic theory they subscribe to.[3] Within such an economy inequality plays a crucial role in stimulating growth, since those lower down the consumption hierarchy are incentivised to work hard and be innovative. As we are beginning to learn in this post-growth era, without such opportunities, or the belief in such opportunities, inequality takes on a much more threatening aspect, a threat to the very social contract that holds societies together. This changes the political dynamic away from that which characterised the period from the end of the Second World War, when the focus of democratic politicians was on increasing the size of the national pie, rather than being concerned

TABLE 8.2 .Real income growth by quintile group under New Labour, 1996–2009

Government	Quintile					
	Poorest	II	III	IV	Richest	Mean
Labour I (1996–97 to 2000–01)	2.4	2.7	2.4	2.5	2.7	3.1
Labour II (2000–01 to 2004–05)	2.6	2.5	2.0	1.6	1.4	1.7
Labour III (2004–05 to 2007–08)	–0.9	0.2	0.5	0.6	1.2	1.1
Whole Labour period (1997-08)	1.6	2.0	1.7	1.6	1.8	2.0

Source: Brewer, M., A. Muriel, D. Phillips, and L. Sibieta. 2009. *Poverty and inequality in Britain: 2009.* London: Institute for Fiscal Studies.

with how that pie was divided up (Glyn, 2006). So long as there was more for everyone, the fact that some were increasing their share much more rapidly than others was not a policy concern. This is in spite of the fact that, as long ago as 1992, Douthwaite provided evidence that there was no connection between a growing economy and greater well-being, and in fact that the relationship between growth and well-being had started to run in reverse as a result of greater stress, higher rates and crime, and the breakdown of relationships, amongst other things.

More recently we have seen clear evidence that this inequality has damaging psychological and physiological consequences. There is understandable anxiety in the medical community surrounding the statistical evidence that those in professional occupations live considerably longer than those in manual occupations. Data from the Office for National Statistics (2005) indicate the persistent trend for those in lower social classes to die younger. Men in the managerial class can expect to live to be 80, more than 7 years of life more than men in the lowest social class. For women the gap is exactly the same, although women in both classes live five years longer than men. And the gap is widening: compared with 1972–76, men in non-manual occupations have seen an increase in their expected years of life of 8 years, while men in manual occupations are living only 6.8 years longer (ONS, 2011). More details are given in Table 8.3.

Research findings indicate that inequality not only impacts negatively on those who are in the lowest social groups, but on all those in society. As explored in the previous chapter, part of the reason for this is the psychological pressure that results from being part of a society where status is derived from material consumption, and therefore from market power. In a ground-breaking and striking study from 1996, US researchers found that inequality is bad for life expectancy across social classes, since the relationship they found between a measure of inequality across society as a whole (measured by the Gini coefficient) and the life expectancy of that society remained after they had controlled for poverty (Kennedy *et al.*, 1996). In an unequal society it is not just life expectancy that suffers, but a whole range of factors, from obesity to premature motherhood

TABLE 8.3 Life expectancy at birth and at age 65 by social class, England and Wales, 2002–05

Class	At birth		At age 65	
	Men	*Women*	*Men*	*Women*
I	80.0	85.1	18.3	22.0
II	79.4	83.2	18.0	21.0
IIIN	78.4	82.4	17.4	19.9
IIIM	76.5	80.5	16.3	18.7
UV	75.7	79.9	15.7	18.9
V	72.7	78.1	14.1	17.7
Unclassified	73.8	77.9	15.1	17.6
All	77.0	81.1	16.6	19.4
Non-manual	79.2	82.9	17.9	20.5
Manual	75.9	80.0	15.9	18.6

Source: ONS, 2005.

and the probability of being attacked or going to gaol: all relate to a person's status in the hierarchy and their level of income (Wilkinson and Pickett, 2009).

However, this policy of targeting economic growth as the main aim of policy-making, and using inequality as a spur to growth, is also misguided for a more fundamental reason. The environmental crisis means that we are reaching, or have already reached, the limit to the size of the national pie. The closing of the planetary frontier increases the salience of political concerns about the distribution of resources. Hence a sustainable economy will need to be an inherently equal economy:

> Henry Wallich, a former governor of the Federal Reserve and professor of economics at Yale, said: 'Growth is a substitute for equality of income. So long as there is growth there is hope, and that makes large income differentials tolerable.' But this relation holds both ways round. It is not simply that growth is a substitute for equality; it is that greater equality makes growth much less necessary. It is a precondition for a steady-state economy.
>
> *(Wilkinson and Pickett, 2009: 221–22)*

So inequality matters because it is destructive of solidarity within society, because it blights lives and causes early deaths, and because it is a central explanation of the pressure on the planet that has resulted in an environmental crisis. The end of the period of boom and the new economic reality of contraction, recession or a period of slow growth adds to the salience of this concern: during the years of expansion it has been possible to sideline debate about the division of the national wealth, leading to a divergence in levels of income. The contraction of the economy that is already taking place, and is likely to continue and even increase in intensity as public-spending cuts reduce aggregate demand, will re-energise debate about the way in which our national wealth is shared, and is likely to lead to an intensification of the struggle over national output.

I have argued that there is an inherent connection between inequality and growth in the late-capitalist economy, and that such a connection drives the pressure on resources and the growth in CO_2 emissions that threaten the health of our planet. We can also consider this question from the other end, by interrogating the relationship between resource use and CO_2 emissions in terms of socio-economic classes. The Joseph Rowntree Foundation has supported research into the social impacts of policies to address climate change, which has indicated that those in high socio-economic groups are responsible for a disproportionate share of CO_2 emissions. Using a dataset comprising 24,207 private households drawn from the Expenditure and Food Survey (EFS) for the period 2004–07, with additional data imput from the English House Condition Survey, the Annual Passenger Survey, and the National Travel Survey, the researchers analysed CO_2 emissions by income decile. The most striking finding of this preliminary report is that:

> Mean average CO_2 emissions are strongly correlated with income: households within the highest equivalised income decile have mean total CO_2 emissions

more than twice that of households within the lowest equivalised income decile. Emissions from private road travel and aviation account for a high proportion of this differential: aviation emissions of the highest income decile are more than six times that of the lowest income decile.

(Fahmy et al., 2011)

Figure 8.2 illustrates mean annual emission of carbon dioxide from all sources across the income deciles. As we move from the lowest 10% to the wealthiest 10% there is a clear increase, class by class, in the amount of CO_2 emissions that are produced; importantly, a larger proportion of the emissions of the richer people in our society are transport-related. The researchers suggest a clear policy imperative and argue that using household energy bills as the focus of increasing the cost of carbon is not only regressive but will also be ineffective. As the data demonstrate that those with more disposable income have a larger carbon impact, we might also conclude that moving towards a more equal society could also facilitate the shift towards a reduction in carbon dioxide emissions.

8.3. A twenty-first-century Domesday

It has already become apparent from the argument in Chapters 5 and 6 that the bioregional citizen will be expected to be considerably more self-reliant and skilful than the twenty-first-century global consumer. The energy profligacy that fuels the

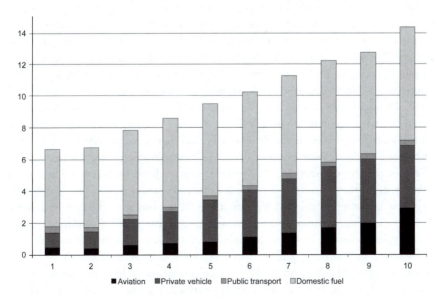

FIGURE 8.2 Mean annual total CO_2 emissions from all sources by equivalised household income decile (metric tonnes), 2004–07

Source: Grateful thanks to Dr. Eldin Fahmy and his team at the School for Policy Studies, Bristol University for their permission to reproduce this graphic free of charge. For further details of their report see: http://www.jrf.org.uk/sites/files/jrf/carbon-reduction-policy-full.pdf.

156 Sharing our common wealth

present supply system will be challenged by policies to address climate change, as well as by the gradual depletion of supplies of fossil fuel, requiring local communities to meet more of their own needs directly. While this will require a reskilling of the population, as well as a developing confidence and more physical labour, it will also require access to the basic resource of a provisioning economy: land.

The story of British land ownership dates back to the most famous date in the schoolboy's history book – 1066 – the last time our land was successfully invaded and the date marking the beginning of the introduction of the feudal system of land use and ownership (Stenton, 1979). The Domesday book is now available online and so we can see plainly the statement of expropriation of land from Saxon nobles by Norman knights that must have been part of its purpose.[4] What preceded the system of feudal land use is fairly unclear, but it appears to have included the open-field system, which survived the conquest across the majority of Britain (Oosthuizen, 2005). This was a complex socio-economic system, where rights and responsibilities intertwined, and where community position was established through a system of duties to those more vulnerable than oneself. Even under Norman rule a range of provisioning rights existed, such as rights to gather wood, to use pastureland and to glean in cornfields: it was this system of common rights that was abolished by the Enclosures from the seventeenth century onwards.

In spite of the theoretical arguments from neoclassical economists that resources need not be a central concern, it appears that this view is no longer shared by the global management consultants. In an interesting historic twist, they are again casting their eyes on 'virgin' land and making arguments about the inefficiency of its use very similar to those made during the period of English enclosures. McKinsey's report *Resource Revolution* considers the change underway globally in land-ownership and land-use patterns to be 'the next agro-industrial revolution'. The report argues that 'Over the past 100 years as a whole, demand for resources grew more slowly than GDP. The reason for this is that a declining share of global income was devoted to resource-intensive consumption' (Dobbs *et al.*, 2011: 22). They identify a new era with a multiplicity of 'resource-related shocks' and rises in commodity prices that will offset the declines in those prices as a result of increased efficiency of extraction.

The analysis of the report is very similar to that offered by green and ecological economists for the past several decades; it is the prescription that is entirely different. In a section of the report called 'the private-sector opportunity', the authors indicate the way that corporations can manage risk and solve the resource challenges identified through increasing productivity: technical and managerial methods will solve the challenge of inefficiency posed by traditional economies in the areas of the world where resources are still plentiful. The role of government is limited to establishing a price for carbon that enables companies to continue to engage in their activities and be subsidised for protecting ecosystem services. No mention is made of the issues of ownership of resources although it is made clear that 'action will be necessary to ensure that sufficient capital is available and to address market failures associated with property rights, incentive issues and innovation' (Dobbs *et al.*, 2011: 3; see also Exhibit 26 on page 87, where property rights are identified as a key barrier to be overcome). Just as in the eighteenth century, those who would seek to privatise resources currently held in common justify this on the basis of greater efficiency. Then, as now, the role of politicians was limited to freeing up the market ('unwinding subsidies'), making capital available, guaranteeing property rights, and providing safety-nets for the 'very poor people' who may lose their livelihoods.

This is a sophisticated and intellectually justified version of what is referred to amongst campaigners and academics alike as 'land grabbing'. Although evidence about exactly how much land is being acquired and how rapidly is extremely poor (World Bank, 2010), it is clear that corporations are rapidly acquiring land for the production of food, fuel or fibre crops for the purposes of export. As we saw in the case of the McKinsey report, the argument on behalf of the corporate purchasers of land is that it can improve the economic opportunities for the poor as well as ensuring greater efficiency, a position that is contested by those whose focus is small-scale sustainable development:

> Some see land grabs as a major threat to the lives and livelihoods of the rural poor, and so oppose such commercial land deals. Others see economic opportunity for the rural poor, although they are wary of corruption and negative consequences, and so call for improving land market governance.
>
> *(Saturnino et al., 2011: 210)*

If we accept McKinsey's arguments that basic resources such as land and water will come under increasing pressure in the remainder of this century, then we are forced to address the question of whether the allocation of those resources should be controlled by corporations within a market system, or whether, as the bioregional economy proposal suggests, they should be considered the property of the local people who inhabit the land. Perhaps the most fundamental basis for making this decision is which system is most likely to meet human need most effectively. As Mellor argues (2006), this requires us to ask fundamental questions about the motivations and relevance of the globalised economy system as currently structured:

> While capitalism is not concerned with supplying the necessities of life, it is based on institutions engaged in denial of access to the means of sustenance for the majority, so that the minority can pursue power and status through predatory competition. Central to capitalism is the privatisation of resources for sustenance. Challenging and changing property ownership and the capitalist economy will not be easy. It is a powerful structure with vested interests, but it is also a structure that has absorbed wants as well as needs.
>
> *(Mellor, 2006)*

If we are to take seriously the proposal to consider that bioregional communities should have ownership of their resources, then an initial policy proposal is the production of a clear system of land registration, perhaps along the lines of a proposal emerging recently from the Public and Commercial Services (PCS) Union. Much as the original Domesday book did, this survey could identify who owns the land of different bioregions, but also its potential uses, whether as grazing or arable land, and so on, as well as the resources it contains. In a country where between 35% and 50% of land is of unknown ownership this is clearly an urgent necessity.

Taking seriously the need for bioregional citizens to have access to land would also require policies of land reform. At present agricultural policies in the wealthier and more developed countries subsidise farmers either to produce crops or to leave their land idle. These subsidies constitute vast amounts of public spending: from 1998 to 2004 US farmers received an annual average of $17bn. (Kirwan, 2009), whereas the EU Common Agricultural Policy involved transfers to farmers of about €55bn. annually (European Commission, 2008). Land remains in the ownership of those who cannot use it profitably, while others who could provide for their own needs directly from that land cannot gain access to it. In contrast, in Latin America the concept of *usufruct*, drawn from Roman Law, is used to argue that land that is not being used productively should be available for use by others. Such a justification has been used by the Brazilian Landless Peasants movement, for example, in their settlement of the land of absentee landlords (Branford and Rocha, 2002). Land Reform need not be the result of such direct action, however: in most cases it arises from the policies of national governments.

In the UK, land reform is usually raised in the media debate only with reference to Zimbabwe, where arguments about efficiency are used to demonstrate that it is irresponsible to partition large-scale farms and enable subsistence farmers access to the land. However, in contrast to these largely rhetorical assertions, a detailed empirical study based on ten years of research of the land reform in Masvingo Province in Zimbabwe indicates that there is neither widespread food insecurity nor a collapse in productivity. Some of the explanation for the poor economic assessment of output is that much of what is being produced is used for direct consumption, rather than being traded in a market, and hence does not feature at all in conventional economic measures (Scoones *et al.*, 2011). The debate about the efficiency or otherwise of small vs. large landholdings is taken up by Michael Lipton (2009). His research covers the land reforms during the 1950s in Japan, Taiwan and South Korea, as well as the land reform in West Bengal in 1969–84. In all cases his study indicates that the weight of evidence is that smallholders produce more per hectare than large-scale farmers.

The UK is unusual in not having undergone significant land reform. In the Czech Republic, by contrast, it was an important response to the achievement of statehood after the break-up of the Austro-Hungarian empire (Cornwall, 1997). The vast estates of the aristocracy were divided between village communities, many of which still enjoy access to forest and arable land today. In the poorer countries of the world land reform is a live issue today, with significant reallocations of land taking place in the Philippines, South Africa (Wily, 2000), Bolivia (Sikor and Müller, 2009) and Brazil (Castañeda, 2006). Closer to my home patch, land ownership and control is an issue that is already being debated in Scotland, where the experience of the Highland Clearances is still remembered and 1066 belongs in somebody else's history book (Wightman, 2010). Outcomes include the Land Reform Scotland Act (2003). As we move towards a world where local resilience becomes increasingly a matter of political concern, the issue of who owns the fundamental national resource can no longer be ignored south of the border.

8.4. Participatory planning for bioregional resources

A book whose vision of a future economy is so radically different from that we live with today would seem incomplete without some attempt to propose an alternative political framework. However, to attempt such an endeavour is clearly beyond my expertise and I do so primarily in the hope that others more skilled and knowledge-able than I am will take this task forward. It is the underlying principle of this chapter that a sustainable economy, limited in its use of energy and materials, will need to be a much more equitable economy. This, I suggest, would require a much stronger role for citizens to be involved in decisions about allocation. In a market system politicians leave most of these decisions to the market, which economists inform them is an efficient mechanism intrinsically. Their only role is to intervene on the rare occasions when the market fails (to be efficient, rather than fair) and to use certain policies to introduce stronger (such as taxation) or weaker (such as 'nudge') incentives.

The data on the ecological crisis presented in Chapter 1 is evidence of where such a system has taken us. In spite of protestations to the contrary by proponents of the market and their political adherents, I would suggest that the critical situation we are in cries out for a more interventionist approach. We face two questions: how might we design a politico–economic system that would best enable us to live sustainably; and how might we find transitional steps to move us from where we are now, in a fully marketised and globalised system of provisioning, to one that is more resilient and more locally based? The priority for transitional policies is, I believe, a renewed emphasis on land, as I have argued in the previous section. Here I explore how allocation might be organised democratically, according to a system of participatory economic planning within self-reliant bioregions. But first I offer a critique of the limitations of the present system of political economy which, on the one hand offers us politicians who are incapable of acting, and on the other allows markets, and the tiny number of people who control them, to exercise the power that our politicians have relinquished.

The past 30 years have seen an abnegation of power by politicians in the developed economies of the West. Politics has been redefined as a process of management, rather than the skill of mediating between conflicting demands and defining and then implementing visions of a better life. The philosophical debate over what constitutes the good life has been superseded by the hegemonic idea of progress, usually con-sidered in a limited and primarily material sense. The role of the politician, reduced to one of tinkering with the capitalist economic machine, has been found wanting since 2008, when the machine demonstrated its inherent design flaws. A whole generation of politicians schooled in the philosophy of self-regulating market systems have proved themselves incapable of action on the scale required.

The apotheosis of the managerialist approach to politics can be found in the politics of 'nudge', so incisively critiqued by Dobson (2011). As he explains:

in liberal-capitalist countries over the past 40 years governments have been increasingly reluctant to govern, in the sense of taking responsibility for a country's political, social and economic direction of travel and offering arguments for preferring that direction of travel to others. Instead, the market is at one and the same time the constraint on, and opportunity and reference point for, policy-making.

(Dobson, 2011: 4)

Dobson makes a strong case for a revival of ethics and dialogue in the political sphere, and for citizens to be guided by ecological principles rather than narrowly materialist inclinations. The bioregional economy will require us to act as the 'ecological citizens' that Dobson and others have described and it will require politicians who both remember their role as interpreters of the good life, and who relearn the skills of mediating between competing demands, rather than defining them out of existence for the sake of managerial convenience. But even if our system of representative democracy were to work ideally, would it be inadequate to enable a peaceful transition towards a world with lower levels of material consumption? The framework for the theories discussed in this book is a world with 90% energy reductions, achieved in a period of some four decades. This represents a process of rapid and radical change unprecedented in the democratic era. Such a process cannot, I would argue, be achieved by a small number of representatives attempting to balance conflicting and disparate material demands. Something more broad-based, more engaged, in short more *participatory*, is required.

Various writers have described societies where allocation is based on social and political decision-making (Polanyi, 1944; Ostrom, 1990; Neeson, 1989; Albert and Hahnel, 1991). Polanyi writes eloquently of the upheavals caused by the 'great transformation' to a market society in the economies of Europe. Yet writers struggle to consider this transformation in reverse: how are we to take millions of global citizens who have been trained to act in a self-interested and 'rational' manner in the economic decision-making and encourage them instead to think of the common wealth and of the protection of the planet we all share?

Perhaps it is easiest if we begin this consideration with a resource that is of relatively recent origination, and for whom claims are still only weakly established. This resource is the 'carbon emission', or more accurately the space in the global atmosphere that this emission will occupy. This is a new resource, which is being effectively enclosed by proposals that suggest the allocation of the right to pollute to energy-intensive industries, as with the EU's Emissions Trading Scheme (Spash, 2010). However, powerful arguments have been made that the earth's atmosphere is the common property of all the earth's people and hence the right to pollute should belong equally to each of the planet's people (Meyer, 2000). At present the decision about how the earth's atmosphere might be shared is being debated at the highest levels by politicians and lobbyists, but even if they were successful in determining national limits, how would this limited resource be shared between citizens?

At present politicians are shying away from engaging the electorate in a debate about the major changes to their lifeways that are urgently required, but various political scientists have argued that the ecological crisis actually requires more politics rather than less. Goodin, in the closing pages of his 1996 paper 'Enfranchising the Earth, and its alternatives', suggests that the process of participatory and deliberative democracy in itself is likely to increase on balance the sense of community and a shared sense of responsibility for pro-environment policy-making. John Barry (1996) and Andy Dobson (2007) have argued that sustainability is such a heavily contested concept that its meaning needs to be determined by a deliberative rather than authoritative process: 'This suggests that where public [environmental] goods are at issue, the appropriate kind of value-articulating institution is not a private survey, but some kind of public forum in which people are brought together to debate before making their judgements. That is, the institution should be *deliberative* in character' (Jacobs, 1997: 220; quoted in Dobson, 2007: 110). For similar reasons, Ward (1999) has proposed citizens' juries as an appropriate mechanism for valuing the environment.

How would such a process operate in practice? I am developing a research project in this area, with the particular intention of taking the question around what a sustainable consumption ethic might look like into some of our poorer communities, where standards of consumption are low but aspirations may be higher. After all, it is one thing to disparage the need for a smart car or a foreign holiday when you have enjoyed these things, quite another to accept that they are things you will never enjoy. This proposal is framed within the Citizens' Jury model but informed by the Needs/Satisfiers Matrix developed by Manfred Max-Neef (2003) as part of his conceptualisation of 'human-scale development'. It seeks to engage directly with citizens and to present them with questions about how our limited energy resources should best be used. It asks them to address consumption decisions not as individuals (selfish utility-maximising individuals, perhaps) but as citizens representative of the needs and preferences of all their fellows.

Green economists have long argued that markets are inherently social institutions, governed by rules that are subject to democratic decision-making (Cato, 2009*a*; Henderson, 2009). While this runs counter to prevailing economic orthodoxy – with its emphasis on 'free' markets – it is actually exemplified by legislation to protect consumers, such as environmental health legislation and building regulations, and more recently by increasing control over the activities of business in relation to climate change. Rather than proposing the replacement of the market system with a planning-based allocation system, this proposed research will explore the potential for democratic processes to adjust the incentives governing the market in a more environmentally benign direction. I plan to adopt an interdisciplinary approach based on findings from social psychology, economics, sociology and anthropology to answer the question of how we, as individuals, determine our needs before questioning how needs might be defined at a societal level, and how conflicts between these two imperatives could be brought into closer alignment through economic policies that create appropriate incentives.

8.5 Conclusion: a commonwealth of all beings?

In this chapter I have made the important link between sustainability and equity: once we include in our economic theorising the reality of a limited supply of resources, the issue of ownership of those resources immediately becomes more salient. This point is, I think, axiomatic. However, I seek to extend the argument to suggest that, in a more imperative sense, justice requires that resources thus limited are viewed as social wealth, not as the preserve of an elite who have legal title to them for historical reasons. This leads us into challenging territory concerning decision-making about how such resources should be allocated. I argue that such decisions would be facilitated by a reduction in the scale of the politico-economic areas within which they are made, an argument for relocalisation that is taken forward in Chapter 10. And finally I suggest that within these narrower boundaries we need a more participatory form of decision-making governing the allocation of resources, a form of participatory economic planning as sketched in the previous section.

A critique that might be made of such a proposal is that it would enhance the potential for conflict between bioregions over resources, especially resources such as water, the boundaries of which cannot be clearly delineated. These arguments should be taken seriously, since the ecologically limited economy will require restraint and that may be resisted both within and between bioregions. However, such conflict is not a direct result of the creation of smaller economic units, nor are larger politico-economic units immune from such conflict. It is a commonplace amongst scholars of security studies that the twenty-first century will be scarred by resource wars (Peters, 2004; Le Billon, 2007), and it seems to me that the best way to avert this is to undertake a radical review of different systems of resource ownership, and techniques for resource allocation.

I began this chapter by exploring how Britain's colonial past has left British politicians with a sense of entitlement when defending their 'permanent interests' around the world. I suggested that a bioregional approach to provisioning radically challenges this historical perspective, proposing instead that the resources of each bioregion belong to the inhabitants of that bioregion as 'common wealth'. How they may be shared, consumed, or left as wilderness should be a matter for deliberation between the citizens of the bioregion. I have self-consciously slipped between the words 'citizen' and 'inhabitant' in this paragraph because I am seeking to raise the question: 'Who is a member of our commonwealth?' While suggesting that all bioregional citizens have an equal right to their bioregion's resources may be radical enough, I would like to end this chapter by raising the question of what the role of non-human animals might be in this debate.

This is another area where I feel that others are better qualified to theorise than I am, and I lean especially on the work of Mary Midgley who, in her short essay 'Granting citizenship to wildernesses', comments on the poor levels of protection that species and habitats have been afforded by the existing system of contract-based economics:

> Even over animals, the legalistic notion of contractual rights works badly. And when we come to such chronic non-litigants as the rain forest and the

Antarctic it fails us completely. If duties are essentially contractual, how can we possibly have duties to such entities?

(Midgley, 2001: 185)

While the suggestion of a 'parliament of all beings' is an attractive one (Seed *et al.*, 1993), at present it is really little more than a thought experiment, helping us to imagine a world where we might consider the needs of non-human animals as in some sense equivalent to our own. Others have called for 'a new covenant with all beings' based on relationship rather than legal contract (Read, forthcoming 2013). These are, it seems to me, live questions that a bioregional economist would have to consider in decisions about the allocation of resources. The sort of embedded economic life that a bioregional citizen would enjoy would entail a different quality of relationship with the local environment, perhaps conceived now in the nature of kinship rather than territory. The processes of participatory planning over resource use would enable the decision to leave areas of land unexploited, a process of 'rewilding' (Hintz, 2007) that is beginning to replace the conservation approach to environmental protection in theory, but is unlikely to be popular within an economic philosophy based on maximising utility.

9

PROVISIONING, EXCHANGE AND SUFFICIENCY

Any country that exposes itself to unlimited foreign competition can be reduced to starvation and therefore, subjection if the foreigners desire it.

M. K. Gandhi

Proposing a new approach to provisioning boundaries creates the need to consider the exchange between the new bioregions on which we will depend to meet the majority of our needs. This chapter begins to clear the ground for considering how such a system of exchange might operate. It begins in Section 9.1 with a critique of the existing trade system and the vulnerability of the current reliance on lengthy supply chains in an era of climate change. Section 9.2 provides a more detailed critique of the theory on which globalisation depends: Ricardo's theory of comparative advantage, which is shown to be obsolete in the face of changing circumstances and to have always been more of a justification for British imperialist expansion than a credible theory of how trade actually operates between nations. Following a brief critical account of the political economy of the existing global trade system, Section 9.3 sketches an alternative global trade and exchange system that includes the perspective of the poorer countries and asks whether, in the context of climate change, they might be better protected by a system that compensates them for their lower levels of consumption and specifically for their lower carbon emissions. I then move on to outline a proposal for a system based within the Contractionand Convergence framework and including consideration of the carbon exchange that implicitly takes place when goods are traded. Section 9.4 considers the nature of trade between bioregions, and how the setting of the new and more local boundaries might balance the need for clear identification and uniformity, with the need to achieve maximum possible self-reliance. Questions are raised about the need to share resources between bioregions and how interregional trade might work based on the concept of 'trade subsidiarity'. It also encompasses a brief discussion of how a world made up of self-reliant bioregions would confront problems of insularity.

9.1. The vulnerability of complexity

We have grown used to a world in which decisions about consumption begin with our desires: we wish for strawberries in January and the interconnected system of global production and trade swings into action and they appear in a supermarket close enough to be reached within minutes and at a price that is well within our means to pay. This is the reverse of the situation that has faced our ancestors for the majority of human history, and that today faces the majority of the world's population, for whom consumption was or is responsive to availability. In Chapter 7 I discussed how consumption is now a means of establishing identity rather than a means to subsistence. While I am not about to propose that we go back to a world of drab routine and limited choices in our consumption, I think it is essential that we face squarely the energy-profligate nature of the system of global supply chains that the contemporary trade system consists of.

The first concerns about the energy cost of the global trade system were framed in terms of 'food miles' (Iles, 2005). Significant sums have been invested by government and corporate players in the food industry to demonstrate that providing for consumers' demands without significant transport of food could require more energy, for example, to heat greenhouses in winter in order to provide the January strawberries (Watkiss, 2005; Gray, 2007). But this is to miss the point. The challenge is not to find the lowest-energy means of providing for consumer demand, but rather to ask consumers to act like citizens and make an adult decision to change their consumption patterns to match the seasonal availability of local food.

Providing for the needs of the world's wealthy citizens is a significant technological feat. The system is so efficient at satisfying our consumption desires that we rely on it for 40% of our food, a figure that is higher than the 30% we imported in the 1980s but lower than our level of dependence on food imports before and after the Second World War (Defra, 2008; see the detailed data from the same report reproduced in Table 8.1). Yet in this era of greater climate, financial and geopolitical insecurity perhaps it would be wise to question the security of a system in which provisioning relies on such long-distance transport networks. Polanyi was doubtful about the security of such a system of global trade networks: 'With free trade the new and tremendous hazards of planetary interdependence sprang into being' (Polanyi, 1944: 190). One practical consideration is the location of the world's major trading ports. The map that is reproduced as Figure 9.1 illustrates the position of the ports on which 90% of the world's trade[1] and 99% of UK food imports depend (Defra, 2006): unsurprisingly they are at sea-level. Although it is air-freighted food that most enrages environmental campaigners, the overwhelming majority of food is transported by sea. A quarter of food imports arrive in bulk form: these are the unprocessed commodities like cereals, fruit, sugar, oils and nuts. The other three-quarters arrives in pre-packaged form.

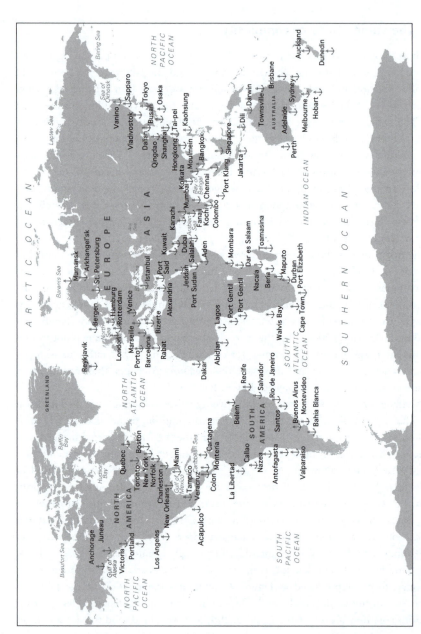

FIGURE 9.1 Map of the world's major trade ports

Source: Original artwork by Imogen Shaw.

With sea-level rise being the most predictable and earliest consequence of global warming, a strategy that relies on a system of ports that are likely to be inundated within 30 years is doing little to guarantee our security. In 2007 the Intergovernmental Panel on Climate Change (IPCC) predicted a 0.35-metre rise in sea levels by the end of the twenty-first century.[2] However, since these figures were released the speed of melting of Antarctic and Greenland icecaps has caused scientists to revise their forecasts: in 2009 they declared that sea-level rise was occurring at twice the rate they had estimated just two years earlier (McCarthy, 2009). Although the adaptability of ports varies, it is difficult to imagine that this will not have a significant impact on the global trade system, and given the unpredictable nature of climatic events, it might result in sudden shocks rather than gradual and predictable adjustments (Becker et al., 2011). In the UK this is exacerbated by the fact that the ports are geographically concentrated in the south-east, an area particularly vulnerable to sea-level rise: 63% of total container volumes were handled by just three ports in the south-east in 2004 (Defra, 2006).

In terms of resilience, which we have already identified as a key defining feature of a sustainable approach to provisioning, this system does not appear to be scoring very well. It is highly concentrated both technologically and geographically. It is also highly energy dependent, relying on precisely the fossil fuels that we know are on the inevitable path to exhaustion and that are responsible for the CO_2 emissions that threaten our climate. As well as being vulnerable to climate change, the global trade system is clearly contributing to its intensity, as a major component of carbon dioxide emissions. International transport – that is, transport relating to trade between rather than transport within countries – is responsible for a third of transport-related emissions, a third of which are accounted for by US trade, which is heavily dependent on air transport. US researchers estimate that the growth in trade that we are likely to see continue as a result of trade liberalisation, and particularly the increasing dependence of the richer countries on China and India to provide their manufactures for them, will contribute to rapid emissions growth (Cristea et al., 2011).

What of the social consequences of greater global trade: can trade help to 'make poverty history'? I have rehearsed these arguments elsewhere (Cato, 2009a: Ch. 8) and have limited space here, but I would report that the conclusions researchers reach on this point are contested. Researchers from the UN Conference on Trade and Development (UNCTAD) asking a similar question found mixed evidence: the larger countries they studied had seen social benefits, but the smaller countries had seen significant social costs, especially in terms of displacement and unemployment amongst the resilient members of the societies. This tallies with what Lines (2008) concludes in his analysis of the economic benefits of trade: the powerful nations who can exercise some control in trade negotiations are seeing some benefits, although these are not fairly shared across the income groups within their societies. Meanwhile, the smaller countries, especially those that are land-locked, produce mainly primary resources, and particularly those in Africa are seeing serious deterioration in their terms of trade.

Closer to home there is a general sense of unease about the movement of the UK from the workshop of the world to a nation whose main export is financial services.

This debate is taking place under the banner of the need for a 'balanced economy', as in the report from the Department for Business, Innovation and Skills titled 'The path to strong sustainable and balanced growth' and released in 2010 (BIS, 2010: 3). This claims that 'The Government's economic policy objective is to achieve strong, sustainable and balanced growth that is more evenly shared across the country and between industries'. The title of this report is less encouraging for a green economist than it might at first appear, since both 'sustainability' and 'balance' have entirely different meanings in our opposing discourses. While some of the concern about the erosion of the UK manufacturing sector arises from intuitive motivations, the energy-intensive nature of the global trading system, its insecurity in the face of unpredictable changes in our weather and climate, and its dependence on a stable geopolitical environment should all give cause for concern to the most rational observer.

9.2. Workshop of the world or nation of shopkeepers?

In this section I am going to consider briefly how the system of global trade arose, and the historical context in which we shifted from assuming domestic provisioning as the norm to becoming dependent on a global trading system. Polanyi identifies this process as a crucial one in the 'great transformation' from a traditional to a market economy:

> Such an event was the universal mobilization of land, implied in the mass transportation of grain and agricultural raw materials from one part of the planet to another, at a fractional cost. This economic earthquake dislocated the lives of dozens of millions in rural Europe. Within a few years free trade was a matter of the past, and the further expansion of the market economy took place under utterly new conditions.
>
> *(Polanyi, 1944: 223)*

Since reversing this process is central to the bioregional proposal it is important to assess how it came about. Polanyi identifies the theoretical work of Ricardo as an intellectual underpinning of this movement:

> External trade is carrying; the point is the absence of some types of goods in the region; the exchange of English woollens against Portuguese wine was an instance. Local trade is limited to the goods of the region, which do not bear carrying because they are too heavy, bulky, or perishable. Thus both external trade and local trade are relative to geographical distance, the one being confined to the goods which cannot overcome it, the other to such only as can.
>
> *(Polanyi, 1944: 62)*

This is a provisioning analysis: the reason for trade is to increase availability, and therefore it focuses on goods that are not available locally – the distance such goods travel depends on their size, weight and perishability. In such a framing strawberries would always be a local commodity, so what changed? Polanyi's account suggests that it was the introduction of trade as part of a competitive market that led to its being focused on arbitrage, that is to say, exploiting the difference in information, labour costs or productive conditions between two markets in order to extract maximum profit; this shift also undermined the focus on trade as supporting domestic provisioning. Continuing his analysis based on the principles of ease of portability, he continues:

> Local exchange between town and countryside, foreign trade between different climatic zones are based on this principle. Such trade need not involve competition, and if competition would tend to disorganize trade, there is no contradiction in eliminating it. In contrast to both external and local trade, internal trade, on the other hand, is essentially competitive; apart from complementary exchanges it includes a very much larger number of exchanges in which similar goods from different sources are offered in competition with one another. Accordingly, only with the emergence of internal or national trade does competition tend to be accepted as a general principle of trade.
>
> *(Polanyi, 1944: 63)*

It is in this context that we must consider Ricardo's most lasting contribution to economic thought: his theory of comparative advantage. Although it has been entirely superseded by economic developments,[3] this theory is still to be found in all introductory economics texts and lies behind much popular discussion of the benefits of trade. In their 'anti-textbook' critique of the view propagated by introductory courses, Hill and Myatt identify that the model omits from consideration: the costs associated with the process of removing tariffs; the unequal distribution of the 'gains from trade'; the impact of trade on wage levels; the impact of technological change on the model of comparative advantage; and the failure of Ricardo's assumption about constant rather than increasing returns to scale in production (see Hill and Myatt, 2010: 224–30). The authors move on to consider the key features missing from the model, in particular the 'externalities' associated with transport, particularly carbon dioxide emissions, as well as more local environmental externalities.

Ricardo's theories replaced the prevailing economic orthodoxy of the time: that of mercantilism. This school of thought focused on the accumulation of specie, usually in the form of gold, which enabled states to defend their interest since they could purchase the materiel necessary for warfare and the control of non-domestic resources (Gee, 2009). The shift made by Ricardo was not to challenge the right to overseas expansion, but rather to change the basis of the accumulation of wealth. The new generation of British privateers used money created through bills of exchange as rewards for and to enable their foreign adventures, rather than the hoarding of cash and issuance of currency against it. The trade system of the twenty-first century relies heavily on the dollar as its form of gold, to the extent that some have argued we are in a new era of mercantilism (Cwik, 2011). The need to acquire dollars has been driving the production and trade patterns of some of the world's largest economies, thus fulfilling Polanyi's critique of the original Ricardian theory: 'Ricardian trade and currency theory vainly ignored the difference in status existing between the various countries owing to their different wealth-producing capacity, exporting facilities, trading, shipping, and banking experience' (Polanyi, 1944: 216). Regardless of the reality of global trading relations and the dominance of the ideology of free trade, what Polanyi refers to as the 'incubus of self-sufficiency' (Polanyi, 1944: 28) is still a powerful influence in most countries. Hence in 2010, following disastrous forest fires that destroyed much of its harvest, the Russian government banned the export of grain,[4] and the French government has been suspected of what is referred to disparagingly as 'economic nationalism' in European Union (EU) policy circles (Castle, 2006). We will return to these questions of self-sufficiency in a later section; first we will explore the extent to which the existing global trade system can be considered 'fair'.

So much for theory. What about the practice of trade in the globalised economy? The governance of global trade is overseen by the World Trade Organization (WTO) which replaced the General Agreement on Tariffs and Trade (GATT), the global body with authority in this area under the tripartite system established at the end of the Second World War, and signed by 23 governments in 1947. Its aim was to replace the chequered history of mercantilist policies based around the protection of national interests that had dominated the early years of capitalism and was considered to have been implicated in the unstable and conflict-ridden history, especially of Europe, in the period leading up to the Second World War (Peet, 2009). The WTO 'does not adopt a neutral stance on trade policy. It is passionately against protectionism and just as profoundly for trade liberalization' (Peet, 2009: 193). In its mission to liberalise trade the WTO has proceeded well beyond the GATT's aim of ensuring efficiency and stability, and follows this imperative even when this 'conflicts with the need for environmental protection in an age of burgeoning production, massive consumption and the use of powerful technologies', and even when the restrictions on trade are intended to 'protect the environment, ensure food quality and safeguard public health'. According to Peet's critical account, the single-minded emphasis on free trade undermines national attempts to ensure environmental protection, and the power of labour to ensure decent working conditions and acceptable levels of pay.

The failure of talks to extend the liberalisation of global trade further, the so-called Doha Round (Scott and Wilkinson, 2011), indicates that the nature of the WTO as a membership organisation has resulted in a political stalemate, with the rising nations of the South refusing to accept the terms of trade that favour the more powerful nations that have traditionally dominated trade talks. Global trade is now governed by a patchwork of bilateral and regional trade agreements, the regional agreements between the countries of Latin America (Mercosur) and South-East Asia (Association of Southeast Asian Nations – ASEAN) being examples of co-operation at different levels that contrast with the continued rhetorical emphasis on *globa*lisation (Baldwin, 2006). More radical is the ALBA trading bloc (Alternativa Bolivariana para las Américas), a developing, socially focused trade bloc enabling the direct exchange of goods between Latin American nations.[5]

The argument made in the preceding chapter around the ownership of resources as 'common wealth' by the citizens of bioregions suggests a wholesale revision of this view of trade, which is dominated by powerful countries and the often more powerful corporations who transcend their boundaries and who are therefore not subject to their democratic authority. In this chapter I think we need to pose a different challenge to the prevailing mindset and switch from the focus on providing in response to the demand of the wealthy and instead switch the focus to local supply. This is inherent in the proposal of bioregions as units of common ownership. If the land of Kenya was conceived as having as its primary function the provision of food for the Kenyan citizens who jointly owned it, we would be unlikely to see Kenyan farmers producing cut flowers while their children went hungry. The profits that accrue from using African land to produce luxury goods for Western tables tend to be concentrated amongst the larger-scale local farmers and those who trade with them, rather than benefiting all Kenyans equally. (This was a key aspect of Stiglitz's – 2002 – critique of globalisation.) As we saw in the previous chapter in terms of land reform, it is precisely the refusal of local farmers who are given their own land to engage in a production-for-export system that is causing contention. From a market viewpoint this is reducing the efficiency of the land, since less of its production is bought and sold. From a bioregional perspective, however, it could be seen as ensuring sustainable local livelihoods with minimal environmental impact.

The critique of a green approach to trade is that it pays no heed to the benefits gained from those in poor countries through the system of export. Conversely, it directly challenges the notion that trade can help to 'make poverty history', and uses the evidence of continuing global poverty in the wake of a massive increase in trade as evidence of this. Rather, the trade system has benefited those in the West:

> countries such as Britain, France and the United States, could never have achieved the rates of material economic growth and affluence they continue to enjoy if they were dependent upon their own native natural resources. The affluent lifestyle enjoyed in these countries is dependent on a disproportionate consumption of world resources.
>
> *(Barry, 1998: Ch. 4)*

In spite of his stance towards the trade system, Barry is critical of the early bioregionalist approach to local self-reliance within bioregions on the basis of its limited purview, ignoring the huge variety in resource endowments between bioregions. Such a radically localist approach, he argues, could be characterised as 'condemning' those in resource-poor bioregions to their fate in a community-individualist approach that does not allow for redistribution of resources between bioregions. This critique has some merit and, in a sense, is a parallel to the critique made in Chapter 4: that radical localisation is not possible in a world where all resources are already owned and powerful economic actors have an established claim on them. Similarly, in an already interconnected world we cannot return to the morally acceptable ignorance of our ancestors who rarely travelled beyond their villages and for whom the consequence of domestic economic policy overseas was obscure.

From an economic point of view, it is important to begin to enumerate and place a value on these resources that are unequally endowed, and to explore how their value is likely to change as we move towards an economy where energy is more expensive and non-fossil-fuel energy is a more significant part of our supply. Just as the industrial revolution led to the migration into cities and areas rich in fossil fuels, we can expect the transition to a sustainable economy to result in the reinhabitation of rural areas, and a movement of people towards areas where renewable energy sources and biofuels are readily available.

The nature of human habitation of the planet has always been responsive to resource endowments. Pre-modern societies inhabit locales where sources of water, food and fuel were plentiful and, where their supply was competitive, positions that could be defended. This pattern can be clearly seen in the Domesday map of Britain, where most of the present settlements already existed and were positioned in river valleys and on hilltops (Darby and Welldon Finn, 1967). The arrival of industralisation and especially of the economic dependence on fossil fuels rapidly changed this pattern of habitation (Hoskins, 1955/1985). Vast populations were sucked into areas where resources such as coal and iron ore could be extracted (Cato, 2004), and equally into areas where factories could now be built away from sources of water-power or human-power. Technological advance facilitated this process, enabling people to change their environment to suit their needs, rather than choosing a habitat where their needs could be met from the natural surroundings (Jahi et al., 2009).

The pattern of habitation that the nineteenth and twentieth centuries have bequeathed to us is not a sustainable one. Populations are located far from their sources of basic resources and rely on a ready supply of cheap fossil fuels for their provisioning. Such a pattern will inevitably face change as the price and availability of fossil fuels change, and part of the transition strategy must be to encourage a change in settlement patterns to minimise fuel use. Hence the question about redistribution of resources is not a question that can be addressed in terms of the resources that we currently consider most valuable. Nor can it be considered solely in terms of the movement of resources. A transition to a lower-energy inhabitation of the world's productive land is likely to result in high rates of migration, which to some degree reverse the pattern of migration that occurred in response to industrialisation. These issues can only be sketched here and are identified primarily as a guide to the need for future detailed study.

9.3. Trade, climate change and global justice

A system of 'free' trade not only undermines the ability of the poorer countries to meet their own needs; it also means that their economies move towards a pattern of ecological impact more similar to that seen in developed Western economies. Writing for UNCTAD, Hoffman (2011: 32) sees a greater focus by 'developing' countries on self-reliance as ecologically and socially beneficial:

> If properly transformed, agriculture can be turned from being a climate-change problem to becoming an essential part of its solution ... The key problems of climate change, hunger and poverty, economic, social and gender inequity,

poor health and nutrition, and environmental sustainability are inter-related and need to be solved by leveraging agriculture's multi-functionality.

He calls for 'regenerative agricultural systems', shifting the focus away from individual crops and towards a systemic approach akin to permaculture. This sort of systemic change is, he argues, a much more fruitful way of approaching both the problems of environment and food insecurity in the poor world than would an increased focus on markets and technology.

In addition to its direct and negative impact on carbon emissions, the trade regime is also impeding attempts to negotiate a global climate change treaty because of the problem of embodied emissions. Although we have seen some reductions in the emissions of the high-emitting nations of the West, this is largely the result of the offshoring of emissions that takes place when domestic productive industries are closed down and demand is satisfied instead by imported goods. Under the current carbon accounting system, the emissions produced in the manufacture of these goods count in the totals of the countries of production, not of consumption; the emissions associated with the goods' transport were omitted from consideration entirely under the Kyoto Protocol (Oberthür, 2003). Table 9.1 provides details of the size of these 'embodied emissions' for a range of countries. It is clear from the figures that the UK and USA are gaining significantly in terms of the consumption per emissions ratio, largely as a result of their having offshored production and the emissions that go with it. In contrast, the significant exporters – including both China and Germany – are carrying a larger balance of emissions than their domestic consumption demands.

We could choose to view these embodied emissions as being part of the trade exchange, alongside the goods and capital that are currently viewed as part of that exchange. As already outlined, the basis of a mercantilist view of trade is that goods pass in one direction and currency flows in the reverse direction. This clearly benefits the countries who produce the currency, especially if they can produce it virtually without cost, either by printing paper or hitting the keys of a computer (Mellor, 2010). This has certainly improved the terms of trade for the dominant banking

TABLE 9.1. Balance of Emission Embodied in Trade (BEET) for selected countries.

Country	BEET MtCO$_2$	BEET as % of production-based emissions
Brazil	2.5	0.8
China	585.5	17.8
Germany	−139.9	15.7
Indonesia	58.1	19
India	70.9	6.9
Mexico	−17.6	−4.5
Russia	324.8	21.6
UK	−102.7	−16.6
USA	−438.9	−7.3

Source: Jiang *et al.* (2008).

nations since the days of gold. However, the recognition of the limitation on our ability to produce carbon dioxide should change the way we envisage the trade system. While goods still flow into the richer Western countries, we could imagine those goods with carbon price-tags attached to them.[6] As well as paying for their imports with money, the richer countries need to find a way of compensating for the carbon cost represented by these embodied emissions.

Once we conceptualise the global trading system in this way we can begin to see how we might link a trade system to a solution to climate change. The Contraction and Convergence model provides a framework within which we can undertake this reconfiguration (Meyer, 2000). It begins with a scientifically determined cap on the level of CO_2 emissions that are compatible with preventing climate change. These emissions are then shared on an equal per-capita basis between all the world's citizens and permits to produce this quantity of CO_2 are allocated to national governments. While the high-consumption countries are overproducing significantly in terms of their global share of what might be considered the 'atmospheric commons' (Starkey, 2011) the countries of the global South are significantly under-producing.

So how could we compensate these countries and make good on our excessive emissions? In order to ensure equity it might be necessary to rethink the basis of what is rather pompously called the 'global financial architecture', perhaps to include a new global trading currency in which carbon emissions are already inherent (see Cato, 2009b). Another proposal is that we reward the poorer countries for their lower emissions not with cash, of whatever form, but rather with technological expertise, especially in renewable energy systems (Pontin and Roderick, 2007). This may enable them to tunnel through the 'environmental Kuznets curve',[7] avoiding the period of fossil fuel-intensive growth that has left the world's industrialised nations with unresponsive and high-energy infrastructure.

9.4. Bioregional specialisation and cosmopolitanism

It is clear from the foregoing discussion that the present way of conceiving of trade is entirely incompatible with a bioregional economy. Within a competitive market framing, the focus of trade is arbitrage. From a provisioning perspective such activity has no rational purpose, and within a limited-energy approach to economics it is both wasteful and destructive. At this point we reach the stage when a neoclassically trained economist will be unable to resist the impulse to reach for another A-word, autarky: the word that describes an economy with no external trade, of which the most commonly cited example is North Korea. I would like to reassure readers that I have no intention of proposing such a future: the bioregional economy is not to be one in which the compulsive staging of rigorously choreographed spontaneous street demonstrations replaces the free availability of fresh fruit and vegetables.

So how are we to assess which trade merits its environmental impact within a bioregional economic approach? Elsewhere I have used the concept of 'trade sub-sidiarity' to help guide responses to this question (Cato, 2009a). The suggestion is that we should take as the guiding principle of provisioning the meeting of our needs from within our own bioregion. Only if this is not possible should we look further afield. In other words it is the devolution of the responsibility for provisioning to the lowest appropriate level, which is taken to be the bioregion in the first instance. A bioregional approach to trade does not assume that demands must always be met, and that the sole factor determining whether or not we may have access to our heart's desire (a pineapple in February, say) is whether we have the money to pay for it. The more participatory approach to the use of resources, especially energy resources, as outlined in the previous chapter, implies that we need to find answers to the question 'How should we determine which needs should be considered worthy of the investment of energy?' and to find answers to such questions as a community.

The discussion of trade subsidiarity, as illustrated in Figure 9.2, helps us to consider different kinds of products and what the appropriate scale of production and market might be in each case. For foodstuffs the discussion is fairly straightforward: a shift in the ethic of consumption towards local and seasonal, with luxury goods being produced under fair trade conditions and imported following the payment of tariffs. Harking back to the discussion of craftwork in Chapter 6, such a model suggests a focus on quality rather than quantity when considering the manufacture of goods that require skill to make but whose raw materials are domestically plentiful. In my own bioregion the local materials to produce such goods as furniture or clothing are available but the skills are lacking because we have increasingly come to depend on cheap labour overseas. The relearning of the ability to make shoes or chairs within our own communities using local raw materials will be part of the reskilling that a bioregional economy requires, and it will also create fulfilling employment. Prices would inevitably rise significantly, but a chair made by a respected acquaintance would have a value and longevity quite distinct from the rapidly assembled, emotionally empty IKEA chair that it replaces.

FIGURE 9.2 Trade subsidiarity grid
Source: Original artwork by Imogen Shaw.

It is a natural consequence of all that I have previously argued that the section of the provisioning space taken up by commodities that cannot be produced within the bioregion will shrink considerably. As a result of the introduction of tariffs as well as the changing nature of the ethic of consumption we can expect demand for luxury goods such as unseasonal fruit and vegetables to decline. Those goods such as coffee and tea that have no substitutes, and which many people regard as essential (what economists might call goods with 'inelastic demand'), are likely to increase significantly in price and so will become a part of a luxury budget whose consumption may require economies elsewhere. From the perspective of the producers of these commodities we could encourage the extension of policies supportive of fair trade, a development that would require a shift in orientation on the part of the global body responsible for regulating trade.

This leaves the final category from my production possibility space: the technological goods with a high degree of design specialisation and high levels of embodied energy. The distribution of such goods is instructive, since the skill to make them is not found in the countries where they predominate (this is illustrated for the case of computers in Table 9.2). This is an example of the international division of labour, where the intellectual property governing the production of a computer, for example, resides in the dominant nations of the West, who also own these goods that are so fundamental to economic success. The citizens of countries whose skilled labour is used to manufacture these products are far less likely to enjoy the fruits of that labour.

Thorbecke (2011) provides useful information on where these high-tech goods are actually made: since 1994 they have dominated exports from East Asia to the rest of the world. This massive market is subject to precise and detailed divisions of labour, with China providing the majority of low-skilled work and thus earning little in

TABLE 9.2. Personal computers per capita for a range of countries, computers per 100 people, 2004

Switzerland	83.0
Sweden	76.0
United States	75.0
United Kingdom	60.0
Korea, Republic of	52.4
Czech Republic	24.0
Chile	13.3
Brazil	13.0
China	4.1
Vietnam	4.0
Swaziland	3.2
Egypt	3.0
Sudan	1.6
India	1.2
Nigeria	0.6
Malawi	0.1

Source: Data from UN.

terms of value added. Thorbecke characterises this as a new form of triangular trade in which multinational corporations based in Japan, South Korea, Taiwan and China 'produce sophisticated technology-intensive intermediate goods and ship them to China and ASEAN for assembly by lower-skilled workers. The finished products are then exported throughout the world' (Thorbecke, 2011: 646). Around a third of these goods (computers and office equipment) find their way to the USA, with just over 20% going to the EU and 8% to Japan. Only 4.4% of these electronic goods are actually destined for the Chinese market.

As the graphic makes clear, we need to consider two aspects of this question of the production of high-tech goods: the resources needed to make them and the level of skill and design knowledge required to make them. It is clear that the reason for the domination of certain countries in the production of cars or computers is the result of the control of 'intellectual property' by the corporations that dominate the supply chain. This seems to be an arbitrage advantage that we can no longer afford in an era of ecological crisis. The expensive materials necessary for production, especially rare earths in the case of many electronic goods, are also the subject of competition and control (Morrison, 2011).

In Chapter 7 I considered at length how our desires and needs arise, and how we have learned to define and articulate them. I concluded that there were social and ecological parameters guiding what in economic theory is defined as 'demand', and I would suggest that social and ecological parameters should similarly guide questions of exchange. For those long schooled in the traditions of individualist consumption and personal freedom this may again raise spectres of uniformity and oppression, whether the Soviet-regulated sausage or the European straight banana. What I have in mind is a more social and negotiated process, which is already beginning in the community where I live. For example, my membership of a CSA means that I have a regular supply of seasonal and local vegetables. They have a greater value for me because they are part of my local soil, and because the farmer is a friend. It is painful to waste parsnips that I know were chipped out of frozen soil in favour of an aubergine produced in a heated Dutch polytunnel or a Kenyan green bean. While we may baulk at recipes such as that for Swede bruschetta which circulate in radical green circles, we could all question whether our desire for a pineapple could be assuaged by one of the 157 varieties of apple native to Gloucestershire, or satisfied only three or four times a year.

This is the soft, social end of changing desires and moulding our consumption patterns as a community. I would suggest that as well as reducing our dependence on lengthy supply chains and the energy that feeds them, it would also build our relationship to our local soil in a way constitutive of a sustainable future. But what of the harder end, of policy constraint? At the turn of the millennium Colin Hines (2000) proposed a GAST – General Agreement on Sustainable Trade – as part of his localisation manifesto. The sorts of policies he proposed there might provide a global framework within which bioregions could flourish. This built on earlier work by Hines and Lang (1993) in which they proposed making regions, rather than the globe, the focus of economic activity, and encouraging local and regional self-reliance. They suggested export restrictions to prevent the export of scarce national resources where they are not managed sustainably and the end of subsidised dumping. Import restrictions would be reintroduced to protect domestic industries, by way of environmental taxes embodying the climate and other environmental costs inherent in the global trading system. They summed up their approach in the phrase 'the new protectionism' and, although it is now nearly 20 years old, it is perhaps more important than ever as part of a new approach to economics (see further deails in Table 9.3).

The sorts of policies suggested by Hines are appropriate for a world of nation-states with clearly defined boundaries. The theorists of bioregionalism tend to favour a softer approach to boundaries, which they argue can be flexible in the provision of any particular good or service. While appealing intellectually, this is problematic when we seek to impose traditional trade policies such as quotas or tariffs, since we need to be able to identify clearly which state or bioregion the good or service originates from. Hines's proposals, which enable democratic authorities to nurture and facilitate local production, consumption and distribution, seem more compatible with this view of a bioregional future, and the inevitable significant increases in the price of fuel, or the cost of producing carbon dioxide, or both.

Two questions arise in connection with this bioregional approach to trade. The first concerns the obvious point that, if bioregions are defined in terms of the uniformity of the land and its species, then they will incline towards the production of

TABLE 9.3. Proposals for a general agreement on sustainable trade

Current rule	Effect	Amended GAST rule
GATT Article I: Most-Favoured Nation Treatment	Discrimination between foreign producers is prohibited	States shall give preferential treatement to goods and services from other states that respect human and animal rights, subscribe to global minimum wage and environmental standards
GATT Article III: National Treatment	Imported and locally produced goods to be treated equally	States are urged to give favourable treatment to domestic products that further goals of decent wages and high environmental standards
GATT Article III: Process and Production Methods	It is unlawful to discriminate against goods because of damaging or unethical production methods	Members are encouraged to make distinctions between products on the basis of their contribution to sustainability
GATT Article XI: Elimination of Quantitative Restrictions	Prohibition of quotas or bans on imports or exports	Quantitative restrictions should be permissible on the basis of social or environmental conditions
GATT Article XX: General Exceptions to WTO Rules	Provides scope for enforcement measures on environmental or health and safety grounds, but narrowly interpreted	Scope of exemptions should be extended and reinforced

Source: Abridged from Woodin and Lucas, 2004.

particular kinds of crops. In other words, the process of defining a provisioning economy based around bioregions itself incurs exactly the sort of risks from specialisation that I have elsewhere suggested lead to vulnerability. The bioregions of most parts of the world are yet to be drawn, and as already mentioned it is unclear how definitely they should be established in the case of any particular product or resource, but it is clear that the desire for a smaller scale of provisioning unit should be balanced by the objective of all necessary resources being available within it. The greater sense of identification and capacity for reconnecting with a known and understood landscape should be balanced against the specificity of the resources that it can provide.

The second issue concerns the appropriate political authority and range of policies necessary to effect the shift towards a trade subsidiarity approach. We have already seen how the establishment of an international trading body with a motivation to support local self-reliance could set a supportive global framework. The role of the national government would be likely to focus primarily on monitoring CO_2 emissions and ensuring that the productive enterprises within its territory did not exceed their carbon budgets. During the transitional period national governments would also play an important role in undertaking redistributive policies between bioregions with varying natural endowments and providing support to those seeking to relocate from one bioregion to another. The responsibility for provisioning, for imposing tariffs on imports and exports, and for enabling the reskilling of local people in production of food and raw materials and in craft production, would fall on the bioregion itself.

Dobson (1989) criticises the bioregional worldview on the basis that there is no guarantee that, if political power is devolved to the lowest level, all bioregions will be democratic and just. This follows the suggestion of the early theorists of bioregionalism, who were heroically optimistic in their requirement for the smallest communities to be responsible for all aspects of political power. I would certainly acknowledge this critique, but current developments in Europe suggest that they are not the most serious threat to democratic governance: the ability of citizens to influence the economic direction their countries are taking is removed as a result of financial calamity; and democratically elected politicians are replaced with the so-called 'technocrats' who seem to arise primarily from the banking sector. What is argued here, rather, is a system of subsidiarity, where bioregional, national and global bodies are empowered to act in matters that are most appropriately dealt with at their level of government. In many parts of the world the failure to regard local resources as common wealth is a key to explaining why democratic power and political accountability is still an unattainable dream for so many.

In Chapter 2 I identified the loss of cosmpolitanism as one of the threats of the bioregional vision, and to me this is a more immediate and serious weakness of the bioregional approach. Barry is critical of early bioregional theorists in their opposition to cultural exchange as representing an invasion of the unique identity of the bioregion. An example is Berg (1981: 25) with his stricture that 'Global Monoculture dictates English lawns in the desert, orange juice in Siberia and hamburgers in New Delhi. It overwhelms local cultures and "raises" them regardless of the effects on cultural coherency or capacities of local natural systems'. While I have proposed identification with local landscapes and their products as an alternative source of social and psychological underpinning in a bioregional vision, fetishisation of the local is unhelpful, and unrealistic. However, the reality of the cultural impact of globalisation has been unlimited global travel for the wealthy, at huge environmental cost, while the world's poor, whether in the West or the South, have been left in ghettos without the benefit of either a secure home culture or a global cosmopolitan culture.

In his plea for a kind of 'aboriginal cosmopolitanism', Nigel Clark suggests that, in an era of rapid change brought by both globalisation and climate change, we might seek inspiration from those who have learned to create their culture in response to the 'dynamic and eccentric rhythms' (Clark, 2008: 737) of the earth:

> if we are to understand the conditions that broadly configure want and plenty, estrangement and emplacement, ontological insecurity and security on this planet, then we must address the injustices that inhere in specific ways of organizing global social life while at the same time accounting for variability that is characteristic of the earth itself.
>
> *(Clark, 2008: 738)*

Clark seeks to learn from the wisdom of those who have stayed in place for hundreds of thousands of years, of which he takes Australian native peoples as an example. His suggestion of an 'aboriginal cosmopolitanism' 'refers to the nomad's openness to the past and future, to the disposition of all those who understand the capacity of their worlds to deterritorialize well enough to know that these events can make strangers of any of us; and who live accordingly' (Clark, 2008: 742). This suggests an approach to culture and place that would typify a bioregional approach to inhabiting the land, and which questions our narrow Western notions of what 'cosmopolitanism' might mean. As Clark notes, to develop a deep relationship with your local place is also to travel, but to travel in depth rather than breadth.

9.5. Conclusion

This chapter has established the vulnerability of Britain's provisioning strategy in an era of oil depletion, rapidly increasing energy prices and the urgent need to curb carbon emissions. Relying on land outside our political control for the production of our necessities undermines self-reliance and diminishes the quality of community life. We have reached this situation by following the strictures of the defunct economists who created the theory of comparative advantage. I have suggested that this theory was based not on empirical findings but rather on the need to justify England's military and politico-economic strategy in the nineteenth century. Its assumptions are outdated and it has become a dangerous millstone diverting us from changing our provisioning systems in a more sustainable and secure direction.

We have also seen how trade, instead of helping to end global poverty, has in fact reinforced it, and how the 'free trade' system put in place by the dominant Western economies and governed by the WTO has led to exploitation of the poor countries and increasing conflict and inequality within and between them. It has also prevented them from following a developmental path that would allow them to use their land to achieve subsistence and to use the 'multifunctionality' of agriculture to ensure that their land has a positive impact on climate change. The Contraction and Convergence framework was proposed as a means of ensuring a balanced approach to the need for global transfers from the wealthy countries to the poorer ones, while also addressing the increasingly pressing problem of achieving an international agreement to reduce CO_2 emissions.

Finally, we looked at proposals to change the framework within which trade takes place, as a precursor to re-imagining a provisioning system based on much smaller areas, the bioregions. The GAST that was proposed would enable the creation of a system of self-reliant local economies, operating within a global structure designed to reduce the volume of global trade. The idea of trade subsidiarity was offered as a way of rethinking the role of trade as one of exception based on climatic or specialist production differences, rather than a primary one based on the desire to generate profits. This framework could facilitate the growth of sustainable local economies based on bioregional boundaries, to which our attention turns in the next chapter.

10

SPACE, LIMITS AND BOUNDARIES

The Eighth Wonder of the World, Beethoven's Tenth, the Eleventh Commandment of the Lord: on all sides one hears hymns of praise to the free market, source of prosperity and guarantee of democracy. Free trade is sold as something new, as if born from a cabbage or the ear of a goat, despite its long history reaching back to the origins of the unjust system that reigns today.

Eduardo Galeano

This is my last substantive chapter, and writing it makes me realise more strongly than ever how this book is more of a clarion call than a complete vision. The areas covered here are some of the most intractable and the questions that I feel least qualified to answer. Applying the bioregional vision to provisioning systems is an important and urgent task I believe, and a broad-ranging one. It is perhaps inevitable, therefore, that in this first book my job is as usual to raise questions as to find solutions. I have approached my subject from the perspective of political economy, but I am aware of raising more political questions than I can easily find answers to. This is particularly so in this chapter, where I begin to propose how the bioregions and their resources might be governed.

The argument of this chapter follows from the conclusions of the previous two. The bioregional economy implies a system of more, and more diverse, local economies, largely self-reliant in providing for their citizens' basic needs. In Chapter 8 I argued that such a proposal would need to rely on a radical re-exploration of how the earth's resources are owned. Then in Chapter 9 I addressed the question of the limits to self-provisioning and the remaining role for exchange between bioregions. In this chapter I develop further the discussion about how a bioregional economy might work as a provisioning unit. I outline a range of policies to support self-reliant local economies and describe how these would result in fundamental changes to our political arrangements. In a bioregional economy, more economic decisions will be made locally, allowing a genuine responsibility for decisions that support the transition to a sustainable future.

The chapter begins in Section 10.1 with a critical account of the popular assumption that larger scale is economically efficient. In Section 10.2 I take a longer historical perspective than elsewhere and pick out a resonant thread running through the history of economic thought: the need for strong local economies as provisioning communities. Section 10.3 begins with a consideration of the issue of boundaries in the global economy, and moves on to consider what is the appropriate scale for the ownership, control and provisioning of basic resources. I identify the market town as a model for sustainable provisioning and a prototype for the transition to low-energy, local economies. In Section 10.4 I explore the transitional politics of moving towards the bioregional economy, as well as introducing some examples of thriving local economies in the unsupportive politico-economic setting of Britain in 2012. Following this consideration of a range of policies that we might introduce now to encourage a shift towards a more local system of self-provisioning economies, Section 10.5 briefly concludes.

10.1. Economies of scale; diseconomies of hope

In his 'sympathetic critique' of the politics of transition, North (2010: 587) suggests that the green economist's penchant for a patchwork of self-reliant local economies may be a simplistic 'reading off' from an observed or idealised conception of nature: 'A variety of local economies mirrors nature's diversity, facilitating experimentation and the development of more effective practices and models'. I think we can do better than that. Those who suggest relocalisation of our supply chains are routinely rebutted with references to 'economies of scale'. Yet the empirical evidence suggests that this totem of popular neoclassical economic theory is flawed. (Even neoclassical economic theory admits diminishing marginal returns to scale.) Beyond the most basic processes, the justification of the value of economies of scale is often provided theoretically, and the popularity of the concept is based more on its constant repetition than on empirical evidence (Hill and Myatt, 2010: 138–39).

The economist Fritz Schumacher turned the arguments about efficiency and scale on their heads: on his account it was the ever-increasing scale of production that was the problem. Large-scale operations are inefficient in their generation of management systems and Parkinsonian bureaucracies – which he considered undermined productivity – and voracious in their use of energy. Schumacher, unlike too many mainstream economists, also considered the social implications of ever-increasing scale. In terms of the problems of vastness he argued:

> most of the sociologists and psychologists insistently warn us of its inherent dangers – dangers to the integrity of the individual when he feels as nothing more than a small cog in a vast machine and when the human relationships of his daily working life become increasingly dehumanized.
>
> *(Schumacher, 1973)*

Much of Schumacher's politico-economic critique in this area was drawn from the writings of the Austrian economist Leopold Kohr. Kohr's masterpiece *The Breakdown of Nations* established a critique of globalisation before it had even been named. He argued that there are natural boundaries to human communities:

> nature puts limits to growth not only on its biological organisms. In particular, it puts them also on its social organisms such as firms, cities, or states. The only difference is that natural instincts which guide the behaviour of animals have become so dulled in the case of the human species as a result of educational sophistication and mechanical progress, that the social and economic implication of the limiting principle impose on growth by function and form is not grasped with half the lucidity with which it has long been recognized in its biological context.
>
> *(Kohr, 1977/1988: 29–30)*

Kohr's model for the ideal community was the small town he had grown up in near Salzburg in Austria, a community which, he argued, was an economically efficient form of life as well as the ideal psychologically and culturally. Modern cities were, by contrast, inefficient and socially destructive. Kohr locates their inefficiency partly in the over-production of two types of goods, the need for which increases as society expands in scale: power commodities and density commodities. The first include such things as 'tanks, bombs or the increase in government services required to administer increased power'; the second are 'rendered necessary as a result of population increases, such as traffic lights, first-aid equipment, tube services, or replacement goods for losses which would never have occurred in less harassed smaller societies' (Kohr, 1957: 146). Local communities would have less need to defend their expansive interests, and hence less need for 'power commodities'. The simplified life that citizens would lead within such locally based economies would not generate the complexity and need for management systems of larger, more interconnected systems typical of a globalised world, and hence less need for 'density commodities'. Although a capitalist, growth-based economy revels in the additional demand that power and density commodities create, from an ecological point of view sustainability tends more towards ecological efficiency.

Ivan Illich was a champion of Kohr's work, particularly of his use of the concepts of 'proportionality' and 'appropriateness'.[1] He quotes Khor as saying that 'bicycling is ideally appropriate for one living in a certain place, like Oberndorf', the community where Kohr grew up. As Illich continues:

> An examination of this statement immediately reveals that 'certain', as used here, is as distant from 'certainty' as 'appropriate' is from 'efficient'. 'Certain' challenges one to think about the specific meaning that fits, while 'appropriate' guides one to knowledge of the Good. Taking both 'appropriate' and a 'certain place' together allows Kohr to see the human social condition as that ever unique and boundary-making limit within which each community can engage

in discussion about what ought to be allowed and what ought to be excluded. To consider what is appropriate or fitting in a certain place leads one directly into reflection on beauty and goodness. The truth of one's resultant judgment will be primarily moral, not economic.

(Illich, 1994)

Illich concludes that it is difficult to fit this concept of 'proportionality' into an 'economic calculus': in spite of the horror many people experience as a result of the consequences of economic growth, it is difficult to argue with economic expansion on purely rational grounds.

The idea of economies of scale conflicts with two other principles of economic theory; in fact the very bases of the market model: the removal of barriers to entry to the market and the unacceptability of undue power in any market. For the market to work efficiently, both demand and supply sides must be free and open so that new, enterprising producers can enter easily, out-compete existing players, and ensure the dynamism on which capitalism prides itself. This should naturally limit the expansion of existing market players, since if they are earning 'supernormal profits', then other firms will enter the market and take a share. However, the reality of capitalist markets is that players engage in strategies precisely to enable the consolidation that allows them market control, whether through mergers, partnerships or expansion. The asserted superiority of the market arises from the assumption on the part of neoclassical economists that the firm is the basic unit of economic analysis. The rationality of market actors and the establishment of clear property rights are also taken as unproblematic, and self-evident. Without these assumptions the superior efficiency of large-scale production and distribution becomes open to question. In the case of private firms the proposition of economies of scale is problematic since, if it generates real efficiencies, then this will encourage the tendency towards consolidation and undermine market competition, the very reason that competitive firms were considered the ideal form of productive organisation.

Critiques of public provisioning, especially of services such as healthcare and education, have similarly focused on the inefficiencies suffered as a result of increasing or excessive scale. This critique has focused on the complacency of single providers such as the UK's National Health Service (NHS) or local authority providers of housing, while also noting the potential for public-sector purchasers to dominate markets precisely because of their scale, acting as what economists would label a 'monopsonist'. Alexandersson and Hultén (2007) explore how in a market with a small number of providers and one dominant provider, in this case the Swedish railway industry, it is possible for outcomes to be based on strategic manoeuvres rather than market competition. This centralised approach to the provision of public goods was undertaken partly in order to generate the economies of scale in provisioning and procurement that would reduce prices. Birner and Wittmer (2004) conducted an empirical enquiry into the 'efficient boundaries' of the state in the area of natural resource management. In this area of profound relevance to the question of bioregional economies, they conclude that nation-state governance may not be most efficient and that co-management systems may work better.

For commons resources the literature suggests that organisations based on co-opera-tion between the users of the resources can have a comparative advantage so long as there exist appropriate institutions for the governance of the commons (Ostrom, 1990):

> Such cooperative types of organizations represent a further governance struc-ture or coordination mechanism which is distinct from markets and hierarchies. Whereas hierarchies have to solve principal-agent problems, cooperatives and membership organizations have to solve the free-rider problem of collective action. Therefore, it appears justified to consider them as a third governance structure besides markets and hierarchies. Hybrid governance structures can then be defined as combinations of different such coordination mechanisms.

My aim in this section has not been to provide a full critique of the link between efficiency and great scale – given the prevalence of this phrase within the catechism of neoclassical economies, that would be a lengthy undertaking – but rather to open this question in the minds of readers. My own conclusion is that sometimes econo-mies of scale prevail, sometimes diseconomies of scale prevail, and sometimes the quest for economies of scale leads to unacceptable social or environmental con-sequences: in view of these variations in optimal outcomes it would seem judicious to adopt a pragmatic approach.

10.2. Ideal and idealised communities

In this section I address the question of the ideal size of human settlement, a question that has engaged the attention of a surprising number of philosophers and political theorists. According to Sale (1980), Plato was fairly specific about the optimum size for a city-state: it should contain 5,040 citizens (male heads of household), so that once the inhabitants Plato considered of lower-status (women, children, slaves) were included the total size would be some 35,000 to 40,000 people. Sale proceeds to list European intellectual luminaries including Leonardo da Vinci, Thomas More, Mon-tesquieu and Rousseau as all recommending the ideal city with a population in the region of 20,000 to 30,000 people.

In a geographical and social setting that could hardly have been more different, both Tolstoy and Kropotkin supported the small-scale community in contra-distinction to the burgeoning cities of their Russian experience. The latter argued for such settlements on the basis of the need for their citizens to show varied and prac-tical skills, as part of a self-provisioning community:

> the greatest sum of well-being can be obtained when a variety of agricultural, industrial and intellectual pursuits are combined in each community; and that man shows his best when he is in a position to apply his usually varied capa-cities to several pursuits in the farm, the workshop, the factory, the study or the studio, instead of being riveted for life to one of these pursuits only.
>
> *(Kropotkin, 1899/1994: 18)*

Throughout the political-economy debate in the English language runs a golden thread that is the desire to create local communities, bound together by shared values and sharing resources they own as common wealth. It surfaces in the work of Ruskin and Morris. Delveaux (2005: 139) has argued that William Morris's idyllic future society of Nowhere was a prototype for an ecological society and a 'bioregional utopia'. During his exploration of the ideal form of human existence Morris's protagonist Guest undertakes a journey from London into my backyard of Gloucestershire. What he discovers is a flourishing rural community forming part of a national patchwork of similar confident and self-reliant communities:

> England has been divided into different regions and decentralized communities, which is reminiscent of Berg's bioregional motto, but these communities are also autonomous in political terms in that they engage directly in political affairs in the context of the Mote, i.e. the meeting of the specific commune, ward, or parish. The objective of this meeting is to discuss questions and decide on matters of common interest to the whole community, e.g. the construction of a bridge or when to start the hay-harvesting. Decisions are taken by consensus, or by majority vote in case of disagreement. Hierarchical power structures are absent and every member of the community has the same rights. In Nowhere, decision-making power flows from bottom upwards rather than from the top down.

This is not an academic or theoretical analysis, more a plea for an ideal system, which challenges the dislocation that Morris saw in Victorian society. Morris's proposal for provisioning also closely resembles the proposals made in this book: 'Similar to the political structure in Nowhere, people are also largely self-sufficient in economic terms, mainly because they produce according to communal needs, not single wants' (Buick, 1990).

According to Pepper (1984: 190), Kropotkin argued against the notion that centralisation was necessary to take advantage of economies of scale: 'But small-scale autonomous industries could overcome disadvantages of market weakness by federating into co-operatives for buying raw materials and marketing goods.' William Morris concurred, suggesting that the high-density communities of the industrial age were a step on the path to his utopia: 'the aggregation of population having served its purpose of giving people opportunity of inter-communication and of making the workers feel their solidarity, will also come to an end'. He described a future utopia where 'the huge manufacturing districts will be broken up, and nature heal the horrible scars that man's heedless greed and stupid error have made'. Efficiency and lower prices would be less important than pleasant and beautiful communities (Morris, 1885/1973: 196).

This lead was followed directly by the guild socialists, weavers of a lost thread of British socialism, whose name itself harks back to the medieval era of organisation within city states. For them the issue of scale was important more for reasons of accountability and resistance to authoritarianism than because of environmental concerns. Much as I have done in Chapter 6, they championed the social and spiritual value of craftwork, and sought to resist the psychological and sociological depradations of the industrial cities of their time (for a more detailed discussion of the links between the guild socialists and the modern green movement see Arthur *et al.*, 2006). Orage, editor of the guild socialist paper *New Age*, was typical of the group, being 'strongly hostile to bureaucracy' and holding that 'men could not be really free as citizens unless they were also free and self-governing in their daily lives as producers' (Cole, 1960: 244).

Two leaders of national freedom movements who had lived at the sharp end of the English market system agreed about the need to build small-scale, self-reliant communities in response. Gandhi's concept of 'swadeshi' required that 'whatever is made or produced in the village must be used first and foremost by the members of the village. Trading among villages and between villages and towns should be minimal, like icing on the cake'. Gandhi thought that such self-reliant villages should almost have the status of a 'republic' and that production was constitutive of community: 'a locally based economy enhances community spirit, community relationships, and community well-being.' Mass production, by contrast, led to the breakdown of communities and social and spiritual dislocation (Kumar, 2001). In Ireland, a country that has a fair claim to be England's first colony, green economist Richard Douthwaite linked 'the Mahatma's message' to what he called De Valera's dream of Ireland as a country of self-reliant communities (Douthwaite, 1992). He made this argument before the rise and fall of the Celtic tiger drew Ireland's young people from the land and left them abandoned in the depressed cities.

A research project funded under the EU scientific framework (Marshall and Lamrani, 2011) suggested a means for judging the ideal size of settlements: 'Theory suggests that if settlements are of a sufficient size to maintain a certain range of facilities, then a settlement can be "self-contained" and inter-urban travel minimised. The same could be applied to any scale: a neighbourhood with a full range of facilities appropriate for that scale could be expected in principle to generate fewer inter-neighbourhood trips than neighbourhoods bereft of facilities.' While this laudably includes consideration of low-energy transport options, it fails to consider the provisioning aspects of settlement design, again assuming the lengthy supply-chains that, at least in my opinion, seem considerably less secure today than they did even a decade ago. Research in psychology attempts to approach this question of ideal community size from the other end, as it were, by attempting to pin down the number of people with whom a human animal can create a meaningful relationship within a network. The research suggests an average network size of 136 to 150 people (Dunbar, 2003). Other research has suggested that the network size is functionally limited by the ability of the human brain to maintain close emotional bonds, and that if the network size increases the intensity of the relationships declines (Roberts *et al.*, 2009).

The emphasis these writers place on community sets them apart from the growing number of voices raised both within and outside academia for a more individualist response to the crises that threaten. The impulse to 'run to the hills' is the diametric opposite of the faith in others that must surely offer us a more positive future.

Morris's mentor Ruskin observed that accountability is impossible to achieve at too large a scale. I think this is a crucial observation for achieving sustainability. We must ensure that the boundaries or our political systems, the areas over which we exercise democratic authority, match our provisioning systems, and that these areas are not too large for us as citizens to take moral responsibility for them:

> The clear implication of Ruskin's analysis, that we need to recognise the consequences of our actions, and be held responsible for them, is that local and nearby economic relations are preferable to those at a distance as it is distance that reduces the efficacy of empathy. Like Thorstein Veblen some years later, this suggests that (what Veblen termed) 'absentee ownership' – the ability through (fragmented) share holdings for owners to distance themselves from the everyday responsibility for their company's actions – contributes to the problems of the market not recognising non-pecuniary values (Veblen 1997 [1923]).
>
> *(May, 2010: 194)*

The market town is an elegant social institution and an efficient economic one. It was the dominant structuring settlement before the discovery of fossil fuels enabled the explosion in transport of resources. In my own bioregion of the Cotswolds Trueman suggests that the distribution of settlements followed this pattern for purposes of energy efficiency: 'Cirencester, Tetbury, Malmesbury, Northleach, Chipping Norton and others are spaced at intervals of ten to twenty miles, that is at such a distance that market centres were within suitable reach of all parts in horse-transport days' (Trueman, 1938: 28). In his plea for a return to human scale Kirkpatrick Sale (1980) identifies the city-state as an ideal form of economic and social organisation for human society. Specifically he singles out the Italian city-state of Lucca, in Tuscany, as an example of a thriving community that was destroyed by its connections with wider economic systems. For 800 years it operated independently and achieved high standards of living for its citizens, even with the levels of technology available at the time:

> It enjoyed a rich and self-sufficient agriculture, with fruits, grains, wine, vegetables, chestnuts, and grazing fields; it was a major banking center from the fourteenth century on … famous for its velvet and other textile manufacturing, was the home of recognized artists, musicians, and writers; and it expressed its prosperity, century after century, in a magnificent array of churches … palazzo, castles, fortifications and townhouses that was extraordinary even for those extraordinary years.
>
> *(Sale, 1980: 413)*

The tale of decline is the result of the imperialist expansion of Spain, and then France, and then the subsuming of Lucca into the Italian state. Today it has a 'shaky industrial base' relying on the production of jute and tobacco, and imports agricultural produce.

Not far from Lucca a group of economists are developing work to analyse the energy efficiency of their own local economy. The SPIn-ECO Project for the Province of Siena is a network of projects designed to measure the sustainability of the territory, made up of the city and its hinterland, including ecological footprint analysis, a greenhouse gas inventory, and emergy and exergy analysis[2] to provide a picture of the relationship between human inhabitants and the natural environment. Pulselli *et al.* observed 'the attitudes of the territorial systems toward resource use as revealed by their patterns of emergy consumption' and offered an analysis of the use of local resources within the Siena territory based within a thermodynamic framework. This yields information about land use intensities that could underpin proposals for more self-reliant provisioning. This is the sort of work that, as it seems to me, economists should be interested in investigating if they are to contribute to building a sustainable future and offers a scientific approach to appraising the bioregional economy.

While this work demonstrates the potential for assessing the thermodynamic advantages of living within a city-state provisioning system, it would be foolish to deny that some of the appeal of this model is simply its attractiveness. Polanyi sees towns as providing a brake on urban expansion as well as guardians of market exchange: 'Towns, insofar as they sprang from markets, were not only the protectors of those markets, but also the means of preventing them from expanding into the countryside and thus encroaching on the prevailing economic organization of society' (Polanyi, 1944: 65). While Morris and Ruskin find an aesthetic and ethical value in this way of life:

> Demonstrating warmth towards the creation of small, self-sufficient and self-governing communities and rural regeneration, the people in Nowhere live in small villages dispersed over the whole country and reap all the benefits of living in a small community: they engage directly in politics, lead a self-sufficient life, co-operate between themselves, and simply enjoy their unalienated labour and life in nature.
>
> *(Delveaux, 2005: 136)*

Morris falls in line with Marx and Engels who argued that the bourgeoisie greatly increased the urban population as compared with the rural, and subjected the country to the rule of the towns (Gould, 1988). While there is an aspect of this argument that is aesthetic, there is also a link to the politico-economic critique of these early socialists:

> Not only is Ruskin's approach a rejection of abstraction, but his political economy is clearly predicated upon a localised, closely known polity, in which responsibility is supported by the inability to avoid (or ignore) the consequences of actions, and therefore it is unsurprising that many of his scattered remarks on directed markets imply a form of civic municipality rather than merely state government.
>
> *(May, 2010: 196)*

The appeal of the city-state model for provisioning is that it returns us to an understanding of the way towns and cities cannot exist in isolation from nature: this is necessary since the suggestion that the limitations of a city's expansion can be removed by a heavy investment of fossil fuels, fails to face up to the reality of life in a climate-changed world facing the imminence of petroleum depletion (Steel, 2008). Herbert Girardet remembers the work of nineteenth-century German economic geographer Johann Heinrich von Thünen, whose book *The Isolated State* described the design of human settlements surrounded by rings of provisioning land, or 'agropolis', which were typical of pre-fossil-fuel habitations. He has revived and updated this in his vision of the 'Ecopolis', illustrated in Figure 10.1, which is a form of 'restorative' urban settlement, integrating human society within its local environment. Provisioning of food is local, and the ecopolis is powered by renewable energy.

The key to the success of the city-state is its complex relationship with its hinterland. The proposal for a bioregional economy does not require all citizens to go 'back to the land', but that they all recognise their ultimate dependence on that land: 'Knowing place for the urban-dweller, then, means learning the details of the trade and resource-dependency between city and country and the population limits appropriate to the region's carrying capacity. It also suggests exploring the natural *potential* of the land on which the city rests' (Sale, 1991: 45). Rather than a destructive economic competition between urban and rural areas, the relationship should be mutually interdependent. In Morris's account the city is trascended:

> Morris offers a visionary symbiosis of city and country that combines the ben-
> efits of both while avoiding their shortcomings. In a process of de-urbanization
> and decentralization, the inhabitants of Nowhere have abandoned the cities
> and gone back to the countryside, so that the whole population in Nowhere is
> equally dispersed in small villages over England.
>
> *(Delveaux, 2005: 134)*

whereas for Sale the advantages of urban and rural life are balanced:

> Human life, to be fully human, needs the city; but it also needs food and other
> raw materials gained from the country. Everybody needs ready access to both
> countryside and city. It follows that the aim must be a pattern of urbanisation
> so that every rural area has a nearby city, near enough so that people can visit it
> and be back the same day. No other pattern makes human sense. Actual
> developments during the last hundred years or so, however, have been in
> exactly the opposite direction: the rural areas have been increasingly deprived
> of access to worthwhile cities. There has been a monstrous and highly
> pathological polarization of the pattern of settlements.
>
> *(Sale, 1991: 114, quoting Schumacher)*

Of all the aspects of this project for a bioregional revisioning of our provisioning systems, this aspect of the provisioning of the world's mega-cities is the one for which I feel my response is the most inadequate, and that finding a response is urgent for the world's people, more than half of whom now live in cities, many of them in the rapidly expanding mega-cities of the South.

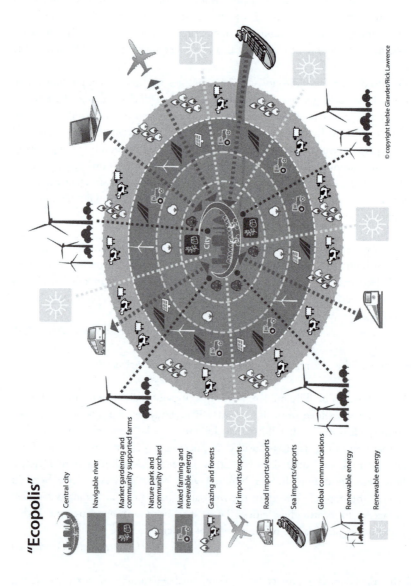

"Ecopolis"

- Central city
- Navigable river
- Market gardening and community supported farms
- Nature park and community orchard
- Mixed farming and renewable energy
- Grazing and forests
- Air imports/exports
- Road imports/exports
- Sea imports/exports
- Global communications
- Renewable energy
- Renewable energy

FIGURE 10.1 The ecopolis as an efficient provisioning settlement
Source: © Herbert Girardet and Gary Lawrence.

10.3. Establishing our boundaries

The late capitalist economy suffers from serious boundary issues. As a result of globalisation the boundaries we used to live within have become porous or have been transcended altogether; yet we have not found new boundaries within which we can feel secure. The two boundaries as recognised by neoclassical economics – the boundary of the firm definitive of *micro*-economics and the nation-state boundary definitive of *macro*-economics – no longer have relevance in the post-globalisation world. Contemporary economic debates take place in a boundary vacuum in spite of the fact that, as discussed in Chapter 2 in connection with Iceland, one thing we have learned from the financial crisis of 2008 is that our economic responsibilities are very much tied to our national territories.

The hegemonic idea of our age is that of the superiority of business, and in discussions of globalisation and its consequences this idea expresses itself in terms of uncritical support, with emphasis on efficiency and mobility, and little reference to cultural and social consequences (the classic example in the popular literature is Friedman, 2005). Critical accounts of the consequences of globalisation use the term 'deterritorialisation' to frame the discussion of the way that human communities have become disembedded from their geographical and sometimes cultural context. Some take a critical stance with regard to the 'overzealous' way that commentators on globalisation have celebrated 'mobility' and 'deterritorialized forms of social interaction' (Bude and Dürrschmidt, 2010: 482). The contemporary form of 'disembodied globalism' (James, 2005) is seen as lacking analytical depth, while the emphasis on technology as capable of annihilating distance is seen to underestimate the importance that human cultures place on their sense of place (Tomlinson, 1999).

The importance of the question of our relationship to geographical places is evident from the proliferation of academic concepts in recent years, although the usefulness of these in interpreting what has happened, still less in guiding ecologically empowered responses, is questionable. Scholte, for example, considers the modern world in terms of a form of 'respatialisation', which he defines as a 'reconfiguration of social geography with increased transplanetary connections between people'. Many authors follow the lead set by Castells in his theorising of a 'network society' where close connections are still possible across vast distances (Castells, 1996). However, this discussion tends to absent the consideration of energy in a way which is, in my view, evidence of the influence of academic and theoretical discussion, which has no need to address the fundamental questions of provisioning that is confidently assumed. More positive in this regard is the proposal for 'glocalization' (Swyngedouw, 1997), an attempt to combine the advantages of embedded local action with global awareness.

The theme of this book is an exploration of the ecological implications of our provisioning strategies, and how these impact on our understanding of our place in the world. In former times citizens might have turned to political leaders to address these questions. Yet as the economic and ecological crises have demonstrated, the political cadre has been infected with a 'learned helplessness', leading to the pitiful performance of hand-wringing by suited men (and less often women) in a range of exotic locations. The ambition of politicians has become so diminished that, when we need political leadership, there is none available. The caustic tone of the response from social critics is perhaps unsurprising:

> The raison d'etre of the state today is the same as that of the financial markets that rule the world and produce nothing but speculation. Subcommandante Marcos, the spokesman for the Indians of Chiapas, described the process aptly: we are witnessing, he said, a striptease. The state takes off everything down to its underwear, that indispensable intimate garment which is repression. The moment of truth: the state exists only to pay the foreign debt and guarantee social peace.
>
> *(Galeano, 1998: 92)*

In the case of the eurozone crisis we are beginning to see that these two residual roles for political authority may become incompatible if the state is not prepared to widen its purview.

A large measure of the appeal of a bioregionalist vision is the discomfort we experience when we live without boundaries. According to McGinnis (1999) we are 'boundary creatures', but the boundaries we respect are, like those of animals, in a constant state of flux. He contrasts these boundaries with the 'boundaries of mechanical life':

> We should recognize that these senses and memories we share with other animals in a community are rapidly fading. Modern institutions make a series of somber choices: to foster the development of formal economies and bureaucracies, to devalue informal economies and diverse communities, to control a 'static' nature as a resource, to develop technological and scientific instruments for making exploitation of the environmental machine more effective and efficient.
>
> *(McGinnis, 1999: 62)*

Yet the process of globalisation has opened up the question of what the appropriate boundaries from a provisioning perspective, or a wider political economy perspective, might be. The traditional boundary of the nation-state is fading, as the forces of globalised corporations transcend its borders and traduce its people's democratic powers (Della Porta, 2005). The bioregional argument suggests that the nation-state never reflected the boundaries we know in our evolutionary selves. Our inner boundaries may be more akin to those of other animals or of nomadic peoples. But how are we to accommodate this inner knowing of wide boundaries with an over-populated world and with private ownership systems?

As I suggested in Chapter 8, one answer may lie in more participatory processes of economic negotiation, rather than in mechanical systems of legality and bureaucracy. McGinnis acknowledges what he calls this 'fundamental border redefinition conflict', which he conceptualises as shown in Figure 10.2. For McGinnis the need for

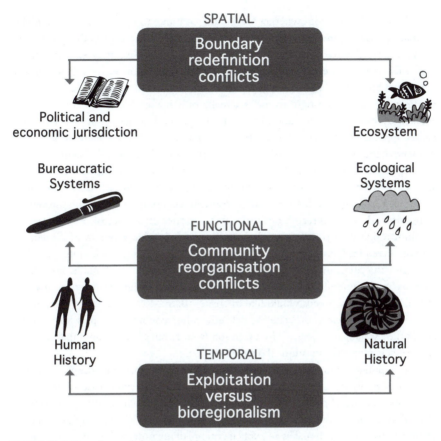

FIGURE 10.2 Boundary redefinition problems
Source: Original artwork by Imogen Shaw, based on McGinnis, 1999.

redefinition has three aspects. The first is the spatial, raising the question of whether we consider our local places in terms of real geographical areas or in terms of politically designated boundaries. The second is functional, and concerns whether or not we resolve our issues of sharing and relating through bureaucratic means (the discourse of laws and rights) or through learning to be ecological citizens. The third type of boundary issue is the temporal, and concerns the extent to which our sense of the area within which we are justified in claiming resources is historically embedded and considers the needs of generations stretching forward indefinitely into the future.

In Chapter 4 I discussed the way that the expansion of the market and the ending of a system of provisioning from within the domestic territory laid the foundation for the globalisation of the economy, and allowed private property rights to dictate ownership, sometimes in opposition to national territorial boundaries. Bioregionalism suggests a different way: a way of deciding boundaries on the basis of negotiation within and between bioregions. McGinnis argues that the present political boundaries appear 'hard' and yet post-globalisation debates have already softened them considerably. He questions whether we should 'continue to rely on top-down, highly centralized markets and bureaucracies' (McGinnis, 1999: 69). As both the graphic and the preceding discussion make clear, this is an area where we may expect conflict, which for some is a reason to resist the bioregional paradigm. However, it seems to me that asking these fundamental questions about our place in space and which resources this gives us a right to use is actually only making explicit a conflict that is entailed by our over-exploitation of nature. I propose bioregionalism as an emancipatory approach to framing this question; the question itself is inevitable if we are to maintain a commitment to social justice within a limited ecological system.

I began this chapter by making explicit the fact that there is a mismatch between areas of democratic accountability, of provisioning systems, and of real human identification. I have argued that if we are to create an economy in which the throughput of resources does not threaten our survival as a species, then control of those resources must reside with the people who use them: this is what a system of bioregional economies requires. For Barry, one of few political economists to discuss bioregionalism at length, this attachment to local economic empowerment exemplifies 'the almost complete monopolization of the [deep] green political imagination by an anarchist vision of the society greens would like to create' (Barry, 1998: 77). Barry characterises the ideal green society as 'stateless, self-governing communities plus solar power equals the "sustainable society"' by extension from Lenin's famous quip that socialism was 'Soviets plus electrification' (Barry, 1998: 77).

Barry's critique of bioregionalism comes from a political base but, since the green position argues repeatedly for a return to political economy and the explicit expression of the intertwined nature of politics and economics, such an approach is entirely appropriate. Barry distinguishes between bioregionalism and Bookchin's 'social ecology' according to the extent to which each makes an explicit critique of the power of the state, the former being characterised as 'weak' eco-anarchism in contrast to the 'strong' eco-anarchism of social ecology. In Barry's analysis, bioregionalists are content to rely on the essential goodness of human nature and the benevolence of natural design to ensure that the local provisioning economies established autonomously across the nation-state will be both ecologically sensitive and socially just. North (2010) makes a similar critique in the context of the Transition Movement, which he finds politically naïve and almost delusional in its expectation that local action will be able to flourish in the context of an accumulative and financialised wider economy, seeking ever more complete extraction of value.

The typical response of a green or an anarchist to such specific questions of ideal structure is that a single answer is not required (Kingsnorth, 2003) or even that 'diversity is nature's way'. However, in this context such a response is insufficient, since the critique is precisely that proponents of local, community responses to an ecologically and socially threatening mode of capitalism are naïve about the extent to which any of their projects for society, no matter how small-scale, will be eroded, if not actively opposed, by a system that by its very design tends towards uniformity and consolidation. Barry attempts to effect a compromise between visions of eco-anarchism and the existence of a state of some sort, but such a compromise between local, self-reliant communities and a globalised form of capitalism is harder to posit.

Summarising the early debate around the limits to economic localisation, Dobson (2007: 96) notes:

> They argue that the green decentralist programme is unrealistic for three reasons. First, not everything that we might reasonably expect from a green society can be produced locally; second, dealing with the environmental problems that the green movement has identified requires the kind of planning and co-ordination that can only be provided by centralized planning structures; and third, such structures are needed to organize the redistribution required by the greens' egalitarian project.

The bioregion has to balance being large enough to provide the majority of resources with being small enough to allow genuine democracy, accountability and participatory planning. It is clear from the previous chapter that I believe that the role of setting sustainable environmental and social standards for economic production, would reside at the global level, and to some extent this would naturally limit trade between bioregions, since energy efficiency would be enforced. So we are left with the question: in such a system, what would be the remaining role of the national government? And perhaps equally importantly, who would take responsibility for ensuring redistribution between richly and poorly endowed bioregions?

This brings us to draw more general conclusions about the appropriate scale for production and for economic decision-making, an argument that needs to be pragmatic rather than ideological, I would suggest. By this I mean that the appropriate scale for the exercise of any particular authority is the scale at which it can be most efficiently exercised (meaning energy efficiency) to achieve the highest level of accountability and responsiveness. I have been helped in developing this pragmatic approach by the work of Alec Nove in his 1983 book *The Economics of Feasible Socialism*. The book was written in the era of disillusionment amongst Western socialists, who had seen their utopian dreams battered by the Hungarian and especially Prague uprisings and who now sought a pragmatic response. Nove's response is that we should seek a diversity of forms and structures, ranging from state-owned enterprises in strategic sectors, through worker co-operatives and small-scale, private enterprises, depending on the relevance or not of economies of scale and the preferences of those working in the sector.

In similar vein, Cumbers and McMaster (2012) have used the nationalisation of the UK banks as a framing argument to reopen the question of the role of the state in economic policy-making. They offer the example of the Danish wind-farm industry as one where political support and economic incentives were able to provide support for a deliberative form of policy-making that resulted in energy infrastructure that was both sustainable and owned by local communities. Between 1980 and 2007 the Danish wind-power industry went from zero to 15% of domestic generation: it now has 50% of the world market, with 85% of the turbines being owned by individuals or co-operatives. The speed of Denmark's transition to renewable electricity generation suggests that this might be a model to follow in our transition to lower-energy and lower-materials economies. They suggest that rapid change requires decentralisation as well as much wider democratic participation.

Figure 10.3 begins to map the different levels at which decision-making might operate for a range of different economic goods and services. It is based on a graphic from a government publication *Open Public Services* (Cabinet Office, 2011), designed to challenge the public ownership of schools and hospitals. I am using it here in a more open way, asking genuine questions about the ideal level of ownership and control for a range of national systems of provisioning. It is constitutive of the bioregional proposal that control over the three strategic resources of a green economy – land, energy and water – passes to the bioregion. These could be designated as belonging to the community of the bioregion, and some redistribution through a process of participatory decision-making could be expected in most bioregions. If a decision is made that some common resources should be managed or administered by private bodies, then this is likely to be via a non-profit arrangement (as in the Glas

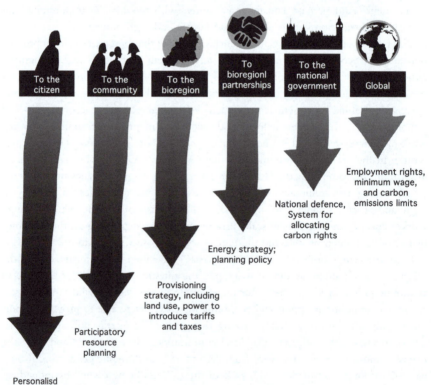

FIGURE 10.3 Appropriate scale for strategic provisioning of necessary resources
Source: Original artwork by Imogen Shaw based on the original in the DWP's publication *Open Public Services*.

Cymru model: see De Bruijn and Dicke, 2006), or in return for a tax to return the value received to the community at large (as is argued in the case of a Land Value Tax: see Wilcox, 2010). Once this reallocation is achieved the bioregional authority could be empowered to ensure provisioning for the community, responsive to local priorities about the competing uses of land for the production of food, fuel or material crops, and the consequent attainable lifestyles. Such decisions could be enforced through planning guidance backed up by land tax systems with variable rates to provide incentives to dedicate land to meet socially agreed priorities. At the community level, people would be encouraged and trained to engage in participatory planning, as discussed in Chapter 8, a practice used in Venezuela (see Azzellini, 2010).

Just as Morris saw the industrial era as a necessary stage for people to learn communitarian values, so the era of globalisation and ecological crisis is a necessary stage for us to recognise our interconnectedness as part of the planetary web of life. So while we claim our right to the resources of our bioregion, this does not allow us to consume excessively when this might threaten the global systems on which we all depend. Hence the basic norms of ecological citizenship should be established on a global and equitable basis, and within the framework of the Contraction and Convergence model outlined in Chapter 9. These would include limits on per-capita carbon emissions, as well as laws regarding employment rights and minimum wages. The GAST, or General Agreement on Sustainable Trade outlined in Chapter 9, would also be enshrined at this global level, within a democratised system of international institutions (see Cato and Mellor, 2012). The bioregion would also acquire the power to protect its own domestic production through systems of import and export tariffs and taxes, as well as the power to raises taxes on resource use and incomes. The need for co-operation between bioregions, especially in matters of planning land use and production, is included in the figure in terms of bioregional partnerships.

So what role would this leave for the nation-state? Its role would be largely one of ensuring the over-arching security within which its bioregions could flourish. This would include facilitating the development of inter-regional energy security policies, as well as allocating and policing carbon allowances. The traditional role of national defence remains at this level, although as provisioning boundaries shift, these military distinctions might also be expected to become more flexible. There may be a role for national governments in effecting redistribution between bioregions. A national welfare and fiscal system automatically brings about a certain level of redistribution, since more taxes are paid in wealthier regions whereas levels of benefits tend to be fixed nationally. The extent of redistribution has been estimated to range between 38% in France to 16% in the USA and Canada, with the UK lying in the middle at 26% (Mélitz and Zumer, 2002). In the UK, policies to adjust housing benefit payments according to local housing costs, and the undermining of national collective bargaining for public-sector workers, is beginning to undermine this implicit solidarity (DWP, 2010).

This issue of the relative wealth of regions will take on a different complexion in a bioregional economy. At present the South-East is the richest area of the UK, including the vast monetary wealth generated in the City of London, which has the highest GDHI (gross domestic household income) of any of the NUTS2[3] areas studied (ONS, 2011). However, if London were required to feed its own population from within its bioregional boundary this would prove impossible. Girardet (2006) has calculated that London currently has a resource footprint equivalent to 80% of the entire UK landmass (see Cato 2011a). Once regions have access only to their own resources the balance of wealth will shift dramatically and those w have lived through creating monetary wealth and using it to accumulate real resources will face a drastic fall in incomes. In contrast, bioregions such as Wales, with widespread availability of fertile land, water and renewable energy resources, will see their natural wealth revalued. So while there may well be a need for supra-bioregional redistribution, it will not follow the same paths as it does currently.

10.4 Transitional policy – transitional politics

This chapter and indeed this whole book is proposing such an entirely different paradigm for provisioning from the globalised capitalist economy of 2012 that, however appealing it may be, taking the first steps to reach it can be daunting. While we have a fairly clear vision of how a future bioregional economy could work, the very distance between this vision and the globalised, growth-driven and inequitable economy of today provides a challenge in terms of policy. When the world you are seeking is different in every respect, and based in a different philosophical paradigm, getting there cannot be a question of one step after another. A journey of a thousand miles may begin with a single step, but a journey to a new paradigm needs to begin with something more akin to the process of teleportation.

This is where the concept of a 'transition', popularised through the Transition Towns movement, can be useful. The Transition Towns began in the south-western UK in 2006 with the aim of mobilising communities to response to climate change (Merritt and Stubbs, 2012). It has provided a new narrative for citizens concerned about the lack of action by public and private sectors in response to climate change. Although its style and approach are new, to some extent it has built on initiatives and projects growing out of Local Agenda 21, a sustainability initiative emerging from the 1992 Rio Earth Summit, and it has rebranded these community sustainability initiatives in a new and exciting way (Cato and Hillier, 2010). It is also practical in its focus, leading Barry (2012) to label it as 'concrete utopian' as opposed to 'abstract utopian'. Experimentation and the 'reskilling' of local people in crafts such as darning and pickling are encouraged, in contrast to the focus on education that has dominated earlier environmentally focused citizen action groups. This practical focus and the emphasis in its economic strand on self-provisioning and community resilience could suggest it as a precursor of a wide move towards a bioregional approach to economic life, arising from the local community.

There are many examples of transitional practice towards the self-provisioning communities that would make up a bioregional economy. As 'barefoot economist' Max-Neef notes, it is easy for policy-makers to overlook these:

> When introducing in public the alternative paradigm for a more humane economy, as described in the previous chapter, people often ask how it would work in practice or how such principles could be articulated into policy. In other words, the concern is about implementation, but in fact such policies are already being implemented in hundreds of places. The point is that policy is generally perceived as a macro top-down process that makes the news, and not as a bottom-up grassroots phenomenon that remains hidden in the consciousness of those directly involved in the actions, and very rarely appears in the media.
>
> *(Max-Neef and Smith, 2011: 172)*

Notwithstanding these flourishing communities of hope, we need some significant changes in the framework of economic and political life in order to facilitate the transition to a sustainable economy. Given the renewed focus on land that infuses my arguments throughout, it is unsurprising that it is to this area that I turn first. Part of the solution is likely to lie in reversing the changes in land-tenure and -use patterns that marked the 'great transformation' from a feudal to a market economy. The enclosure of common land, removing the majority of the population from the basis of their provisioning activities, led to a range of social problems that have remained unsolved throughout the history of capitalism. Polanyi identifies three consequences of the growth of the market system specifically in the conversion of arable land to pasture to enable the growth of the wool trade: 'the destruction of a definite number of houses, the scrapping of a definite amount of employment, and the diminution of the supplies of locally available food provisions' (Polanyi, 1944: 40). Interestingly, all three of these problems continue today, with housing shortage, unemployment and food insecurity continuing to trouble policy-makers.

In one part of the UK, the country of Wales, an interesting social experiment is underway that may offer clues to a way to reverse this move away from locally based security to global insecurity. The clue lies in the One Planet Development section of the Wales Assembly Government's latest rural development policy. In July 2010 the Welsh government published a technical advice note (TAN 6) called 'Planning for Sustainable Rural Communities', which provided further detail of this policy. Self-reliant communities are accorded favourable treatment within planning law: 'Land based One Planet Developments located in the open countryside should, over a reasonable length of time (no more than 5 years), provide for the minimum needs of the inhabitants in terms of income, food, energy and waste assimilation'.[4] This is a radical approach to the rehabitation of the countryside, which could form a supportive environment for the transition to a bioregional economy.

The Welsh policy is in line with the One Planet Living approach pioneered by the London-based consultancy Bioregional. The approach has 10 principles, including zero approaches to waste and carbon together with sustainable policies for transport, materials and water, and two over-arching aims of 'equity and local economy' and 'health and happiness'. Two of the 10 points are particularly relevant to a bioregional approach to provisioning as proposed here: a focus on land use and wildlife; the prioritisation of local and sustainable food, and a bringing to the fore a focus on culture and heritage of the local area. As an example of the latter, Bioregional have revived the lavender fields of south London through a partnership between the local Downview prison, Sutton Council and the perfume manufacturer Yardley, launched in 1996. Since 2003 the project has been run by the social enterprise Carshalton Lavender. In the same year Bioregional began a larger-scale project on the North Surrey Downs. This has become a commercial venture called Mayfield Lavender, which is reviving a cottage industry that flourished 100 years ago. This project exemplifies the bioregional emphasis on local connection between people, land, and production. Perhaps this is best demonstrated by the three acres of lavender planted at a local allotment site, which is available for local people to 'pick their own' at an annual harvesting event held on the last weekend in July.

Another practical manifestation of this desire for relocalisation can be found in the degrowth movement (Schneider *et al.*, 2010), whose 'objectives are to have an economy that sustainably fulfils the food, health, education and housing needs for everybody' (Kallis *et al.*, 2009: 23). While much of the talk of degrowth is still at the level of theory (Latouche, 2009), it finds its practical expression in movements to foreground quality and quantity of life rather than material excess, of which the Slow Food movement is perhaps the best known. The focus of the movement on pleasure rather than restraint offers a positive vision of post-growth consumption to challenge the conventional stereotype of the hair-shirted environmentalist (Sassatelli and Davolio, 2010).

There is also some recognition of the need for local political authorities to respond to the potential food insecurity that might result from rapidly changing climatic patterns and over-reliance on extended supply chains. London has taken a prominent role, under the leadership of then Mayor and Deputy-Mayor: Ken Livingstone and Jenny Jones, respectively. In spite of a change of democratic authority the process is being sustained, with increased emphasis on food production and food security (Reynolds, 2009). Other cities such as Bristol and Brighton are also developing strategies that involve local people growing their own food in gardens and on allotments, as well as exploring the scope for shortening supply chains and regenerating cities through the use of their land for labour-intensive food production.

Food has provided a central activity for the many Transition Towns, and several have also created community currencies as a means of underpinning local economic self-reliance. Totnes as the first to originate a new circulating currency (as opposed to time banks or electronic LETS systems). North (2010) details these small-scale experiments aimed at increasing the velocity of circulation of local money and thus underpinning local production and exchange. All those arising in Transition Towns have struggled to compete with the pound sterling, and yet they have emancipated their home communities from the notion that banks create money, and led them to see money as a genuine means of exchange that responds to local productive energies, rather than a powerful force that arises outside their community and extracts its value. Just as the craftsmen I celebrated in Chapter 6 struggle to compete with the wage rates of Chinese workers, these currencies struggle to survive in the battle with their global competitors, and a criticism often made of the Transition communities is that they are not sufficiently political in their analysis (Trapese, 2008). The Transition Movement needs to take seriously the need for significant changes in the global framework within which local economies operate. Examples were given in Chapter 9, in terms of radical reorganisation of the system of global trade. Other suggestions made in Chapter 8 concerned the reclaiming of rights over their resources by local communities; we might also add the need for national legislation to prioritise the tax-raising powers of local, rather than central, government.

Without a politico-economic analysis, the activities of communities such as the Transition Towns can seem homespun, fantastical even. It is perhaps the inevitable consequence of taking a single step towards a new paradigm. But perhaps the most important of these initiatives gain their significance from their potential to operate as transitional demands, in Trotsky's meaning of demands that, while appearing mainstream in the context of the existing paradigm, could – if they were put into operation on a wider basis – create the conditions for the new paradigm to flourish (Trotsky, 1938). We might use as an example the demand for land for growing food. In the context of climate change this seems a mild enough request, and one that is a legal right as a result of the Smallholdings and Allotments Act 1908.[5] However, if all the inhabitants of even a single city made this demand, it would raise questions about land ownership that would challenge the existing political order of private ownership, and would undermine the market system of food production for profit. They may thus be the means of transcending one worldview and replacing it with another: transition in praxis as well as in practice.

10.5. Conclusion: a rural idyll for all?

The appeal of the small, rural community is a powerful one. It is remarkable how many of those who have achieved wealth and power as a result of their encouragement of the globalisation of economic systems choose for themselves to live in the leafy villages of England – or at least spend weekends there after a Friday night drive in the four-by-four. When researching the Chipping Norton commons I was amazed to discover that petrol-head and scourge of the green movement Jeremy Clarkson lives nearby, far from the madding crowd for whom he created his celebrity persona.[6] For many the rural idyll is not unwelcome but rather, they think, unattainable. Part of the purpose of the bioregional economy proposal is to counter this poverty of imagination: to propose the ideal life that many strive for, where we can have responsive and mutually reinforcing communities and where our relationship to the land can be fruitful and strong.

William Morris was not afraid to dream of such a utopia, and even to imagine the disappearance of the dark satanic mills that surrounded him and their replacement with productive fields and workshops:

> We turned away from the river at once, and were soon in the main road that runs through Hammersmith. But I should have had no guess as to where I was, if I had not started from the waterside; for King Street was gone, and the

highway ran through wide sunny meadows and garden-like tillage … There
were houses about, some on the road, some amongst the fields with pleasant
lanes leading down to them, and each surrounded by a teeming garden. They
were all pretty in design, and as solid as might be, but countrified in appearance,
like yeoman's dwellings.

(Morris, 1890/2008: 21)

Morris's own idyllic home at Kelmscott Manor was not far from the Chipping
Norton that now provides escape for our power-brokers. However, rather than an
escape from the *hoi poloi*, or a green and pleasant life for himself provided by the
labour of those who lived in poverty in his own backyard or in the global backyard,
Morris imagined rural peace and prosperity for all. This is a dream that, in spite of the
appeal of technology, refuses to die. This is, I would argue, because we are creatures
of place and creatures of the land, and without a clear connection with a place in
space we experience a sense of loss that no amount of material possessions can heal:
'In contrast to the apparently unlimited, global character of the technologically
mediated world, the sensuous world – the world of our direct unmediated interactions – is always local' (Abram, 1996: 266).

In a way that I believe is appropriate to a book whose central message is about
cultural as well as geographical embedding, I have self-consciously rooted my argument within my own national and bioregional boundary. However, as I have sought
to argue elsewhere, I do not believe that it is a narrow or parochial vision. Hence I
would like to end with a quotation from the culture that is rapidly becoming the
apotheosis of global industrial success. Here is fifth-century BCE philosopher Lao-Tzu's
prescription for a happy human life:

Let your community be small, with only a few people;
Keep tools in abundance, but do not depend upon them;
Appreciate your life and be content with your home;
Sail boats and ride horses, but don't go too far;
Keep weapons and armour, but do not employ them;
Let everyone read and write,
Eat well and make beautiful things.
Live peacefully and delight in your own society;
Dwell within cock-crow of your neighbours,
But maintain your independence from them.

('Utopia', verse 80 of the *Dao de Jing*)

As the twentieth-century saying goes: it's not rocket science.

11

LIVING THE FULL CIRCLE OF LIFE

I don't want to achieve immortality through my work; I want to achieve it through not dying.

Woody Allen

The purpose of this book is to create the vision of a life lived differently, a life where economic growth, competition and material consumption are replaced as the central objectives of society by a renewed sense of spiritual meaning, and social and environmental harmony. In short, the bioregional economy as described offers a life in which quality replaces quantity as the driving force of the economic system. As described by Dobson, this is an ecologically focused alternative to the techno-scientific future as currently conceived:

> While most post-industrial futures revolve around high-growth, high-technology, expanding services, greater leisure, and satisfaction conceived in material terms, ecologism's post-industrial society questions growth and technology, and suggests that the Good Life will involve more work and fewer material objects.
>
> *(Dobson, 2007: 189)*

The book is ambitious in questioning most of the underpinning assumptions of our economic life as currently structured. While I do not apologise for this, I am aware of the fact that I have left aside many important questions, some because I have not found space for them and some because I feel I do not have the expertise to answer them. One area that I feel has been particularly cursorily treated is that of electronic production and internet communications. This is the area where most young people come alive and, while it should not become a substitute for human relationships, it can obviously offer much that can facilitate a transition to sustainable consumption patterns. The task of redesigning the world of the internet so that, rather than stimulating the need for travel, it removes such a need; for example, through improvements in systems for teleconferencing and virtual meetings, is an urgent task. This way the breadth and scope of knowledge currently offered by the internet can be made available within a low-energy framework; so the task is an important one, but one for which I do not myself have sufficient knowledge. Although I have touched on ways to reduce the extent of production of technological goods in Chapter 9, and in Chapter 7 I have described how changing the structure of our economy will remove the need for relentless redesign and repurchase of cars, computers, TVs and the like, this is another area where my aspiration is greater than my knowledge. I hope that others, younger and better qualified than me, will be sufficiently inspired by the wider bioregional vision, to take up this challenge.

In this concluding chapter I will explore the implication of shifting the focus in the bioregional economy towards quality rather than the quantity of life. In the final section I develop the notion of 'full-circle living' to encapsulate a way of living that accepts the limited nature of our tenure on life and encourages us to live what we have more fully. To live life in balance with nature and to acknowledges death as an intrinsic part of life: this requires a fundamental change in the dominant mind-set, which is perhaps the first step in the transition towards a bioregional future. I discuss how we might begin to think differently in Section 11.2. In Section 11.3 I reprise some of the arguments made in the third part of this book, concerning the way in which a limited and locally based economy will require a different relationship with our local places. Then in Section 11.4 I tackle the big questions: those of life and death, and attempt to re-evaluate the balance between quantity and quality of life. First, in Section 11.1, I consider the urgent need for the human species to reinhabit our world, unpicking the colonial mentality (in terms of other peoples and other species) that underlies current attitudes to economic life. What I call 'falling in love with your native soil' is constitutive of the bioregional worldview and can offer a fulfilment deeper and more satisfying than material consumption.

11.1. Falling in love with your native soil

Throughout this book I have attempted to include the perspectives of people distant from us in time and space who have expressed their identity as people of the land. During my own explorations of what this phrase might mean I have been astonished by how prevalent such an understanding is amongst human societies that are in many superficial ways entirely different. The bioregional economy assumes that we have much to learn from this conception of human life as intrinsically relational, and that we can learn again to find our place within a community of diverse creatures and within an ecosystem that is complex and diverse.

The price we will pay for taking our place amongst equals will be the abandonment of a sense of superiority, a relinquishing of the God-given right to dominion that we have assumed for several millennia. In environmentalist critiques, an attitude of dominion is said to arise as a result of the Biblical command to 'fill the earth and subdue it; and have dominion over the fish of the sea and over the birds of the air and over every living thing that moves upon the earth' (Gen. 1:28). It implies a superior and separate position for the human animal, made in the image of God, and given the right – or perhaps even the duty – to assume authority over the earth and its creatures. In some fundamentalist interpretations this requires the denial of ecological crisis, or even its acceleration to hasten the second coming and eternal heavenly bliss. While few outside the US evangelical community would be that extreme, the argument is that this approach has dominated the modern scientifico-technical paradigm, displacing a more organic and earth-centred understanding of our place in the world (Merchant, 1980).

A bioregional approach to life means re-inhabiting our world, knowing our way around the world, not in the sense of a weekend break in St. Petersburg and a winter yoga retreat in Hawaii, but rather by recreating an intimate relationship with our own backyard. As I argued in Chapter 7, an important route to such a reconnection and a deeper knowledge of the abundance that our bioregion has to offer can be through establishing and cherishing a new ethic of consumption. The local food and slow food movements and the recent enthusiasm for foraging and for enjoying wild and seasonal foods are all encouraging signs that this sort of reconnection is already underway. Similarly, projects to build experiential learning into environmental education support the idea of reconnection as a physical process (Cato and Myers, 2010).

I am writing this book at a time of great insecurity and fundamental change: the social and economic contract that we have lived with since the 'great transformation' of the late eighteenth century is being questioned. The economic dominance of Europe is waning and the strategies we have used to ensure secure livelihoods are being rapidly undermined. The shift in the balance of economic power away from Europe and towards the countries of the East and South could push us into an aggressive, appropriative response. Bioregional thinking suggests a different way: a way of reappraising what we really value and recreating a utopian future that begins with the local, because the costs of the global competition are too high and because it does not serve the interests of the majority very well.

This is not a proposal recommending insularity or selfishness: in fact the reverse. It is not surprising that the proposal for 'one-planet living' discussed in Chapter 9 has come from an organisation called Bioregional. If we are to recognise our place within a global society then we need to ensure that we do not consume more than a fair share of resources, and a bioregional approach to provisioning enables us to keep within those limits. It is not a proposal that we create a fortress Britain or a fortress Europe and ignore the needs of those in the poorer countries of the global South; rather that we propose for all the earth's inhabitants an economic policy based around the same sense of local embedding and thrifty and respectful use of resources that we prove ourselves capable of following. I am making the novel proposal that we, the Europeans who have had all the material and educational advantages, begin to set an example that is not about technology or science, but rather about insight and wisdom.

11.2. Learning to be reasonable

Even those of us who have enjoyed the benefits of an excellent post-Enlightenment education and consider ourselves experts in ratiocination should be aware of our ability to project our pre-existing understandings onto our observations. Hale reports a tart remark from Marx that should give all academics pause for thought:

> Having just read On the Origin of Species (1859), Karl Marx was prompted to write to Friedrich Engels regarding the ideological assumptions at the heart of Darwin's work: 'It is remarkable how Darwin rediscovered, among the beasts and plants, the society of England with its division of labor, competition, opening up of new markets, "inventions", and Malthusian "struggle for existence"'.
>
> *(Hale, 2003: 253)*

I offer this quotation to remind us that, in spite of scientific advancement, we all still have a tendency to see the world as we believe it to be. While this requires us to accept a little intellectual humility, it also offers great hope, because if we can begin to believe the world is different, then we have taken the first step to making it so.

After two centuries of predominance, the view of the world invented by the English classical economists that is parodied by Marx is running out of steam. The superiority we have claimed for the system of market competition, pioneered in England and later exported under the banner of 'free trade' (and sometimes at the point of a gun), is no longer assured. On the one side, the countries that were once our colonies have seen through our rhetoric and learned to out-compete us. On the other side, the earth, which was the exploited victim of this economic system in a more fundamental sense than the colonised peoples of the lands we conquered, has been sickened and wounded to such a degree that we are undermining our own strategy of exploitation.

If we truly are *Homo sapiens* then we need to use our powers of reason to do more than simply catalogue our own demise; actually to think our way into a different relationship with the earth and find a different answer to the question of what life is for if not the accumulation of material possessions at the earth's expense. Economists have shown themselves to be particularly inadequate to this task, seeking to misrepresent the nature of our relationship with the earth and to use the power of reason to justify an economic system that is not only ecologically destructive but also unjust: 'The history of scholarly economic thought can be understood as a process of boundary keeping, a process of rationalising argument that either ignored entirely or entailed gross simplifications about the natural world and broader questions of right and wrong' (Kallis *et al.*, 2009: 19).

The pseudo-science of economics may be the clearest and most immediate failure, but across the scientific disciplines we see the hubris of the scientifico-technical paradigm (Koppa, 2011). Dawkins presents a splendid example, in his attempt to attack God while creating a God in his own image: the Godhead of the scientist. Elsewhere, in a Swiss laboratory a mere 25 miles from where Mary Shelley wrote *Frankenstein*, the scientists of CERN have invested $9bn (McSmith, 2008) in seeking what has been dubbed the 'God particle'. Both of these are glaring examples of the category error perhaps most neatly exemplified by Galton's (1872) essay on 'A scientific exploration into the efficacy of prayer'.

A similar criticism has been made of Dawkins's discovery of the 'selfish gene', the central concept of the pseudo-science of socio-biology, which, as Midgley notes, is despised by geneticists themselves. Her own verdict is hardly more respectful. Rather than a rejection of religion she finds in the writings of the sociobiologists the worship of a very particular deity: power:

> Sociobiology is a false light because it is 'reductive' in the sense of ruling out other enquiries, of imposing its own chosen model as the only norm ... To balance the austere renunciation of religious ideas and of a normal view of human standing in the biosphere, which Wilson and Dawkins denounce, they offer us a mystique of power, various indeed but evidently, from the fervent tone which celebrates it, none the less exciting for that.
>
> *(Midgley, 1985/2002: 154)*

It is beyond the scope of this book to provide an analysis of how we think and how we come to know what we know, but writing from a discipline in which the past few years have been a demonstration of the revenge of the unknown unknowns, I cannot avoid the conclusion that such a consideration does merit some attention. The intellectual world we inhabit was transformed by the Enlightenment, and the comfortable and sophisticated lives we enjoy would have been impossible without that revolution in the way we both related to the natural world and valued the process of our own minds.

According to Porter (1990) the Enlightenment represented a shift in power in the relationship between the spiritual and the rational, between the intellect and the soul, and between man and nature. Before the period of intellectual upheaval thus labelled, European intellectuals undertook their thinking within an Aristotelian framework that had remained unchanged for 2,000 years. According to this schema:

> Theory (episteme or scientia) was certain knowledge based on the logical syllogism and geometrical demonstration. Practice (praxis or experientia), on the other hand, could be of two kinds – things done and things made. Things done were comprised of human knowledge such as history, politics, ethics, and economics. Praxis was studied in the particular (by collection of experiences); it could not be formed into a deductive system, and thus was not as certain as theory. The other type of practice was comprised of things made, or techne, that involved bodily labour. Techne had nothing to do with certainty but instead was the lowly knowledge of how to make things or produce effects, practice by animals, slaves and craftspeople.
>
> *(Smith, 2004: 17)*

The revolutionary thought that launched the huge surge in knowledge that the Enlightenment represented was that we should learn by focusing on the material. In medicine this led to anatomy and in chemistry to the division of the world of matter into a table of elements and ultimately the division of those elements themselves. By analysing and subdividing the physical, man might learn the secrets of nature and thence manipulate natural systems to achieve his ends.

Nature lost her place as a source of mystery and awe and became subject to dissection and experimentation. The knowledge discovered through this new 'scientific method' was then exploited by the new economic methods that followed rapidly in its wake. With reference to the link between the growth of London's City and the role of the Royal Society in propagating a scientific approach to all aspects of life, Lewis Mumford wrote that, 'The power that was science and the power that was money were, in the final analysis, the same kind of power: the power of abstraction, measurement, quantification' (Mumford, 1934/1963: 25). Through this process of abstraction and quantification we lost what Feyerabend (2001) refers to as the abundance of nature, together with the wealth that comes from ambiguity and uncertainty. The need for taxonomies and categorisation, while supremely effective in enabling us to manipulate nature for our own ends, reduced the inherent complexity of natural systems and thus limited our understanding of the sacred whole.

Greens are often wrongly criticised as being anti-science or dismissed as latterday Luddites when, in reality, our knowledge of the ecological crisis is derived from scientific analysis, much more than from our everyday experience. Greens' critique, rather, is of the dominance of the one form of scientifico-technical knowledge to the exclusion of others, and, more fundamentally, of the dominance of reason to the exclusion of other ways of knowing. The ecological crisis is, as identified by Plumwood (2001), at least in part a crisis of reason. The urge to leave behind the superstition of the medieval world ushered in an era of knowledge without responsibility and without humility. The bioregional worldview, by contrast, sees the basis of real knowledge as physically embedded. This is not to suggest that abandonment of the knowledge that we have acquired (we are not seeking, as is often charged, to 'uninvent the atomic bomb' or to 'go back to the horse and cart'), but rather to accept that the pendulum has swung too far in the direction of the reductive, subdivision of reality and needs to move back towards seeing the wood as well as the trees. In short, we need to relearn a view of reality that is inherently relational:

> This seems true not only of culture, but also of knowledge, person, nature, performance and other terms found in academic critical vocabularies. Equally it seems applicable not only to anthropology but to other ethnological and phenomenological disciplines, as well as to philosophers and scientists interested in consciousness, embodiment and other issues. Placing humans within a community of persons rather than at its peak challenges claims to human uniqueness (whether expressed in religious, 'creationist' or scientific, 'evolutionist', discourse).
>
> *(Harvey, 2005: xix)*

To support the calls from Feyerabend and others for a balancing of scientific and rationalist argument with an acceptance of the importance of intuitive understandings and even spiritual values is an essential part of the reordering of our relationship with nature. We might hope that particularly in the field of economics, which has been most eager to claim its status as a science and where hubris has been most clearly evident in recent years, this call for widening the nature of study will be heard most clearly.

11.3. Learning to know our place

In earlier chapters I have critiqued the idea of the spaceless, weightless economy, which is found unrealistic and undermining of a sustainable future. But where did the temptation arise for us to divorce our identity from our physical selves and the places they inhabit? For Abram, the loss of a direct relationship with nature resulted from the development of literary culture:

> We may better comprehend this curious development – the withdrawal of mind from sensible nature and its progressive incarceration in the human skull – by considering that every human language secretes a kind of perceptual boundary that hovers, like a translucent veil, between those who speak that language and the sensuous terrain they inhabit. As we grow into a particular culture or language, we implicitly begin to structure our sensory contact with the earth that surround us in a particular manner, paying attention to certain phenomena while ignoring others, differentiating textures, tastes, and tones in accordance with the verbal contrasts contained in the language. We simply cannot take our place within any community of human speakers without ordering our sensations in a common manner, and without thereby limiting our spontaneous access to the wild world that surrounds us.
>
> *(Abram, 1996: 255)*

While living with a connected sense of oneself in place is far distant from the experience of a modern, intellectual person, it survives in the lived practice of the remaining cultures which are collected under the anthropological term 'animism'. According to Harvey (2005: xvii), 'Animisms are theories, discourses and practices of relationship, of living well, of realising more fully what it means to be a person, and a human person, in the company of other persons, not all of whom are human but all of whom are worthy of respect'. While this worldview might be hard for many rationalists and academics to stomach, it does hint at a route out of our impasse in terms of the rebalancing of concepts such as dominion and reverence, which find a place in discussions of our place in the natural order in the world's religions, but are anathema to the discourse of science.

Our culture admires the material, and particularly those who triumph over material constraint: in the case of Britain I offer as evidence the national idolisation of Isambard Kingdom Brunel, who achieved second place in a 2002 poll of the Greatest Britons (BBC, 2002). The question of why we admire the Brunels, father and son, is instructive in terms of our project to reinhabit our world in a way that permits our continued flourishing as a species. They were, after all, dedicated to finding ways of thwarting nature at every turn in order to achieve man's superior project and can be made to stand as iconic representative of the nineteenth-century hubris. Sennett tells the tale of their war with nature: 'The Brunels treated natural resistance as their enemy, and tried to defeat it'. Their 1826 project to build a road tunnel under the Thames resulted in the deaths of several miners and serious injury to the younger Brunel. His confidence was undimmed: 'The picture many people know of him is a photograph in which he poses, cigar in hand, top hat tipped back, slightly crouching as if ready to spring, against a background of massive chains hanging from the great iron-sided ship he created. It is the image of a heroic fighter, a conqueror, overcoming whatever stands in his path. But in his case, aggressive combat proved inefficient' (Sennett, 2008: 216–17). Brunel's battles with nature met with mixed success, his early death from a stroke at just 53 being his worst outcome. My purpose here is not to challenge his achievements in civil engineering but to question a culture that idealises a man whose approach to nature was one of conquest rather than accommodation.

What a contrast to the medieval world that the modern scientifically informed paradigm replaced and where, 'For medieval people, reality consisted in the supernatural realm while the material world was transient and insubstantial' (Sale, 1991: 47). Again, I would not wish readers to infer that I am proposing a return to a world where threats of damnation from an overdressed clergyman could achieve instant and supine submission. Rather, I hope to indicate how plastic is our human understanding of our place in the world, and how far it has changed in the past five or six centuries, a period that is the mere twinkling of an eye in evolutionary terms.

Even when we can begin to learn some respect for nature, we characterise our relationship as grateful employer, as implied by the concept of 'ecosystem services'. Or else we create a medical model of Gaia, the sickly patient whom medical science can heal:

> This medical imagery at once made it much easier for scientists to accept the notion of Gaia. When the point is put in medical terms, they begin to find it plausible that the earth does indeed in some way function as an organic whole, that its climate and oceans work together with living things to maintain a normal balance, and that what gravely upsets any part of the system is liable to upset others. They can see that, for such a whole, the notion of health is really quite suitable. And of course they find the patient Gaia, lying in bed and politely awaiting attention, much less threatening than that scandalous pagan goddess.
>
> *(Midgley, 2001: 181)*

Perhaps the reason for addressing the ecological crisis as a medical problem is that it is in medicine that we have made the most impressive advances in our ability to control our inner natures and the relationship between our bodies and the natural world. Medicine has moved beyond the healing of sickness to become, in the slogan of a German pharmaceutical company, 'Science for a better life'. As we will see in the following section, this has impacted significantly on our understanding of the boundaries of a human life, and has supported our modernist attempts to sequester and deny the power of death, or the role of death as a part of life.

Medical management of life has extended in numerous directions: drugs can help us to deal with a range of social problems, which are now redefined as medical problems, including shyness, grief, boredom, anxiety and so on: a process known as 'medicalization' (Conrad 1992; 2005). Even the social aspects of the problem of impotence can be ignored and are not enquired into before Viagra is prescribed. The medical 'management' of the female hormone cycle is, to date, the greatest example of the ability of science to take control over matters of life and death. It provides an example of the great benefits and also the hubristic nature of the modern approach to medicine. The contraceptive pill was developed in 1952 and will celebrate its half-century the year this book is published (Chadwick *et al.*, 2012). Becoming widely prescribed through the 1960s, it offered women an escape from the fear of constant pregnancy, and its dangerous consequences. The development of this easy and cheap contraceptive was hailed as a salvation for women and it has been one of the most widely taken drugs of all time; the social consequences of the possibility of sexual activity between men and women without the possibility of pregnancy was less widely discussed, and are generally framed in terms of women's liberation – to join their male colleagues in the workplace.

11.4. The matters of life and death

Having started at the beginning and worked our way through an exploration of an economy for life, we now reach the end: the question of death, and the need to face this honestly and boldly. In his studies of traditional, reciprocal economies Polanyi identified a changed relationship to death as a key characteristic of the transformation to a market economy. In traditional economies that he had studied, Polanyi found that:

> Man accepted the reality of death and built the meaning of his bodily life upon it. He resigned himself to the truth that he had a soul to lose and that there was worse than death, and founded his freedom upon it. He resigned himself, in our time, to the reality of society which means the end of that freedom. But, again, life springs from ultimate resignation. Uncomplaining acceptance of the reality of society gives man indomitable courage and strength to remove all removable injustice and unfreedom.
>
> *(Polanyi, 1944: 268)*

Giddens's identification of the sequestration of aspects of reality that remind us too closely of our less exalted, more earth-bound natures has already been discussed in connection with our unwillingness to admit the vulnerability of our provisioning strategies. According to Willmott (2000), 'A distinguishing feature of modernity, Giddens (1991: 156) argues, is its "purchasing" of ontological security through institutions and routines that protect us from direct contact with madness, criminality, sexuality, nature and death'. Consideration of death is particularly unwelcome in our everyday lives because of its ability to 'render absurd and futile, the projects and the institutions that endow lives with meaning and value' (Willmott, 2000: 650). The modern person is unable to maintain a sense of a dignified existence in the face of his own imminent annihilation.

In his account of the unsustainability of our present approach to life (and death) Barry sees the refusal to allow death to be part of our everyday reality as a symptom of our cultural rejection of vulnerability. He quotes Sontag's (2001) judgement of modern culture's designation of death as an 'offensively meaningless event'. Barry writes that:

> To be modern is to defy death, to live in a world where illness has been if not eradicated, then made curable, and if not curable then to be hidden away ... death, pain and illness are all part of the human condition. They are meaningful and meaning-imparting, constitutive elements of what it means to be human. Therefore, there does seem to be something inherently wrong when a culture or an individual persists in avoiding according these their proper place in the human experience. Equally wrong is an attitude which regards them with such unmitigated and unqualified horror that we respond with an unhealthy denial of these features.

For Barry, the taboo that we have placed on death is evidence of our cultural inability to accept our own vulnerability and, more widely, our place in a natural order within which our powers – like our physical existence itself – are limited. Again we find a contrast in the world-view of traditional societies, such as the Maori: 'In discussing "animism" with several Maori scholars I have been challenged to explain why anyone would ever consider separating "life" from its seeming opposites (death and inanimation in particular)' (Harvey, 2006: 54).

In Chapter 3 I discussed how the move from a cyclical to a linear view of time has radically changed our relationship with the earth and with life itself. This is surely part of the explanation for our clinging to life, since death is literally the end of the line, a point of no return, the ultimate destination of a pointless and futile existence. How differently we might perceive death if it were part of a full circle of life, if we could see ourselves becoming ancestors, and returning to our mother, the earth. Some of the oldest temple complexes in the world, those at Ggantija in Gozo, Malta, seem to have been constructed in the shape of the goddess figurines that also abound at the site, leading to the hotly contested idea that they represent the idea of mother earth welcoming the dead back into her womb (Fleming, 1969). If this religious imagery is too much for the more scientific amongst you, I am sure that Richard Dawkins would be able to provide a more scientific version of a similar story, focusing on the potential of the human cadaver to offer a welcome supply of nutrients to a range of biological life-forms.

Dobson (2007: 184) summarises ecofeminist Mary Mellor's discussion of how a more ecologically embedded life would change our attitude to time:

According to Mellor's version of materialist ecofeminism, women have a special relationship with what she calls 'biological' or 'ecological' time. She defines these as follows: 'Ecological time is the pace of ecological sustainability for non-human nature. Biological time represents the life-cycle and pace of bodily replenishment for human beings' (1997: 189). In the biological realm, women undertake usually unacknowledged work related to the reproduction of human life, and in the ecological realm – particularly in subsistence societies – they are often responsible for nurturing life from the land and for ensuring its sustainability.

Willmott, too, connects the modernist project of the sequestration of death and the denial of our earth-bound reality as a source of tension and dis-ease. The ontological and existential anxieties we suffer, he argues, 'are not universal, or endemic, to the human condition but, instead, are expressions of the socially organized privileging of a separation between wo/man and world. As this separation occurs, the sense of the self as an independent entity becomes institutionalized and largely taken-for-granted' (Willmott, 2000: 657). The perception of oneself as an individual, rather than oneself as part of a community of humans and other species, gives rise to a form of existential angst that invalidates any possibility of a meaningful existence as a modern, cultured person.

If the pharmaceutical industry conceives of itself as harnessing science in service of a better life, then nowhere is this more evident than in extreme old age, where the aim appears to be extending life indefinitely. Rather than a natural part of human existence, death is reframed as a medical failure, even when it occurs at an age when quality of life has severely diminished and which would have been extremely unusual even a century ago. Paradoxically, in parallel with the grasping after ever more life and record rates of life expectancy, the quality of life for the very old is often very poor. In fiscal terms, those in late middle age who are expecting pensions to support an acceptable lifestyle as their lives extend are portrayed as threatening social terrorists, holding the demographic timebomb. In the 1960s Paul Ehrlich's *Population Bomb* was held by the young, and especially the young in poorer countries. Today the discussion of population is more likely to be a couched in demographic terms: an imbalance in our country between different age groups. At the level of tabloid discussion, population is not a problem of the young having too many children, but of the old refusing to die.[1]

Those members of our community born into the post-war years of security and plenty have always been a noisy generation and, as they reach their old age and death, it is unsurprising that they are bringing to the fore discussion about how to grow old without losing power and how to make a decent end. This is surely where we must place the discussion around voluntary euthanasia, or its managerialised cousin 'assisted dying'. While the greatest profits are made from those who submit to the machinery and the drugs, those who spend what Charles II called 'an unconscionable time a-dying', the baby boomers appear to be seeking a different route, where they maintain their strident self-confidence to the end. The report from the Commission on Assisted Dying, with its recommendation to reach a humane consensus around the right of everybody to choose the time and manner of the death, is the latest emanation from this debate (Demos, 2012).

A research study commission by the UK-based charity Help the Hospices asked some difficult questions about what a good death might be. From their conversations with those approaching death they discovered, unsurprisingly, that 'Most of what we most value in life – love, friendship, respect, recognition, care – comes from relationships' (Leadbetter and Garber, 2010: 83). Sadly, for many in highly developed societies today, death is medicalised, the importance of relationship being diminished and replaced with expensive machinery and isolation. This may be part of the reason we fear the process of dying so much: because in it we lose what we value most about life.

The authors of the report commend by way of contrast the system of palliative care in the Indian state of Kerala, which is highly social and community-based. It relies on the involvement of the friends and family of the liminal person, where this is available. They conclude:

> Our research suggests that further extending the lifespan would be a mistake unless we can provide people with much better quality of life at the end of life. The goal for the twenty-first century should be to improve quality of life, learning to live well, including at the very end of life: quality should become more important than further quantity; better years rather than more years. Death is not a failure. Far from it – the prospect of death, the point beyond which our reputations are irrevocable and personal reparations are impossible, helps us understand what makes life worth living, what we owe to others and hope for them.
>
> *(Leadbetter and Garber, 2010: 84)*

From a perspective of ecological responsibility one can only echo 'Amen' to this sentiment.

11.5. Conclusion: living the full circle

At the same time that we acknowledge the reality of death as a rightful part of life, we should restore the true value to life. The discussion of the financialisation of society draws attention to how, in a world where money is accorded supreme value, the value of all other aspects of life is diminished (Leyshon and Thrift, 2007). In a bioregional economy, life becomes more real, more immediate, more fleshly. Hence we accept our human vulnerabilities and the inevitability of our death, but rather than undermining the quality of our life this actually enhances it. This goes beyond the shallow recognition of the need to 'seize the day', towards an approach to life that is full-bodied and hot-blooded. This is what I mean by 'living the full circle of life'.

For all our technology and the vertiginous nature of our consumption, we live mean lives. In his last book, the great commentator on twentieth-century life Ivan Illich bemoaned the loss of our senses, by which he did not mean that we had taken leave of our senses – although he might have done – but that we have lost much of the sensory richness our ancestors enjoyed. He gives as an example that 'Dozens of words expressing the nuances of perception have fallen into disuse. In terms of the sense of smell, the victims of this process have been enumerated: of the 150 German words that indicated variations on smell that were used by the contemporaries of Durer, only 32 are still in use today' (Illich, 2004: 197).

And for all our presumption of what Val Plumwood has called a 'mastery over nature' we are still thoroughly dependent on the productivity and cycles of the natural world. We take the phrase 24/7 to be an expression of our hubristic conquest of time, of being a civilisation that never sleeps. In reality, however, it demonstrates precisely the reverse. To choose a year of seven-day weeks and 24-hour days is an attempt to force some kind of uniformity on the free-flowing pattern of seasons. The non-Gregorian calendars (such as the Hebrew and Chinese calendars) combine lunar and solar cycles, while the Islamic calendar follows the lunar cycle precisely, meaning that the months do not match the seasons (Steel, 2001). The need in the Gregorian calendar for an intercalary day every four years demonstrates the problem of trying to accommodate the cycle of the moon with the cycle of the sun, and provides further evidence of nature's refusal to fit within the rational, orderly systems through which we choose to arrange our lives. And this is to say nothing of the position of Easter: a festival whose ability to retain its meandering pattern through our spring is the most cheering vestige of a time when seasons ruled our lives.

As well as knowing our place in this celestial sense, the proposal of a bioregional economy means finding our place here on earth. Theoretically it demands the reintroduction of place into political economy; personally it is about learning about our place in the world and in our local landscape. Throughout the book I have discussed how the relearning of ourselves in relationship with our local places might impact on the understanding of political economy. In this chapter I have argued how a relearning of ourselves in place and in relationship with each other might support our ability to accept spatial and temporal boundaries.

I have made it clear throughout this book that I consider the establishment of a closer connection with our local natural environment to be constitutive of a sustainable society, and would suggest that, while Shakespeare belongs to my part of the world, everybody finds their own local place to be a 'blessed plot'. However, I would argue that the precise piece of the globe where I am writing this has a particular responsibility for the economic system that now dominates the world, and therefore for the environmental destruction it has trailed in its wake. According to Polanyi:

> Market society was born in England – yet it was on the Continent that its weaknesses engendered the most tragic complications. In order to comprehend German fascism, we must revert to Ricardian England. The nineteenth century, as cannot be overemphasized, was England's century. The Industrial Revolution was an English event. Market economy, free trade, the gold standard were English inventions. These institutions broke down in the twenties everywhere – in Germany, Italy, or Austria the event was merely more

political and more dramatic. But whatever the scenery and the temperature of the final episodes, the long-run factors which wrecked that civilization should be studied in the birthplace of the Industrial Revolution, England.

(Polanyi, 1944: 32)

It is difficult, when reading the words of an exiled Hungarian about one's home country, not to experience an intense mixture of pride and revulsion. Just as London offers a tale of two cities, one a place of ingenuity, compassion and cultural diversity, the other the origin of financial exploitation and colonial oppression, so the economic history of England places on its academics and intellectuals a peculiar authority matched by a particular responsibility. For while our elites and their apologists created the market system that has oppressed millions and devastated the planet, their radical opponents inspired democratic revolutions and the social responsibility for universal welfare. The courage to imagine better futures is bred in the bone in our country, as truly as is the engineering imagination of which we are so proud.

If you have stayed with me this far I would guess that you are inspired by their example; and game for a challenge. As I have said repeatedly throughout this book, the bioregional economy is my proposal for a 'low carbon high life', to quote the slogan of Transition Stroud: a vision of resilient local economies made up of empowered and productive citizens enjoying a joyful and convivial life that is closely in tune with the natural world. This is only one vision, and since part of the message of the green movement is about the need to welcome diversity, I hope it will inspire others to produce visions of their own. Any design for a social and economic system that is able to live comfortably and respectfully within planetary limits is to be encouraged. I look forward to reading what you have to offer.

NOTES

1 Why bioregional economics?

1 This discussion owes much to the programme on Weber's concept of disenchantment hosted by Laurie Taylor in his *Thinking Allowed* series, and in particular contributions from Professor Linda Woodhead of Lancaster University.

2 I particularly valued a joke from one of the farmers employed on the CSA in Stroud, in relation to the need to insure our farm machinery. When asked whether we had insurance in place he replied calmly: 'We have our own form of insurance; we call it "prayer"'.

2 Visioning the bioregional economy

1 There cannot be a precise percentage. This number is based on estimates in the *Zero Carbon Britain* (Kemp and Wexler, 2010) report about what we need to do to achieve global equity by 2050. The exact figure requires assumptions about how energy intensive it is to construct and maintain renewable energy generation facilities; the likelihood of technological advances increasing energy efficiency vs. rebound effects; the contribution to carbon sequestration made by changing land use; and many other factors that cannot be convincingly quantified.

2 The first scholarly account of such delusions in modern times appears to be Mackay, C. (1869), *Memoirs of extraordinary popular delusions* (London: George Routledge and Sons).

3 For more on bioregional planning in the antipodes visit the relevant government websites for Australia (www.environment.gov.au/parks/nrs/science/bioregion-framework/ibra/index. html) and New Zealand (www.legislation.govt.nz/act/public/1991/0069/latest/DLM23026 5.html).

4 The results of their exercise can be found at www.naturalengland.org.uk/ourwork/ landscape/englands/character/areas/default.aspx (downloaded 10 March 2012).

5 Trueman's account helps me to validate my own sense of coming home when I moved from West Wales to Stroud some five years ago, a process I like romantically to think of as coming to dwell in my own land. The fact that the countryside and the stone itself felt so familiar is simply explained by the position of Stroud, perched on the edge of the Cotswold belt, and its familiarity to somebody like me who grew up in Bath, on the southern edge of the same geological formation.

6 The repeating nature of many of our river-names in the British Isles form a direct link with our bioregional ancestors – names such as the Avon (meaning river in Celtic languages), the Tees, the Tay and the Frome.
7 See more details at the website: www.salmonnation.com/place/more_maps.html (downloaded 10 March 2012).

3 The economist as shaman

1 It could be argued that the great economist John Maynard Keynes literally gave his life for the sake of the post-war economic settlement that enabled at least one generation of his fellow citizens to live without concern for their material survival. He died in Easter 1946, exhausted by his negotiations with US politicians and financiers (Skidelsky, 2003).
2 These arguments have been developed in a paper published by the *Journal of Philosophical Economies* (Cato, 2012).
3 Routledge and Zed both publish series on the work of heterodox economics; Routledge's series is called *Advances in Heterodox Economics*.
4 Thanks to Ioana Negru for bringing this quotation to my attention.
5 I do not intend to spend much time here engaging with the debate about precisely what sustainability means. Its meaning is clearly shifting through time (McManus, 1996) and differs depending on the political perspective and personal intention of the person using it. It should be sufficient for me to identify myself with a strong defintion of sustainability (Neumayer, 2003, meaning that I do not believe that other forms of capital can be used as substitutes for natural capital. Elsewhere (Cato, 2008) I have written at length about how I identify 'green economics' as distinct from neoclassical economics and other schools of economics that give a central place to the environment. It should be clear from what I have already said about my working definition of sustainability that this is a characteristic of an ecological approach to economics. What makes green economists distinct, I have argued, is their shared critique of capitalism and their placing of social justice as an equivalent objective alongside sustainability.
6 Project Merlin was an attempt by the top executives of some of the UK's leading banks, under the directorship of former Barclay's CEO John Varley, to take control of the public debate over the future of banks and to offer proposals, especially on the subject of bonuses, to assuage public anger following the 2008 financial crisis and public bailout. For more information see the response from the Treasury: www.hm-treasury.gov.uk/press_17_11.htm.
7 More information is available from the campaign website: mottainai.info/english/

4 Firms, farms and factories

1 Recent research suggests a more pressing reason to follow natural diurnal rhythms: evidence from Denmark has demonstrated the negative health consequences of being exposed to light during the night, which has led to successful damages claims by shift-workers who have been afflicted with breast cancer (Hansen, 2006).
2 According to Pepper (1984: 190), 'Kropotkin thought that capitalists did not amalgamate and centralise for technical reason (i.e. greater economic 'efficiency') – rather they did so in order to dominate markets'.
3 Source: permaculture.org.au/what-is-permaculture/

5 Provenance and provisioning

1 *Piers The Plowman*, Passus VII, p. 62. Downloaded from the Harvard University literature respository, 5 September 2011: www.people.fas.harvard.edu/~chaucer/special/authors/langland/pp-pass7.html

2 'You see, I really have wanted to make it so that people get the idea that these folk, who are eating their potatoes by the light of their little lamp, have tilled the earth themselves with these hands they are putting in the dish, and so it speaks of manual labor and – that they have thus honestly earned their food. I wanted it to give the idea of a wholly different way of life from ours – civilized people. So I certainly don't want everyone just to admire it or approve of it without knowing why.' (Van Gogh letter 497) I was not able to reproduce a picture of The Potato Eaters due to copyright restrictions: to gain some sense of what Van Gogh was trying to communicate please find the image online.

3 A notable exception is the Bristol Food Plan, which focuses on the concept of resilience; Sheffield also has a food plan, although this has a stronger health focus, no doubt reflecting the sources of its funding in public health rather than economic development. See www.bristol.gov.uk/page/food-bristol and www.sheffieldfirst.net/the-partnership/health-and-well-being-partnership/food-plan.

4 More detail can be found on a dedicated website: www.orthorexia.com.

5 For those who can read French, a short report *Les Produits de Terroir: Comprendre et Agir* by Laurence Bérard et Philippe Marchenay (2007) perfectly summarises the ambition of a bioregional approach to provisioning, particularly the note on the image of the Charolais cow: *une race, un produit, des savoir-faire, un paysage* ('a breed, a product, skill, landscape') (Centre national de la recherche scientifique, Alimentec, Bourg-en-Bresse); available here: www.ethno-terroirs.cnrs.fr/IMG/pdf/CNRSTerroirComprendreAgir.pdf (Downloaded 21 September 2011).

6 For an economist, 'opportunity cost' is a relative way of looking at costs in terms of other opportunities foregone. According to Black (1997: 332), it means 'The amount of other goods and services which could have been obtained instead of any good'.

7 this section draws on discussion in Cato (2011*a*).

6 Work as craft

1 A 'bodger' is a woodworker who uses natural rather than mechanical motive power. The website can be found at: www.stuartking.co.uk/index.php/chair-bodgers-of-buckin ghamshire/

2 With great aplomb the burghers of Chesterfield have managed to turn this disaster into a triumph of marketing, as have other members of the Association of Twisted Spires of Europe.

3 Philip Clissett was a renowned maker of chairs who lived in Bosbury near Ledbury in Herefordshire in the nineteenth century. More information about his craft and examples of his chairs can be found at the Ledbury Heritage Centre.

7 What about my iPad?

1 I note with interest that the title of this changed from iPod to iPad during the course of the two years I was writing this book. Perhaps by now the iPad will also have been superseded as an iconic consumption artefact.

2 Two films have been particularly useful in developing ideas for this chapter: The Light-Bulb Conspiracy by Cosima Dannoritzer (www.imdb.com/title/tt1825163/) and Adam Curtis's series The Century of the Self (vimeo.com/24959321).

3 The quotation is apparently 'We made the buttons on the screen look so good you'll want to lick them', as quoted in *Fortune* magazine, 4 January 2000.

4 When speaking to the Occupy Wall Street protesters and quoted at the Disinformation website disinfo.com, 11 October 2011.

8 Sharing our common wealth

1 The famous painting of this title by F. M. Bell-Smith of Threadneedle Street, the Bank of England and the Royal Exchange envisages these financial institutions as central to the imperial project: Ramsay, E. L. (2003), Modernity and Post-colonialism: *The Heart of the Empire* (1909) by F.M. Bell-Smith. *Labour/Le Travail*, 52: 27 pars. 8 Feb. 2012 (www. historycooperative.org/journals/llt/52/ramsay.html).

2 I use the word 'Britain' here to describe the islands of the British Isles, whose constitutional boundaries changed during the period under discussion.

3 Peter Mandelson's tasteless comment during the first New Labour government that they were 'intensely relaxed about people getting filthy rich' (Adams, 2008). Interestingly, Mandelson has recently expressed the view that he was 'misinterpreted', and that he underestimated the relationship between globalisation and inequality, in his Foreword to Straw and Glennie (2012).

4 See www.domesdaybook.co.uk/.

9 Provisioning, exchange and sufficiency

1 According to the World Table of International Shipping Associations; figures like this refer to bulk shipping of goods. The proportion by value is much lower, as a result of trade in 'invisibles' such as financial and insurance services.

2 IPCC Working Group I, the Physical Science Basis, available here: www.ipcc.ch/public ations_and_data/ar4/wg1/en/ch11s11-9-4.html (Downloaded 22 February 2012).

3 See my critique in Cato, 2006.

4 As reported by the BBC in August: www.bbc.co.uk/news/business-10879138 (downloaded 2 April 2012).

5 See more at the Venezuelan Analysis website: venezuelanalysis.com/analysis/339 (Downloaded 16 March 2012).

6 While this might seem somewhat fanciful, it is exactly what the House of Lords is attempting to do in its exploration of the possibility of consumption-based emissions reporting: www.parliament.uk/business/committees/committees-a-z/commons-select/ energy-and-climate-change-committee/news/con-2/

7 I am grateful to Ernst Ulrich von Weiszacker for this idea.

10 Space, limits and boundaries

1 Since this book is all about rooted connection I cannot refrain from mentioning my two connections of place with Leopold Kohr, who taught at the University of Aberystwyth, where I studied for my PhD, and developed his ideas in meetings with Illich, Schumacher and John Papworth in a house in the Slad Valley near Stroud.

2 Emergy analysis enables researchers to measure the qualitative change in energy as it is transformed from one form to another in processes in the ecosystem; within this sort of systems approach 'exergy' is the energy that is available to be used. Both concepts are due to Howard Odum.

3 NUTS (Nomenclature of Territorial Units for Statistics) are regions of various sizes defined by Eurostat. The UK has 37 NUTS2 regions.

4 Source: www.wales.gov.uk/docs/desh/policy/100722tan6en.pdf, p.11.

5 Available online here: www.legislation.gov.uk/ukpga/1908/36/pdfs/ukpga_19080036_ en.pdf (Downloaded 6 March 2012).

6 According to Hanning and Bell (2011), as well as the afore-mentioned Clarkson, the area attracts the likes of Rebekah Brooks and Matthew Freud, who mingle freely with PM David Cameron and perhaps rub shoulders with the host of celebrity hangers-on and members of the elite who own property nearby.

11 Living the full circle of life

1 In this connection, Stroud FM presenter Tim Mars has suggested that the pension should be retitled the Death Seeker's Allowance.

REFERENCES

Abram, D. (1996), *The Spell of the Sensuous* (Vintage: New York).

Adams, J. (1995), *Risk* (London: UCL Press).

Adams, T. (2008), 'The comeback kid: Peter Mandelson', *Observer*, 21 Dec.

Agarwal, A. (2001), 'Common Property Institutions and Sustainable Governance of Resources', *World Development*, 29/10: 1649–72.

Albert, M. and Hahnel, R. (1991), *The Political Economy of Participatory Economics* (Princeton, NJ: Princeton University Press).

Alexandersson, G. and Hultén, S. (2007), 'High and Low Bids in Tenders: Strategic Pricing and Other Bidding Behaviour in Public Tenders of Passenger Railway Services', *Annals of Public and Cooperative Economics*, 78/2: 161–94.

Amin, A. (1997) 'Placing Globalisation', *Theory, Culture and Society*, 14/2: 123–37.

Anderson, V. (1991), *Alternative Economic Indicators* (London: Routledge).

Andruss, V., Plant, C., Plant, J. and Wright, E. (1990) (eds), *Home! A Bioregional Reader,* (Philadelphia: New Society Publishers)

Angell, M. (2011), 'The Epidemic of Mental Illness: Why?', *New York Review*, 23 June.

Arthur, L., Cato, M. S., Keenoy, T. and Smith, R. (2006), 'Green or Red: An Exploration of the Cooperative Environmental Niche in Wales', *Journal of Cooperative Studies*, 39/2: 29–40,

Azzellini, D. (2010), Partizipation, Arbeiterkontrolle und die Commune: Bewegungen und soziale Transformation am Beispiel Venezuela (Hamburg: VSA Verlag).

Baggiani, J. (2011), 'How Steve Jobs changed capitalism', *Guardian*, 6 Oct.

Bagias, C. (2003), *Withy, Rush and Reed: A Somerset Levels Legacy* (Tiverton: Halsgrove).

Balcomb, A. (2009), 'Re-enchanting a Disenchanted Universe – Post Modern Projects in Theologies of Space', *Religion and Theology*, 16/1–2: 77–89.

Baldwin, R. E. (2006), 'Failure of the WTO Ministerial Conference at Cancun: Reasons and Remedies', *The World Economy*, 29/6: 677–96.

Bardsley, D. (2003), 'Risk alleviation via in situ agrobiodiversity conservation: drawing from experiences in Switzerland, Turkey and Nepal', *Agriculture, Ecosystems and Environment*, 99: 149–57.

Barry, J. (1996), 'Sustainablity, Political Judgement and Citizenship: Connecting Green Politics and Democracy', in B. Doherty and M. de Geus (eds), *Democracy and Green Political Thought: Sustainability, Rights and Citizenship* (London: Routledge).

Barry, J. (1998), *Rethinking Green Politics: Nature, Virtue and Progress* (London: Sage)

Barry, J. (1999), *Environment and Social Theory* (London: Routledge).

Barry, J. (2012), *The Politics of Actually Existing Unsustainability* (Oxford: Oxford University Press).

Basso, K. (1992), *Western Apache Language and Culture: Essays in Linguistic Anthropology* (Tucson: University of Arizona Press).

Basso, K. (1996), *Wisdom Sits in Places: Landscape and language among the Western Apache* (Albuquerque, NM: University of New Mexico Press).

Batra, A. (2007), 'Structure of Comparative Advantage of China and India: Global and Regional Dynamics', *China & World Economy*, 15/6: 69–86.

Bauman, Z. (2005*a*), *Work, Consumerism and the New Poor* (Maidenhead: Open University Press).

Bauman, Z. (2005*b*), 'Identity for Identity's Sake is a Big Dodgy', *Soundings*, 29: 12–20.

BBC (2002), 'Churchill Voted Greatest Briton', 24 Nov.: news.bbc.co.uk/1/hi/entertainme nt/2509465.stm (downloaded 28 March 2012).

Berle, A. and Means, G. (1932), *The Modern Corporation and Private Property* (New York: Transaction).

Beck, U. (1992) *Risk Society: Towards a New Modernity* (London: Sage).

Becker, A., Fischer, M., Schwegler, B. and Inoue, S. (2011), 'Considering Climate Change: A Survey of Global Seaport Administrators', Centre for Integrated Facility Engineering Working Paper 128 (Stanford, CA: Stanford University).

Bell, A. (1939/2009), *Men and the Fields* (Wimborne Minster: The Dovecote Press).

Ben-Ami, D. (2010), *Ferraris for All: In Defence of Economic Progress* (Bristol: Policy Press).

Bernays, E. (1928), *Propaganda* (New York: Ig Publishing) pp. 47–48.

Birner, R. and Wittmer, H. (2004), 'On the "efficient boundaries of the state": the contribution of transaction-costs economics to the analysis of decentralization and devolution in natural resource management', Environment and Planning C: Government and Policy 2004, 22/5: pp. 667–85.

BIS (2010), 'The path to strong, sustainable and balanced growth' (London: BIS).

Black, J. (1997), *The Oxford Dictionary of Economics* (Oxford: Oxford University Press).

Blythe, R. (1972), *Akenfield* (Harmondsworth: Penguin).

Borras Jr., S. M., Hall, R., Scoones, I., White, B. and Wolford, W. (2011), 'Towards a better understanding of global land grabbing: an editorial introduction', *Journal of Peasant Studies*, 38:2, 209–16.

Bradley, M. (2009), 'Down with the Fences: Battles for the Commons in South London', *The Land*, issue 7, summer.

Bramwell, A. (1989), *Ecology in the Twentieth Century* (New Haven, CT: Yale University Press).

Branford, S. and Rocha, J. (2002). *Cutting the wire: the struggle of the landless movement in Brazil* (London: Latin America Bureau).

Brewer, M., Muriel, A., Phillips, D., and Sibieta, L. (2009), *Poverty and Inequality in Britain: 2009* (London: Institute for Fiscal Studies).

Britnell, R.H. (1987), 'Forstall, forestalling and the Statute of Forestallers', *English Historical Review*, 102: 89–102.

Brown, L. (2011), *World on the Edge* (London: Routledge).

Bude, H. and Dürrschmidt, J. (2010) 'What's wrong with globalization?: Contra "flow speak" – towards an existential turn in the theory of globalization', *European Journal of Social Theory*, 13: 481–500.

Buick, A. (1990), 'A market by the way – The economics of nowhere', in S. Coleman and P. O'Sullivan (Eds.), *William Morris & News from Nowhere. A vision for our time* (Bideford (Devon): Green Books) pp. 151–68.

Bunyard, P. and Morgan-Grenville, F. (eds) (1987), *The Green Alternative* (London: Methuen).

Busby, J. W. (2007), 'Bono Made Jesse Helms Cry: Jubilee 2000, Debt Relief, and Moral Action in International Politics', *International Studies Quarterly*, 51/2: 247–75.

Cabinet Office (2011), *Open Public Services*, www.openpublicservices.cabinetoffice.gov.uk/ (downloaded 31 March 2012).

Callicott, J. Baird (1980), 'Animal Liberation: A Triangular Affair.' *Environmental Ethics* 2: 311–38.

Campbell, C. (1987), *The romantic ethic and the spirit of modern consumerism* (Oxford: Basil Blackwell).

Campbell, M. and Campbell, I. (2011), 'Allotment waiting lists in England 2011', Transition Town West Kirby in conjunction with the National Society of Allotment and Leisure Gardeners, www.transitiontownwestkirby.org.uk/files/ttwk_nsalg_survey_2011.pdf

Capra, F. (1995), *The Web of Life* (New York: Harper Collins).

Carod-Artal, F.J. and Vazquez-Cabrera, C. (2007), 'An anthropological study about head-ache and migraine in native cultures from Central and South America', *Headache: The Journal of Head & Face Pain*, 47/6: 834–41.

Carr, M. (2004), *Bioregionalism and Civil Society: Democratic Challenges to Corporate Globalism* (Vancouver: University of British Columbia Press).

Castañeda, J. G. (2006), 'Latin America's Left Turn', *Foreign Affairs*, 85/3.

Castells, M. (1996), *The Rise of the Network Society* (Oxford: Blackwell).

Castle, S. (2006), 'Barroso attacks France and Spain over "absurd economic nationalism"', *Independent*, 22 Mar.

Cato, M. S. (2004), *The Pit and the Pendulum: A Co-operative Future for Work in the South Wales Valleys* (Cardiff: University of Wales Press).

Cato, M. S. (2006), *Market, Schmarket: Building the Post-Capitalist Economy* (Gretton: New Clarion Press).

Cato, M. S. (2008), 'Emancipation from Monetary Exploitation: Owen's Vision in Practice Around the World Today', in Cato, M.S. and Bickle, R. (eds), *New Views of Society: Robert Owen for the 21st Century* (Glasgow: Scottish Left Review Press).

Cato, M. S. (2009*a*), 'A New Financial Architecture Based on a Global Carbon Standard', *Ecopolitics*, 3: 61–78; reprinted in Barry, J. and Leonard, L. (eds), *Advances in Ecopolitics*, iii. *The Transition to Sustainable Living and Practice* (Bingley: Emerald).

Cato, M. S. (2009*b*), *Green Economics: An Introduction to Theory, Policy and Practice* (London: Earthscan).

Cato, M. S. (2010), 'Metric measurements divorce us from the natural world', *The Ecologist*, 19 March.

Cato, M. S. (2011*a*), 'Home Economics: Planting the Seeds of a Research Agenda for the Bioregional Economy', *Environmental Values*, 20: 481–501.

Cato, M. S. (2011*b*), 'Defensive Localism or Creative Localisation', a response to the gov-ernment's Localism Bill (Weymouth: Green House).

Cato, M. S. and Hillier, J. (2010), 'How could we study climate-related social innovation? Applying Deleuzean philosophy to Transition Towns', *Environmental Politics*, 19/6: 869–87

Cato, M. S. and Mellor, M. (2012), 'Supplanting the Holy Trinity: Creating a New Global Architecture that Serves People and Planet', *Capitalism, Nature, Socialism* (forthcoming).

Cato, M. S. and Myers, J. (2010), 'Education as Re-Embedding: Stroud Communiversity, Walking the Land and the Enduring Spell of the Sensuous', *Sustainability*, 3/1: 51–68.

Cato, M. S. and North, P. (2012), 'A Suitable Climate for Political Action? A Sympathetic Review of the Politics of Transition', in Pelling, M., Manuel-Navarrete, D. and Redclift, M. (eds), *Climate Change and the Crisis of Capitalism: A Chance to Reclaim Self, Society and Nature* (London: Routledge).

Cato, M. S., Arthur, L., Keenoy, T. and Smith, R. (2006), 'Green or Red: An Exploration of the Cooperative Environmental Niche in Wales', *Journal of Cooperative Studies*, 39/2: 29–40.

Chadwick, K. D., Burkman, R. T., Tornesi, B. M. and Mahadevan, B. (2012), 'Fifty Years of "the Pill": Risk Reduction and Discovery of Benefits Beyond Contraception, Reflec-tions and Forecast', *Toxicological Sciences*, 125/1: 2–9.

Chan, A. (2003), 'Racing to the bottom: international trade without a social clause', *Third World Quarterly*, 24/6: 1011–28.

Chatwin, B. (1988), *The Songlines* (London: Penguin).

Christensen, J. and Murphy, R. (2004), 'The Social Irresponsibility of Corporate Tax Avoidance: Taking CSR to the bottom line', *Development*, 47/3: 37–44.

Clark, N. (2008), 'Aboriginal Cosmopolitanism', *International Journal of Urban and Regional Research*, 32/ 3: 737–44.

Clifton, S.-J. (2009), *A Dangerous Obsession: The Evidence against Carbon Trading and for Real Solutions to Avoid a Climate Crunch* (London: Friends of the Earth).

Cobbett, W. (1830/1985), *Rural Rides* (Harmondsworth: Penguin).

Cole, G. D. H. (1953–60), *Socialist Thought* (London: Macmillan); the volumes consulted here are vol i, *The Forerunners 1789–1850* (1954), vol ii, *Marxism and Anarchism 1850–1890* (1957), and vol. iii, *The Second International 1889–1914* (1960).

Cole, G. D. H. (1920), *Guild Socialism Restated* (1920).

Cole, G. D. H. (1930), *Social Theory* (London: Methuen).

Conford, P. (2001), *The Origins of the Organic Movement: Getting Back to Our Roots* (Glasgow: Floris).

Connor, S. (2009), 'Warning: Oil supplies are running out fast', *Independent*, 3 Aug.

Conrad, P. (1992), 'Medicalization and Social Control', *Annual Review of Sociology* 18: 209–32.

Conrad, P. (2005), 'The Shifting Engines of Medicalization', *Journal of Health and Social Behavior*, 64/1: 13–14.

Constantine, S. (1987), 'The Buy British Campaign of 1931', *European Journal of Marketing*, 21/4: 44–59.

Cornwall, M. (1997), '"National Reparation?" The Czech Land Reform and the Sudeten Germans 1918–38', *Slavonic and East European Review*, 75/2: 259–80.

Craig, D. M. (2006), *John Ruskin and the Ethics of Consumption* (Charlottesville, VA: University of Virginia Press).

Creeger, G. R. (1956), 'An Interpretation of Adam Bede', *English Literary History*, 23/3: 218–38.

Cristea, A. D., Hummels, D., Puzzello, L. and Avetisyan, G. (2011), 'Trade and the Greenhouse Gas Emissions from International Freight Transport', NBER Working Paper No. 17117, June 2011.

Crook, T. (2009), 'Craft and the Dialogics of Modernity: The Arts and Crafts Movement in Late-Victorian England and Edwardian England', *The Journal of Modern Craft*, 2/1: 17–32.

Cumbers, A. and McMaster, R. (2012), 'Revisiting Public Ownership: Knowledge, Democracy and Participation in Economic Decision-making', *Review of Radical Politics Economics* (forthcoming).

Cutter, S. L., Burton, C. G., and Emrich, C. T. (2010), 'Disaster Resilience Indicators for Benchmarking Baseline Conditions', *Journal of Homeland Security and Emergency Management*, 7/1: 51.

Cwik, P. F. (2011), 'The new Neo-Mercantilism: Currency Maniupulation as a Form of Protectionism', *Economics Affairs*, 31/3: 7–11.

Daly, H. (1977), *Steady State Economics* (New York: W. H. Freeman).

Daly, H. (1996), *Beyond Growth* (New York: Beacon).

Daly, H. (1999), 'Uneconomic growth in theory and in fact', the first annual FEASTA lecture, Trinity College, Dublin.

Daoud, A. (2011), 'The *Modus Vivendi* of Material Simplicity: Counteracting Scarcity via the Deflation of Wants', *Review of Social Economy*, 1470–1162, 7 April.

Darby, H. C. and Welldon Finn, R. (1967), *The Domesday Geography of South-West England* (Cambridge: University Press).

Davies, G. (1997), *A History of Money from Ancient Times to the Present Day* (Cardiff: University of Wales Press).

de Botton, A. (2004) *Status Anxiety* (Harmondsworth: Penguin).

De Bruijn, H. and Dicke, W. (2006), 'Strategies for Safeguarding Public Values in Liberalized Utility Sectors', *Public Administration*, 84/3: 717–35.

de Graaf, J., Wann, D. and Naylor, T. (2001), *Affluenza: The All-Consuming Epidemic* (San Francisco: Berrett-Koehler).

de Grazia, V. (2005), *Irresistible Empire: America's Advance through Twentieth-Century Europe* (Cambridge, Mass: Harvard University Press).

Deakin, R. (2007), *Wildwood: A Journey through Trees* (London: Hamish Hamilton).

Defra (2008), *Ensuring the UK's Food Security in a Changing World* (London: TSO).

Defra (Food Chain Analysis Group) (2006), *Food Security and the UK: An Evidence and Analysis Paper* (London: TSO).

Deleuze, G. and Guattari, F. (2004), *A Thousand Plateaus*, trans. B. Massumi (London: Continuum).

Della Porta, D. (2005), 'Globalizations and Democracy', *Democratization*, 12/5: 668–85.

Delveaux, M. (2005), '"O me! O me! How i love the earth": William Morris's News from Nowhere and the birth of sustainable society', *Contemporary Justice Review*, 8:2, 131–46.

Demos (2012), *The Commission on Assisted Dying* (London: Demos).

DWP (Department for Work and Pensions) (2010), Changes to the Local Housing Allowance to be Introduced in 2011–12 (London: DWP website).

Diamond, J. (2011), *Collapse: How Societies Choose to Fail or Survive* (Harmondsworth: Penguin).

Disch, D. (2010), 'A comparative analysis of the "development dividend" of Clean Development Mechanism projects in six host countries', *Climate and Development*, 2/1: 50–64.

Dobbs, R., Oppenheim, J., Thompson, F., Brinkman, M. and Zornes, M. (2011), *Meeting the Worlds' Energy, Materials, Food and Water Needs* (Chicago: McKinsey Global Institute).

Dobson, (1989), *Justice and the Environment: Conceptions of Environmental Sustainability and Theories of Distributive Justice* (Oxford: Clarendon Press).

Dobson, A. (2003), *Citizenship and the Environment* (Oxford: Oxford University Press).

Dobson, A. (2007), *Green Political Thought*, 4th edn. (London: Routledge).

Dobson, A. (2011), *Sustainability Citizenship* (Weymouth: Green House).

Douthwaite, R. (1992), *The Growth Illusion* (Totnes: Green Books).

Douthwaite, R. (2006), *Closed Circuit: Strengthening Local Economies for Security in an Uncertain World* (Totnes: Green Books).

Drenthen, M. (2009), 'Ecological Restoration and Place Attachment: Emplacing Non-Places?', *Environmental Values*, 18/2: 285–312.

Driver, S. (2008), 'Poverty, social justice and the Labour government', 1997–2007'. *Benefits*, 16/2: 157–67.

DuBois, T. A. (2011), 'Trends in contemporary research on shamanism', *Numen*, 58: 100–128.

Duffy, A. (2008), 'Indigenous Peoples' Land Rights: Developing a *Sui Generis* Approach to Ownership and Restitution', *International Journal on Minority and Group Rights*, 15/4: 505–38.

Dunbar, R. (2003), 'The Social Brain: Mind, Language and Society in Evolutionary Perspective', *Annual Review of Anthropology*, 32: 163–81.

Ehrenfeld, J. R. (1997), 'Industrial ecology: a framework for product and process design', *Journal of Cleaner Production*, 5/1–2: 87–95.

Ekins, P., Hillman, M. and Hutchinson, R. (1992), *Wealth Beyond Measure: The Prospects for Green Growth* (London: Routledge).

Eliot, G. (1859/2008) *Adam Bede* (Oxford: Oxford University Press).

European Commission (2008), *The Common Agricultural Policy Explained* (Brussels: European Commission Agricultural and Rural Development).

European Commission (2011), 'Reform of the Common Fisheries Policy', COM (2011) 417.

Evanoff, R. (2007), 'Bioregional and Cross-Cultural Dialogue on a Land Ethic', *Ethics, Place and Environment*, 10, 2, June, 141–56(16).

Ewen, S. (2001), *Captains of Consciousness: Advertising and the Social Roots of the Consumer Culture* (New York: Basic Books).

Fahmy, E., Thumim, J. and White, V. (2011), 'The distribution of UK household CO_2 emissions: Interim report' (York: Joseph Rowntree Foundation).

Fairlie, S. (2009), 'A Short History of Enclosure in Britain', *The Land*, issue 7, summer.

Feagan, R. B. and Morris, D. (2009), 'Consumer quest for embeddedness: a case study of the Brantford Farmers' Market', *International Journal of Consumer Studies*, 33/3: 235–43.

Feldstein, M. (1999), 'Reducing poverty, not inequality', *The Public Interest*, 137: 33–41.

Feyerabend, P. (2001), *The Conquest of Abundance: A Tale of Abstraction Versus the Richness of Being* (Chicago, IL: University Press).

Fine, B. (2001) *Social Capital versus Social Theory: Political Economy and Social Science at the Turn of the Millennium* (London: Routledge).

Foresight (2008), *Powering our Lives Sustainable Energy Management and the Built Environment*, available at: www.foresight.gov.uk/Energy/EnergyFinal/final_project_report.pdf

Foucault, M. (2007). *Territory, Population; Lectures at the College de France, 1977–1978*, edited by Michel Senellart, (New York: Palgrave Macmillan).

Foucault. M. (2008) *The Birth of Biopolitics; Lectures at the Collège de France, 1978–79* (New York: Palgrave Macmillan).

Fourier, C (1803), Lettre de Fourier au Grand Juge, available online: www.marxists.org/reference/archive/fourier/works/ch04.htm (downloaded 2 April 2012).

Freedman Lustig, D. (2004), 'Baby pictures: family, consumerism and exchange among teen mothers in the USA', *Childhood*, 11 (2), 175–93.

Friedman, T. (2005), *A Brief History of The Twenty-first Century* (New York: Farrar Straus Giroux).

Friedman, T. (2008), *Hot, Flat and Crowded: Why We Need a Green Revolution – And How It Can Renew America* (Harmondsworth: Penguin).

Fukuyama, F. (1992), *The End of History and the Last Man* (Harmondsworth: Penguin).

Galbraith, J. K. (1958/1970), *The Affluent Society* (Harmondsworth: Penguin).

Galeano, E. (1998), *Upside Down: A Primer for the Looking Glass World* (New York: Picador).

Galton, F. (1869), *Hereditary Genius: An Inquiry into its Law and Consequences* (London: Macmillan).

Galton, F. (1872), 'Statistical Inquiries into the Efficacy of Prayer', *The Fortnightly Review*, 68 NS.

Gandhi, M. K. (1936), 'Causes of decline of village industries', *Harijan*, 20 June; republished in *Village Industries* (Ahmedabad: Navajivan Publishing House).

Garland, K. (1994), *Mr Beck's Underground Map* (London: Capital Transport).

Gee, T. (2009), The World System is Not Neo-Liberal: The Emergence of Structural Mercantilism, *Journal of Socialist* Theory, 37/2: 253–59.

Georgescu-Roegen, N. (1971), *The Entropy Law and the Economic Process* (Cambridge, MA: Harvard University Press).

Giddens, A. (1991), *Modernity and self-identity: Self and society in the late modern age* (Cambridge: Polity Press).

Girardet, H. (2006), *Creating Sustainable Cities*, Schumacher Briefing no. 6 (Totnes: Green Books).

Girardet, H. (2011), *Creating Regenerative Cities* (Berlin: Heinrich Böll Foundation).

Glass-Coffin, B. (2010), 'Anthropology, Shamanism, and Alternate Ways of Knowing–Being in the World: One Anthropologist's Journey of Discovery and Transformation', *Anthropology and Humanism*, 35/2: 204–17.

Glyn, A. (2006), *Capitalism Unleashed: Finance, Globalization and Welfare* (Oxford: Oxford University Press).

Godwin, M. and Lawson, C. (2009), 'The Working Tax Credit and Child Tax Credit, 2003–8: a critical analysis', *Benefits*, 17:1, 3–14.

Goodin, R. E. (1996), 'Enfranchising the Earth, and its alternatives', *Political Studies* XLIV 835–49.

Gould, P. (1988). *Early green politics. Back to nature, back to the Land, and socialism in Britain, 1880–1900* (Sussex and New York: Harvester and St. Martin's Press).

Gowdy, J. M. and Hubacek, K. (2000), 'Land, Labour and the Anthropology of Work: Towards Sustainable Livelihoods', *International Journal of Agricultural Resources, Governance and Ecology*, 1/1: 17–27.

Grantham, J. (1997), *Regulated Pasture: A History of Common Land in Chipping Norton*; a short history of Chipping Norton commons can be found online: www.chippingnortontown. info/CHIPPINGNORTON/TOWNHISTORY/tabid/213/Default.aspx

Gray, R. (2007), 'Greener by miles', *Daily Telegraph*, (downloaded 27 February 2012).

Greenspan, A. (1996), Remarks made at the Annual Dinner and Francis Boyer Lecture of The American Enterprise Institute for Public Policy Research, Washington, DC, 5 Dec.

Griffiths, J. (1999), *Pip Pip: A Sideways Look at Time* (London: Flamingo).

Griffiths, J. (2007), *Wild: An Elemental Journey* (London: Hamish Hamilton).

Grundle, S. (2009), *Glamour: A History* (Oxford: Oxford University Press).

Haddad, B. M. (2003), 'Property rights, ecosystem management, and John Locke's Labor Theory of Ownership', *Ecological Economics*, 46: 19–31.

Hale, P. J. (2003), 'Labor and the Human Relationship with Nature: The Naturalization of Politics in the Work of Thomas Henry Huxley, Herbert George Wells, and William Morris', *Journal of the History of Biology* 36: 249–84.

Hall, D. (2011): 'Land grabs, land control, and Southeast Asian crop booms', *Journal of Peasant Studies*, 38:4, 837–57

Hamilton, C. (2009), 'A new era for steel – drivers, implications and risks', *Ironmaking & Steelmaking*, 36/4: 255–58.

Hamilton, C. and Denniss, R. (2005), *Affluenza: When Too Much is Never Enough* (London: Allen & Unwin).

Hanning, J. and Bell, M. (2011), 'Rebekah, Dave, and the Chipping Norton set: Where power in Britain lies', *Sunday Independent*, 10 July.

Hansen, J. (2006), 'Risk of Breast Cancer After Night- and Shift Work: Current Evidence and Ongoing Studies in Denmark', *Cancer Causes and Control*, 17/4: 531–37.

Harrison, J. (2008), 'The Vagaries of Vegetarianism', *Ratio*, 21/3: 286–99.

Harvey, D. (2010), *The Enigma of Capital: And the Crises of Capitalism* (London: Profile).

Harvey, G. (2006), *Animism: Respecting the Living World* (Columbia: Columbia University Press).

Heater, D. (1999), *World Citizenship: Cosmopolitan Thinking And Its Opponents* (London: Continuum).

Henderson, H. (2009), *Ethical Markets: Growing the Green Economy* (White River Junction, VT: Chelsea Green).

Henderson, Hazel (1996), *Creating Alternative Futures: The End of Economics* (West Hartford: Kumerian Press).

Hersh, J. and Voth (2009), 'Sweet Diversity: Colonial Goods and the Welfare Gains from Trade after 1492', Economics Working Papers no. 1163, Department of Economics and Business, Universitat Pompeu Fabra, Spain.

Hill, C. (1961/2002), *The Century of Revolution, 1603–1714* (London: Routledge).

Hill, R. and Myatt, T. (2010), *The Economics Anti-Textbook: A Critical Thinker's Guide to Microeconomics* (London: Zed).

Hines, C. (2000), *Localization: A Global Manifesto* (London: Earthscan).

Hintz, J. (2007), 'Some Political Problems for Rewilding Nature', *Ethics, Place and Environment*, 10/2: 177–216.

Hirsch, F. (1976), *The Social Limits to Growth* (Cambridge: Harvard University Press).

Hobson, S. G. (1914), *National Guilds: An Inquiry into the Wage System and the Way Out* (London: G. Bell and Sons).

Hocking, S. (2010), Cuts and the Equality Act, *Public Finance*, 1st Oct., opinion.publicfinanc e.co.uk/2010/10/cuts-and-the-equality-act-by-stephen-hocking/ (Accessed 26 April 2011).

Hodgson, G. M. (2003), 'The hidden persuaders: institutions and individuals in economic theory', *Cambridge Journal of Economics*, 27: 159–75.

Hoffman, U. (2011), 'Assuring Food Security in Developing Countries under the Challenges of Climate Change: Key Trade and Development Issues of a Fundamental Transformation of Agriculture', UNCTAD Discussion Paper No. 201 (UNCTAD/OSG/DP/2011/1).

Holmgren, D. (2002), *Permaculture: Principles and Pathways Beyond Sustainability* (Hepburn, Vic.: Holmgren Design Services).

Hopkins, R. (2008), *The Transition Handbook: From Oil Dependency to Local Resilience* (Totnes: Green Books).

Hume, C. (2008), *Wetland Vision Technical Document: overview and reporting of project philosophy and technical approach* (Sandy, Beds.: The Wetland Vision Partnership).

Humphries, J. (1990), 'Common Rights, and Women: The Proletarianization of Families in the Late Eighteenth and Early Nineteenth Centuries' *The Journal of Economic History*, 50/1: 17–42.

Hussen, A. M. (2000), *Principles of Environmental Economics: Ecology, Economics and Public Policy* (London: Routledge).

Icelandic Agricultural Information Service (1997), *Icelandic Agriculture* (Reykjavik: IAIS).

Iles, A. (2005), 'Learning in Sustainable Agriculture: Food Miles and Missing Objects', *Environmental Values*, 14/2: 163–83.

Illich, I (1994), *Resurgence*, Issue 180, 18.

Illich, I. (2004), *La perte des sens* (Paris: Fayard).

Inglis, B. (1971), *Poverty and the Industrial Revolution* (London: Hodder and Stoughton).

Ingold, T. (2000), *The Perception of the Environment* (London: Routledge).

Ingold, T. (2010), 'The Textility of Making', *Cambridge Journal of Economics*, 34: 91–102.

Jackson, T. (2009), *Prosperity without Growth: Economics for a Finite Planet* (London: Earthscan).

Jacobs, M. (1997), 'Environmental valuation, deliberative democracy, and public decision-making institutions', in J. Foster (ed.), *Valuing Nature? Economics, Ethics and Environment* (London: Routledge).

Jahi, J. M., Aiyub, K., Arifin, K. and Awang, A. (2009), 'Human Habitat and Environmental Change: From Cave Dwellings to Megacities', *European Journal of Scientific Research*, 32/3: 381–90.

James, O. (2007), *Affluenza* (London: Vermilion).

James, P. (2005), 'Arguing globalizations: propositions towards an investigation of global formation', *Globalizations*, 2/2: 193–209.

Jiang, K., Cosbey, A. and Murphy, D. (2008), 'Embodied Carbon in Traded Goods', paper prepared for the Trade and Climate Change Seminar, Copenhagen, Denmark, 18–20 June (Winnipeg, Manitoba: International Institute for Sustainable Development).

Jones, J. (2011), 'How Steve Jobs made the world more beautiful', *Guardian*, 6 Oct.

Kallis, G., Martinez-Alier, J. and Norgaard, R. B. (2009), 'Paper assets, real debts: An ecological-economic exploration of the global economic crisis', *Critical Perspectives on International Business*, 5/1–2: 14–25.

Keat, R., Whitely, N. and Abercrombie, N. (eds) (1994), *The Authority of the Consumer* (London: Routledge).

Keen, S. (2001), *Debunking Economics: The Naked Emperor of the Social Sciences* (London: Zed Books).

Kemp, M. and Wexler, J. (2010), *Zero Carbon Britain 2030: A New Energy Strategy*, the second report of the Zero Carbon Britain project (Machynlleth: Centre for Alternative Technology) pp. 50–52.

Kennedy, B.P., Ichiro K. and Prothrow-Stith D. (1996), 'Income distribution and mortality: cross sectional ecological study of the Robin Hood Index in the United States', *British Medical Journal*, Vol. 312, pp. 1004–7.

Keynes, J. M. (1936), *The General Theory of Employment, Interest and Money* (Cambridge: Cambridge University Press)

Kingsnorth, P. (2003), *One No Many Yeses: A Journey to the Heart of the Global Resistance Movement* (New York: Free Press).

Kirwan, B. (2009), 'The Incidence of US Agricultural Subsidies on Farmland Rental Rates', *Journal of Political Economy*, 117/1: 138–64.

Kohr, L. (1957), *The Breakdown of Nations* (London: Routledge and Kegan Paul).

Kohr, L. (1977/1988), *The Overdeveloped Nations: The Diseconomies of Scale* (Schocken Books).

Koppa, T. (2011), 'Co-operative Entrepreneurship and the New Humanism', presentation to the ICA global research conference New Opportunities for Co-operatives, 25 August; www.helsinki.fi/ruralia/ica2011/presentations/Koppa.pdf.

Kropotkin, P. (1899/1994), *Fields, Factories and Workshops*, ed. Ward, C. (London: Freedom Press).

Kumar, S. (2001), 'Gandhi's Swadeshi – The Economics of Permanence' in Mander, J. and Goldsmith, E. (eds), *The Case Against the Global Economy – and for a turn toward the local* (London: Earthscan).

Lamoreaux, N. R., Levenstein, M. and Sokoloff, K. (2004), 'Financing Invention During the Second Industrial Revolution: Cleveland, Ohio 1870–1920', NBER Working Paper 10923.

Lang, C. and Hines, T. (1993), *The New Protectionism: Protecting the Future Against Free Trade* (London: Earthscan).

Large, M. (2010), *Common Wealth: For a Free, Equal, Mutual and Sustainable Society* (Stroud: Hawthorn Press).

Latouche, S. (2009), *Farewell to Growth* (Bristol: Polity Press).

Layard, R. G. (2006), *Happiness: Lessons from a New Science* (Harmondsworth: Penguin).

Le Billon, P. (2007) 'Scales, Chains and Commodities: Mapping Out "Resource Wars"', *Geopolitics*, 12/1: 200–205.

Leadbetter, C. and Garber, J. (2010), *Dying for Change* (London: Demos).

Lee, L. (1985), 'Apples', from *Selected Poems* (Harmondsworth: Penguin).

Leopold, A. (1949/1966), *A Sand County Almanac* (New York: Ballantine Books).

Levitas, R. (2010), *The Concept of Utopia* (Pieterlen: Peter Lang).

Leyshon, A. and Thrift, N. (2007), 'The capitalization of almost everything: the future of finance and capitalism', *Theory, Culture and Society*, 24: 97–115.

Lines, T. (2008), *Making Poverty: A History* (London: Zed).

Lipton, M. (2009), *Land Reform in Developing Countries: Property Rights and Property Wrongs* (London: Routledge).

Lohman, L. (2006), 'Carbon Trading: A critical conversation on climate change, privatisation and power', *Development Dialogue* No. 48, September 2006 (Uppsala: Dag Hammarskjöld Centre).

Lowe, E. A. and Evans, L. K. (1995), 'Industrial ecology and industrial ecosystems', *Journal of Cleaner Production*, 3/1–2: 47–53.

MacGregor, N. (2010), 'Chinese bronze bell', *A History of the World in 100 Objects* (London: Allen Lane).

MacMillan, F. and Cockcroft, D. (2008), 'Food Availability in Stroud District: Considered in the context of climate change and peak oil' (Stroud: Local Strategic Partnership: Think Tank on Global Changes).

Maconie, S. (2007), *Pies and Prejudice: In Search of the North* (London: Ebury).

Mankiw, G. (2009), 'Smart Taxes: An Open Invitation to Join the Pigou Club', *Eastern Economic Journal*, 35: 14–23.

Marshall, S. and Lamrani, Y. (2011), *Synthesis Report: Land Use Planning Measures*, key action City of Tomorrow of the Plume Project.

Max-Neef, M. S. (2003), *Human Scale Development* (London: Apex Press).

Max-Neef, M. and Smith, P. B. (2011), *Economics Unmasked* (Totnes: Green Books).

May, C. (2010), 'John Ruskin's Political Economy: "There is No Wealth but Life"', *British Journal of Politics and International Relations*, 12: 189–204.

McCarthy, M. V. (2009), 'Sea levels rising twice as fast as predicted', *The Independent*, 11 Mar.

McGinnis, M. V. (1999), 'Boundary creatures and bounded spaces', in McGinnis, M. V. (ed.), *Bioregionalism* (London: Routledge).

McManus, P. (1996), 'Contested Terrains: Politics, Stories and Discourses of Sustainability', *Environmental Politics*, 5/1.

McSmith, A. (2008), 'CERN special: The 9 billion dollar question', *The Independent*, 10 Sept.

Mélitz, J. and Zumer, F. (2002), 'Regional redistribution and stabilization by the center in Canada, France, the UK and the US: A Reassessment and New Tests', *Journal of Public Economics*, 86: 263–86.

Mellor, M. (1997), 'Women, nature and the social construction of 'economic man', *Ecological Economics* 20, 129–40.

Mellor, M. (2006), 'Ecofeminist political economy', *International Journal of Green Economics*, 1/1–2: 139–150.

Mellor, M. (2010), *The Future of Money: From Financial Crisis to Public Resource* (London: Pluto).

Merchant, C. (1980), *The Death of Nature: Women, Ecology and the Scientific Revolution* (London: Harper Collins).

Meredith, D. (2005) 'The bioregion as a communitarian micro-region (and its limitations)', *Ethics, Place and Environment*, 8(1), 83–94.

Merritt, A. and Stubbs, T. (2012), 'Incentives to Promote Green Citizenship in UK Transition Towns', *Development* (2012) 55/1: 96–103.

Meyer, A. (2000), *Contraction and Convergence: The Global Solution to Climate Change* (Totnes: Green Books).

Midgley, (1996), *Utopias, dolphins and computers: problems of philosophical plumbing* (London: Routledge).

Midgley, M. (1985/2002), *Evolution as Religion* (London: Routledge).

Midgley, M. (2001), *Science and Poetry* (London: Routledge).

Mies, M. (1998) *Patriarchy and Accumulation on a World Scale* (London: Zed Press).

Mies, M. (1999), 'Women and the World Economy', in Cato, M. S. and Kennett, M. (eds), *Green Economics: Beyond Supply and Demand to Meeting People's Needs* (Aberystwyth: Green Audit).

Milani, B. (2000), *Designing the Green Economy: The Postindustrial Alternative to Corporate Globalization* (Lanham, MD: Rowman and Littlefield).

Millennium Ecosystem Assessment (2005), *Ecosystems and Human Well-Being: Synthesis* (Washington, DC: Island Press).

Mirowski, P. (2010), 'The Great Mortification: Economists' Responses to the Crisis of 2007–(and counting)', *Hedgehog Review*, 12/3, available online here: www.iasc-culture.org/publications_article_2010_Summer_mirowski.php

Monbiot, G. (2006), *Heat: How to Stop the Planet Burning* (Harmondsworth: Penguin).

Monopolies Commission (1951), *Report on the Supply of Electric Lamps* (London: Competition Commission) (Downloaded from the website 3 February 2012).

Montgomerie, J. and Williams, K. (2009), 'Financialised Capitalism: After the Crisis and Beyond Neoliberalism',*Competition and Change*, 13/3: 99–107.

Morris, W. (1885/1973), 'Useful Work vs Useless Toil', in A. L. Morton (ed.), *Political Writings of William Morris* (London: Lawrence and Wishart) pp. 86–108.

Morris, W. (1890/2008), *News from Nowhere* (London: Forgotten Books); www.marxists.org/archive/morris/works/1890/nowhere/index.htm (downloaded 24 February 2012).

Morrison, W. M. (2011), *China-US Trade Issues*, Congressional Research Service, 7–5700, RL33536.

Mumford, L. (1934/1963), *Technics and Civilization* (New York: Harcourt, Brace & World).

Mumford, L. (1938), *The Culture of Cities* (New York: Harcourt, Brace).

Naess, A. (1986/1989), *Ecology, Community and Lifestyle* (Cambridge: Cambridge University Press).

Naples, M. I. and Aslanbeigui, N. (1996), 'What does determine the profit rate? The neoclassical theories presented in introductory textbooks', *Cambridge Journal of Economics*, 20: 53–71.

Natural Environment Research Council (2010), 'Finding the wisdom in teeth', *Planet Earth Online: Environmental Research News*, available online at: planetearth.nerc.ac.uk/features/story.aspx?id=675 (downloaded 21 September 2011).

Neeson, J. M. (1989), *Commoners: Common Right, Enclosure and Social Change in England, 1700–1820* (Cambridge: Cambridge University Press).

Neumayer, E. (2003), *Weak versus Strong Sustainability*, 2nd edn. (Aldershort: Edward Elgar).

Nolan, P., Zhang, J. and Liu, C. (2007), 'The global business revolution, the cascade effect, and the challenge for firms from developing countries', *Cambridge Journal of Economics*, 32/1: 29–47.

Norberg-Hodge, H. (2000), *Ancient Futures: Learning from Ladakh* (London: Random House).

Norberg-Hodge, H. (2009), *Ancient Future: Lessons from Ladakh for a Globalizing World* (San Francisco, CA: Sierra Club Books).

Norgaard, R. B. (2011), 'Economism and the Night Sky', post on the International Society for Ecological Economics website: www.ecoeco.org/content/2011/01/economism-and-the-night-sky/ (downloaded 4 Nov. 2011).

North, P. (2010), 'Eco-Localisation as a Progressive Response to Peak Oil and Climate Change: A Sympathetic Critique', *Geoforum*, 41/4: 585–94.

North, P. (2010), *Local Money: How to Make it Happen in Your Community* (Totnes: Green Books).

Nove, A. (1983), *The Economics of Feasible Socialism* (London: Allen & Unwin).

Oberthür, S. (2003), 'Institutional interaction to address greenhouse gas emissions from international transport: ICAO, IMO and the Kyoto Protocol', *Climate Policy*, 3/3: 191–205.

O'Connor, J. (1988), 'The Second Contradiction of Capitalism', *Capitalism, Nature, Socialism*, 1.

Odum, H. (2001), *A Prosperous Way Down: Principles and Policies*, with Elisabeth C. Odum (Boulder, CO: University Press of Colorado).

OECD (2011), *Divided We Stand: Why Inequality Keeps Rising* (Paris: OECD).

Ólafsson, S. and Kristjánsson, A. S. (2010), 'Income inequality in a bubble economy: The case of Iceland 1992–2008', paper presented to the Luxemburg Incomes Study Conference, 28–30 June.

Olivier De Schutter (2011), 'How not to think of land-grabbing: three critiques of large-scale investments in farmland', *Journal of Peasant Studies*, 38:2, 249–79

ONS (2011), 'Regional Gross Disposable Household Income (GDHI) 1995–2009, available from the ONS website here: www.ons.gov.uk/ons/dcp171778_227345.pdf (downloaded 31 March 2012).

Oosthuizen, S. (2005), 'New Light on the Origins of Open-field Farming?', *Medieval Archaeology*, 49: 165–93.

Ormerod, P. (1994), *The Death of Economics* (London: Faber).

Ostrom, E. (1990), *Governing the Commons: The Evolution of Institutions for Collective Action* (Cambridge: Cambridge University Press).

O'Sullivan, P. (1990). 'The ending of the journey – William Morris, News from Nowhere, and ecology'. In S. Coleman and P. O'Sullivan (eds), *William Morris & News from Nowhere. A vision for our time.* (Bideford (Devon): Green Books) pp. 169–81.

Packard, V. (1957/1981), *The Hidden Persuaders* (Harmondsworth: Penguin).

Panayotakis, C. (2003), 'Capitalism's "Dialectic of Scarcity" and the Emancipatory Project', *Capitalism Nature Socialism*, 14/1: 88–107.

Panayotakis, C. (2011), *Remaking Scarcity: From Capitalist Inefficiency to Economic Democracy* (London: Pluto).

Parkin, S. (2010), *The Positive Deviant: Sustainabilty Leadership in a Perverse World* (London: Earthscan).

Pearce, D. W. (1993), *Economic Values and the Natural World* (Cambridge, MA: MIT Press).

Pearson, M. (2006), *In Comes I: Performance, Memory and Lanscape* (Exeter: Exeter University Press).

Peet, R. (2009), *Unholy Trinity: The IMF, World Bank and WTO* (London: Pluto).

Penty, A. (1906), Guild socialism: Arthur Penty (1906), *Restoration of the Gild System* (London: Swan, Sonnenschein), strobertbellarmine.net/books/Penty–Restoration_Guild_System.pdf

Pepper, D (1984), *The Roots of Modern Environmentalism* (London: Croom Helm).

Perraton, J. (2006), 'Heavy Constraints on a "Weightless World"? Resources and the New Economy', *American Journal of Economics and Sociology*, 65/3: 641–91.

Perrons, D.C. (1981), 'The role of Ireland in the new international division of labour: A proposed framework for regional analysis', *Regional Studies*, 15/2: 81–100.

Peters, G. P. and Hertwich, E. G. (2008), 'CO_2 Embodied in International Trade with Implications for Global Climate Policy', *Environmental Science and Technology*, 42/5: 1401–7.

Peters, S. (2004), 'Coercive western energy security strategies: "resource wars" as a new threat to global security', *Geopolitics*, 9/1: 187–212.

Plumwood, V. (2001), *Environmental Culture: The Ecological Crisis of Reason* (London: Routledge).

Polanyi, K. (2001/1944), *The Great Transformation: The Political and Economic Origins of Our Time*, 2001 edn. (Boston, MA: Beacon Press).

Ponsford, R. (2011), 'Consumption, resilience and respectability amongst young mothers in Bristol' *Journal of Youth Studies*, 14/5: 541–60.

Pontin, J. and Roderick, I. (2007), *Converging World: Connecting Communities in Global Change*, Schumacher Briefing 13 (Totnes: Green Books).

Porritt, J. (2005), *Capitalism as if the World Matters* (London: Earthscan).

Porter, R. (1990), *The Enlightenment* (Basingstoke: Macmillan).

Power, D. and Hallencreutz, D. (2007), 'Competitiveness, Local Production Systems and Global Commodity Chains in the Music Industry: Entering the US Market', *Regional Studies*, 41/3: 377–89.

Power, E., (2005), 'The unfreedom of being other: Canadian lone mothers' experiences of poverty and "life on the cheque"', *Sociology*, 39(4), 643–60.

Pretty, J. (2007), *The Earth Only Endures: On Reconnecting with Nature and our Place in it* (London: Earthscan).

Priestley, J. B. and Hawkes, J. (1955), *Journey Down a Rainbow* (Harmondsworth: Penguin).

Prince, R. (2008), 'Councils told to stop being cavalier over prospect of service cuts', *Telegraph*, 13 Oct.

PCS (Public and Commercial Services Union) (n.d.), *An Alternative Vision for the Land Registry*, www.pcs.org.uk/download.cfm?docid=A85BD38B-9092-4B28-A33E964E08200823.

Pulselli, F. M., Ciampalini, F., Leipert, C. and Tiezzi, E. (2008), 'Integrating methods for the environmental sustainability: The SPIn-Eco Project in the Province of Siena (Italy)', *Journal of Environmental Management*, 86: 332–41.

Pulselli, R. M., Pulselli, F. M. and Rustici, M. (2008), 'Emergy accounting of the Province of Siena: Towards a thermodynamic geography for regional studies', *Journal of Environmental Management*, 86: 342–53.

Quah, D. (1999), 'The Weightless Economy in Growth', *The Business Economist*, 30/1: 40–53.

Quarantelli, E. L. and Dynes, R. R. (1977), 'Response to Social Crisis and Disaster', *Annual Review of Sociology*, 3: 23–49.

Rabin, M. (1998), 'Psychology and economics', *Journal of Economic Literature*, 36: 1, 11–46.

Reinhoff, C. M. and Rogoff, K. (2009), *This Time is Different: Eight Centuries of Financial Folly* (Princeton, NJ: Princeton University Press).

Reynolds, B. (2009), 'Feeding a World City: The London Food Strategy', *International Planning Studies*, 14/4: 417–24.

Richardson, G. (2001), 'A Tale of Two Theories: Monopolies and Craft Guilds in Medieval England and Modern Imagination', *Journal of the History of Economic Thought*, 23/2: 217–42.

Rigsby, B. (1999), 'Aboriginal people, spirituality and the traditional ownership of land', *Journal of Social Economics*, 26/7-8-9: 963–73.

Robbins, L. (1962), *An Essay on the Nature and Significance of Economic Science* (London: Macmillan).

Roberts, S., Dunbar, R., Pollet, T. V. and Kuppens, T. (2009), 'Exploring Variation in Active Network Size: Constraints and Ego Characteristics', *Social Networks*, 31: 138–46.

Robertson, J. (1985), *Future Work: Jobs, Self-employment, and Leisure after the Industrial Age* (London: Gower).

Robertson, J. (1990), *Future Wealth* (London: Cassell).

Romer, C. D. (1992), 'What Ended the Great Depression?', *Journal of Economic History*, 52/4: 757–84.

Ross, A. (1967), *Pagan Celtic Britain* (London: Routledge and Kegan Paul).

Rust, M.-J. (2008), 'Consuming the Earth: Unconscious Processes in Relation to Our Environmental Crisis', Lecture given to CAPPP Conference, Bristol, Sept., available at: www.mjrust.net/downloads/Consuming%20the%20Earth.pdf (Accessed 3 February 2012).

Sachs, J. (2008), *Common Wealth: Economics for a Crowded Planet* (Harmondsworth: Penguin).

Saffer, H. and Dhaval, D. (2002), 'Alcohol Consumption and Alcohol Advertising Bans', *Applied Economics*, 34/11: 1325–34.

Saffer, H. and Chaloupka, F. (2000), 'The effect of tobacco advertising bans on tobacco consumption', *Journal of Health Economics* 19: 1117–37.

Sagan, C. (1977), *The Dragons of Eden: Speculation on the Evolution of Human Intelligence* (New York: Random House).

Sahlins, M. (1972), *Stone Age Economics* (Chicago, IL: Aldine Atherton).

Sale, K. (1980), *Human Scale* (London: Secker & Warburg).

Sale, K. (2000/1991), *Dwellers in the Land: The Bioregional Vision*, (Athens, GA: University of Georgia Press).

Saler, M. (1999), *The Avant-Garde in Inter-War England: Medieval Modernism and the London Underground* (Oxford: Oxford University Press).

Salvatore, D. and Sgarbi, S. (1997), 'Specialization and Comparative Advantage of Central European Nations', in Orlowski, L. T. and Salvatore, D. (eds), *Trade and payments in Central and Eastern Europe's transforming economies, Handbook of Comparative Economic Policies*, vi (Westport, CT: Greenwood Press).

Sanchez Bajo, C. and Roelants, B. (2011), *Capital and the Debt Trap: Learning from Cooperatives in the Global Crisis* (Houndsworth: Macmillan).

Sassatelli, R. and Davolio, F. (2010), 'Consumption, Pleasure and Politics', *Journal of Consumer Culture*, 10/2: 202–32.

Schama, S. (1995/2004), *Landscape and Memory* (New York: Harper Collins).

Schneider, F., Kallis, G., Martinez-Alier, J. (2010), 'Crisis or opportunity? Economic degrowth for social equity and ecological sustainability', *Journal of Cleaner Production*, 18/6: 511–18.

Schumacher, E. F. (1973), *Small is Beautiful* (London: Abacus).

Schumacher, E. F. (1979), *Good Work* (London: Abacus).

Scoones, I., Marongwe, N., Mavedzenge, B., Murimbarimba, F., Mahenehene, J. and Sukume, C. (2011), 'Zimbabwe's land reform: challenging the myths', *Journal of Peasant Studies*, 38:5, 967–9.

Scott, J. and Wilkinson, R. (2011), 'The Poverty of the Doha Round and the Least Developed Countries', *Third World Quarterly*, 32/4: 611–27.

Seed, J., Macy, J., Flemming, P. and Naess, A. (1993), *Thinking Like a Mountain: Towards a Council of All Beings* (Gabriola Island, BC: New Society Publishers).

Sennett, R. (2008), *The Craftsman* (Harmondsworth: Penguin).

Seymour, J. (1984), *The Forgotten Arts: A Practical Guide to Traditional Skills* (London: Dorling Kindersly).

Sikor, T. and Müller, D. (2009), 'The Limits of State-Led Land Reform: An Introduction', *World Development*, 37/8: 1307–16.

Simon, H. (1957), 'A Behavioral Model of Rational Choice', *Models of Man, Social and Rational: Mathematical Essays on Rational Human Behavior in a Social Setting* (New York: Wiley).

Skidelsky, R. (2003), *John Maynard Keynes: 1883–1946: Economist, Philosopher, Statesman* (London: Macmillan).

Slade, G. (2006), *Made to Break: Technology and Obsolescence in America* (Cambridge, MA: Harvard University Press).

Smith, P. (2004), *The Body of the Artisan* (Chicago, IL: University of Chicago Press).

Smith, R. (2011), 'Boundarity Rationality: Towards a Theory of the Co-operative Firm', forthcoming in *Journal of Co-operative Studies*.

Snyder, G. (1990), *The Practice of the Wild* (Berkeley, CA: Counterpoint).

Sontag, S. (2001) *Illness as Metaphor, and, AIDS and its Metaphors*, (New York: Picador).

Soper, K. (2008), 'Exploring the relationship between growth and wellbeing', Thinkpiece for the SDC Seminar: Living Well – within Limits, Feb. 2008 (London: Sustainable Development Commission), www.sd-commission.org.uk/pages/redefining-prosperity.html.

Spash, C. (2010), 'The Brave New World of Carbon Trading', *New Political Economy*, 15/2: 169–95.

Spencer, D. A. (2009), 'Work in utopia: Pro-work sentiments in the writings of four critics of classical economics, *The European Journal of the History of Economic Thought*, 16/1, 97–122.

Starkey, R. (2011), 'Assessing common(s) arguments for an equal per capita allocation', *The Geographical Journal*, 177/2: 112–26.

Stavrakakis, Y. (2011), 'Objects of Consumption, Causes of Desire: Consumerism and Advertising in Societies of Commanded Enjoyment', *Gramma*, 14: 83–106.

Stearns, P. N. (2006), *Consumerism in World History: The Global Transformation of Desire* (London: Routledge).

Steel, C. (2008) *Hungry City: How Food Shapes our Lives* (London: Chatto & Windus).

Steel, D. (2001), *Marking Time: The Epic Quest to Invent the Perfect Calendar* (London: Wiley).

Stenton, F. M. (1979), *The First Century of English Feudalism, 1066–1166* (Westport, CT: Greenwood Press).

Stephens, P. H. G. (2001), 'Blood, Not Soil: Anna Bramwell and the Myth of "Hitler's Green Party"', *Organization and Environment*, 14/2: 173–87.

Stern, N. (2007), *The Economics of Climate Change*, The Stern Review (Cambridge and New York: Cambridge University Press).

Stiglitz, J. (2002), *Globalization and Its Discontents* (Harmondsworth: Penguin).

Straw, W. and Glennie, A. (2012), 'The Third Wave of Globalisation', Report of the IPPR review on the Future of Globalisation led by Lord Mandelson (London: IPPR).

Street, S. (2008), *British National Cinema* (London: Taylor & Francis).

Sullivan, S. (2010), '"Ecosystem Service Commodities" – A New Imperial Ecology? Implications for Animist Immanent Ecologies, with Deleuze and Guattari', *New Formations*, 69: 111–28.

Sullivan, S. (2012), *An Ecosystem At Your Service? Culture, Nature and 'Service Provision' in Global Environmental Governance* (forthcoming).

Swain, F. (2011), 'Susan Greenfield: Living online is changing our brains', *New Scientist*, 3 August.

Swyngedouw E (1997), 'Neither global nor local: "Glocalization" and the politics of scale', in K Cox (ed.) *Spaces of Globalization* (New York: Guilford) pp. 137–66.

Taçon, P. (2005), 'Chains of connection', *Griffith Review*, 9: www.griffithreview.com/images/stories/edition_articles/ed9_pdfs/taoned9.pdf

Talani, L. S. (2011), *Globalization, Hegemony and the Future of the City of London* (Houndsmill: Macmillan).

Thayer, R. L. (2003), *Life-Place: Bioregional Thought and Practice* (Berkeley, CA: University of California Press).

Thomashow, M. (1999), 'Toward a cosmopolitan bioregionalism', in M. Thomashow (ed.) *Bioregionalism* (London: Routledge) pp. 121–32.

Thompson, F. (1939/2000), *Larkrise to Candleford* (Harmondsworth: Penguin).

Thompson, E. P. (1963), *The Making of the English Working Class* (London: Gollancz).

Thompson, E. P. (1976) *William Morris: Romantic to Revolutionary* (London: Merlin Press).

Thompson, N. W. (1996), *Political Economy and the Labour Party* (Abingdon: Taylor & Francis).

Thorbecke, W. (2011), 'An empirical analysis of East Asian computer and electronic goods exports', *Journal of the Asia Pacific Economy*, 16/4: 644–57.

Thorpe, A. (2005), 'Unhealthy appetites', *Times*, 20 August.

Tietenberg, T. (2000), *Environmental and Natural Resource Economics* (Reading, MA: Addison-Wesley).

Tolstoy, L. (1877/2012), *Anna Karenina* (London: Sovereign).

Tomlinson. J. (1999), *Globalization and Culture* (Cambridge: Polity).

Toprowski, J. (2009), 'The Economics and Culture of Financial Inflation', *Competition and Change*, 13/2: 145–56.

Trapese Popular Education Collective (2008), *The Rocky Road to a Real Transition*; available from the Trapese website here: trapese.clearerchannel.org/resources/rocky-road-a5-web.pdf (Downloaded 28 March 2012).

Trotsky, L. (1938), 'The Death Agony of Capitalism and the Tasks of the Fourth International: The Mobilization of the Masses around Transitional Demands to Prepare the Conquest of Power', available online here: www.marxists.org/archive/trotsky/1938/tp/index.htm (downloaded 6 March 2012).

Trueman, A. E. (1972/1938), *Geology and Scenery in England and Wales*, revised by J. B. Whittow and J. R. Hardy for rev. edn. (Harmondsworth: Penguin).

Turner, F. J. (1932), *The Significance of Sections in American History* (New York: Holt).

Tussie, D. and Aggio, C. (n.d.), 'Economic and Social Impacts of Trade Liberalization', UNCTAD report available here: www.unctad.info/upload/TAB/docs/TechCooperation /fullreport-version14nov-p106–19.pdf (Downloaded 27 February 2012).

Tye, L. (2002), *The Father of Spin: Edward L. Bernays and the Birth of PR* (Greenwich, NY: Owl Books).

Van Koppen, C. S. A. (2007), 'Social learning for sustainability in a consumerist society', in Wals, A. E. J. (ed.), *Social Learning Towards a Sustainable World* (Wageningen: Academic Publishers) pp. 369–82.

Veblen, T. (1899/1994), *The Theory of the Leisure Class* (Mineola, NY: Dover).

Wade, R. (1988), *Village republics: Economic conditions for collective action in South India* (Oakland, CA: ICS Press).

Wade, R. H. (2009), 'Iceland as Icarus', *Challenge*, 52/3: 5–33.

Wade, R. H. and Sigurgeirsdottir, S. (2011), 'Iceland's Meltdown: The rise and fall of international banking in the North Atlantic', *Real-World Economics Review*, 56: 58–70.

Ward, C. (2002), *Cotters and Squatters: Housing's Hidden History* (Nottingham: Five Leaves).

Ward, H. (1999), 'Citizens' Juries and Valuing the Environment: A Proposal', *Environmental Politics*, 8/2: 75–96.

Watkiss, P. (2005), *The Validity of Food Miles as an Indicator of Sustainable Development: Final report*, AEA Technology Environment. Report for Department of the Environment, Food and Rural Affairs (UK) July.

White, R. (1996), 'Are You an Environmentalist Or Do You Work For A Living?: Work and Nature', in W. Cronon (ed.), *Uncommon Ground. Rethinking the Human Place in Nature.* (New York and London: W.W. Norton & Co.).

Whitefield, P. (2004), *The Earth Care Manual: A Permaculture Handbook for Britain and other Temperate Climates* (East Meon: Permanent Publications).

Wightman, A. (2010), *The Poor Had No Lawyers: Who Owns Scotland (And How They Got It)* (Edinburgh: Birlinn).

Wilcox, C. (2010), *Taxing Natural Rents:* Special Issue of *Tax Justice Network* newsletter, 6/1 (London: Tax Justice Network).

Wilkinson, B., Gamble, J., Humphrey, J., Morris, J. and Doug, A. (2001), 'The New International Division of Labour in Asian Electronics: Work Organization and Human Resources in Japan and Malaysia', *Journal of Management Studies*, 38/5: 675–95.

Wilkinson, R. and Pickett, K. (2009), *The Spirit Level* (London: Penguin).

Willi, B. (2011), 'Ben Law's Camp Fire Mythology', *Permaculture*, 11 May.

Willmott, H. (2000), 'Death. So what? Sociology, sequestration and emancipation', *Sociological Review*, 48, 4: 649–665.

Wily, L. (2000), 'Land tenure reform and the balance of power in eastern and southern Africa', ODI *Natural Resource Perspectives*, 58, June 2000.

Woodin, M. and Lucas, C. (2004), *Green Alternatives to Globlization* (London: Pluto).

World Bank (2010), 'Rising global interest in farmland: can it yield sustainable and equitable benefits?' (Washington, DC: The World Bank).

World Food Programme (2009), *Annual Report 2009* (Rome: World Food Programme).

World Health Organisation (2008), *WHO European Action Plan for Food and Nutrition Policy 2007–12* (Copenhagen: WHO).

Wunder, S., Luckert, M. and Smith-Hall, C. (2011), 'Valuing the Priceless: What are Non-Marketed Products Worth?', in A. Angelsen *et al.* (eds), *Measuring Livelihoods and Environmental Dependence: Methods for Research and Fieldwork* (London: Earthscan).

Zapata, D. and Schielman, S. (1999), 'Indigenous peoples, globalisation, and transnational corporations', in M. S. Cato and M. Kennet (eds), *Green Economics: Beyond Supply and Demand to Meeting People's Needs* (Aberystwyth: Green Audit) pp. 234–43.

Zinn, H. (1980), *A People's History of the United States* (New York: Harper & Row).

INDEX